D1716917

Pioneering television news

A first hand report on a revolution in journalism

Acknowledgements

My chief sources have been my recollections, my diaries, and the ITN film registers, script records and press cuttings, to which the ITN management has given me generous access. I am particularly indebted in this regard to my successors as Editor of ITN - Nigel Ryan, Sir David Nicholas and Stewart Purvis. Where I have drawn on published sources, I have made acknowledgement in the text.

I owe much to the recollections and records of those who shared in these events, particularly to Lord Clark and Lord Bernstein, Aidan Crawley, Arthur Clifford, John Cotter, Sir Robin Day, Martin Gray, William Hodgson, Cyril Page and Robert Verrall. Bernard Sendall, who was Deputy Director General of the ITA (later to become the IBA, then the ITC) during much of the period covered by this book, gave me invaluable support. At ITN David Warner, Jim Green and Suzy Spragg have given great help with the illustrations, as did Jon Lane. The photographs have been reproduced with kind permission of ITN, or of the individuals who own them. Jackie Gumpert once again did miracles in turning my handwriting into typescript.

I am proud to be associated with John Libbey's exciting publishing house. Manuel Alvarado has not only been a skilled editor of my manuscript, but has brought to the book the expertise of an active lecturer and researcher in modern media studies.

Pioneering television news

A first hand report on a revolution in journalism

Geoffrey Cox

John Libbey

LONDON · PARIS · ROME

British Library Cataloguing in Publication Data

Cox, Geoffrey
  Pioneering Television News
  I. Title
  070.195

ISBN: 0 86196 484 5

By the same author:
The Defence of Madrid
The Red Army Moves
The Road to Trieste
The Race for Trieste
See It Happen – The Making of ITN
A Tale of Two Battles.
Countdown to War

This book contains some portions of an earlier book, *SEE IT HAPPEN – The Making of ITN*, published in hardback by The Bodley Head, 1983.

Published by

John Libbey & Company Ltd, 13 Smiths Yard, Summerley Street,
London SW18 4HR, England.
Telephone: +44 (0)181-947 2777: Fax +44 (0)181-947 2664
John Libbey Eurotext Ltd, 127 rue de la République, 92120 Montrouge, France.
John Libbey - C.I.C. s.r.l., via Lazzaro Spallanzani 11, 00161 Rome, Italy

Printed in Great Britain by Whitstable Litho Ltd, Whitstable, Kent, UK.

Contents

Foreword

Sir Robin Day

Sir Geoffrey Cox is the greatest television journalist we have known in Britain. He was Editor of Independent Television News in the years when television was becoming the dominant news medium. His enduring achievements at ITN are landmarks in the history of broadcasting and make a gripping story in themselves.

As the resolute upholder of accuracy and impartiality, as the tutor, trainer and talent-spotter of a whole new generation of journalist–broadcasters, Sir Geoffrey Cox has been one of the two or three most important individual influences in British broadcasting since Sir John Reith. During his twelve years as Editor, he made ITN a resounding success, both highly popular and respected, thus proving that television journalism did not have to be trivial or yellow to win an audience. In 1967 he created the half-hour *News at Ten* against stiff resistance from within ITV, thus proving that the public may not know what they want until it is offered to them.

Those of us who entered television news in the mid 1950s, found ourselves in the van of a journalistic revolution. Within the next decade and a half, the domination of daily journalism by the printed and broadcast word was to be challenged by television's magic box. By 1967, when ITN's *News at Ten* ushered in the era of half-hour news, television had supplanted the press and radio as the main source of daily news for the mass of people in this country. In the United States, the establishing of half-hour TV news in 1963 was hailed by Theodore H. White 'a date as significant in American history as the Golden Spike that linked the Union Pacific and Central Pacific to give America its first continental railway in 1869'.

In Britain the trail had been blazed in these revolutionary developments by Independent Television News. This was a brand new national organ of news. ITN was the news service of the commercial television network launched in 1955. The smashing of the BBC's broadcasting monopoly in that year was the most memorable (some would say the *only* memorable) reform of the last Churchill administration. Unencumbered by the constraints which inhibited the BBC's move into TV news coverage, ITN moved boldly to exploit the 16mm film camera as a powerful new instrument of journalism. ITN also made exciting use of the new freedom which competition had opened up in broadcasting – freedom to probe, explain and illustrate the news of the day. Politicians and public figures were challenged in a way that BBC radio journalism had never attempted. The ban on the broadcasting of elections was swept aside.

After the brief founding editorship of Aidan Crawley, ITN was led for twelve years by Geoffrey Cox. In 1966 he was knighted for his part in pioneering the new journalism. The years of his editorship, vividly described in this book, were years of crossing new frontiers, of breaking new ground, of non-stop revolutions in TV technology, of heated controversies which raged around ITN as television became part of life and part of politics.

The achievement of Sir Geoffrey Cox in this revolution was not only to deploy skilfully the new technology and the new freedom to bring news vividly to the screen, but also to make the new journalism a responsible and trustworthy element in the democratic process. ITN rapidly gained a reputation for swift news-gathering and incisive interviews. In parallel, ITN won a reputation for fairness and accuracy, for upholding these standards as firmly as had the BBC, yet with spunk and spark and personality.

But for the editorship of Sir Geoffrey Cox, ITV's news service could have gone down a very different path, the mucky path of sensationalist, strident yellow journalism. And if ITN had gone yellow, had gone into the gutter, the consequences for the main medium of mass communication in our parliamentary democracy would have been ugly. If the news on ITV had gone down-market, everything – even the BBC – could have gone down market. As ITN's Editor for twelve years, Sir Geoffrey Cox held the high ground. He knew that television news, unless under principled leadership, could succumb to the tabloid temptations – distortion, superficiality, trivialization, sensationalism.

By creating *News at Ten*, Britain's first half-hour TV news, Sir Geoffrey laid a firm foundation for the future to uphold his editorial standards – vigorous, thrusting news coverage, responsibly and impartially presented in popular style.

It was not an easy task. In the early formative days, he had to inculcate a belief in impartiality into the mixed group who came together in 1955 to form the first television journalists of ITN. There was a small core of newsmen, mostly ex-BBC, headed by Arthur Clifford, the brilliant News Editor, who were trained in the discipline of impartiality. Others had no such background. There were cameramen and film editors from the cinema newsreels, where coverage had often been blatantly propagandist. There were journalists from Fleet Street, where proprietors expected their views to shape the contents as well as the policies of their newspapers. There were writers who believed that news should be seasoned by opinion. There were refugees from radio news, where the beauty of the announcer's voice seemed to matter more than the boring bulletins he was reading, and greenhorns like myself (who had been a barrister) with little or no media experience. For some of us in that original ITN team forty years ago, those early days were the happiest and most exciting time of our lives. We could feel a revolutionary thrill. As the poet said (admittedly about a somewhat bigger and bloodier revolution) 'Bliss was it in that dawn to be alive, but to be young was very heaven'.

Under Sir Geoffrey's shrewd and strong editorship, ITN steadily enhanced its reputation for getting news swiftly and for presenting it fairly. He sustained that reputation in later years when the very idea of impartiality came under attack. Opinionated journalism captured a strong foothold in TV current affairs programmes and doc-umentaries. The concepts of truth and fairness often came to be derided and disregarded. But in ITN, Sir Geoffrey held firmly to his profound belief that these principles – truth and fairness – do not inhibit but inspire great journalism. He implanted that belief in a younger generation of TV journalists. Not least of his achievements was to select and train many journalists whose talent and potential he had discerned, such as Ian Trethowan, Alastair Burnet, Sandy Gall, Nigel Ryan, Peter Sissons, Peter Snow, David Nicholas, Gerald Seymour. I was *not* one of Sir Geoffrey's discoveries. He was lumbered with me when he took over ITN. But he did not sack me. He gave me golden opportunities even though I gave him grievous trouble on occasions.

The creation of ITN in 1955 was a landmark in British journalism and broadcasting. As it grew and flourished under the leadership of Sir Geoffrey Cox, ITN succeeded in com-bining the challenge and sparkle of Fleet Street with the accuracy and impartiality re-quired by the Television Act.

To television news in its early years, Sir Geoffrey brought a wealth of experience. He had been a Fleet Street foreign correspondent in the gathering storm of pre-war Europe. The war brought him experience of soldiering, as an infantry officer in the New Zealand Army in campaigns in Greece, Crete, North Africa and Italy. In 1943 he was posted to Washington as a diplomat. As New Zealand *chargé d'affaires*, he had the heady experience at the age of 32 of representing his country on the Pacific War Coun-cil at the same table as President Roosevelt and Prime Minister Winston Churchill. After the war, as political correspondent of the *News Chronicle*, he gained intimate knowl-edge of British politics – and of British politicians. Many whom he knew as young MPs were to emerge as the nation's leaders when Sir Geoffrey was Editor of ITN. At a time when Fleet Street's competition was in its fiercest post-war phase, he became Assistant Editor of the *News Chronicle*. All this constituted a breadth of experience rare then, and rarer still now, amongst broadcast journalists. It gave Sir Geoffrey the capacity not only to develop with skill this new medium of television journalism, but also to be con-scious of the good – and the harm – it could do to the democratic process.

In this important book, Sir Geoffrey tells the story of those early, exciting ITN years with insight and clarity. He paints vivid pen portraits of the strong personalities who gathered round the ITN standard. This is a slice of history written by someone who helped to shape that history. For the general reader, this is a book which tells the story of how television news came to play such a large part in his life. For those who study the media in schools and universities, this is a source book of great value, describing not only what happened but what it felt like at the time it happened, by one who made it happen.

It is a story of how television's coverage of world events has been totally transformed from the primitive days of monochrome, when the 16mm film camera was the TV reporters's notebook, when there was no video-recording, no satellites, no Electronic News Gathering, no hi-tech graphics to explain election results, no glorious colour to show the blood of war or the dead babies of famine.

In September 1955, less than a quarter of a million homes were equipped to receive ITV. In forty years, the audience has multiplied into many millions. Morning, noon and night, television is taken for granted in every home.

The faster the advance of technology, and the greater television's impact on events, the greater has been the need to uphold the principles preached and practised by Sir Geoffrey Cox so consistently and courageously.

Like the great Roman poet, he could justly say '*Exegi monumentum aere perennius*'. But, as a great New Zealander, he is much too unostentatious to say anything of the sort.

1

Recorder – and shaper – of history

A t eleven o'clock on the morning of 19 August 1991, a column of ten tanks drew up in front of the Russian Parliament building in Moscow. They had been sent by the coup plotters as a first step towards seizing the building and arresting Boris Yeltsin, the Russian President. Yeltsin countered with a master stroke. He strode up to the leading tank, shook its commander by the hand, and clambered on to its turret. There he proclaimed his defiance of the plotters, and called upon workers to go on strike in protest. His action presented a marvellously symbolic image. Here was the powerfully built, grey haired, elected leader with his foot planted firmly on the neck of the monster sent against him, rallying his fellow countrymen to the battle. Not only did it show that Yeltsin was still free, and full of fight, but the fact that the tank crew had let him use their vehicle as a platform of protest cast doubt – rightly, as it happened – on how far the plotters could rely on the troops to fulfil their will.

Yeltsin's move was an act of daring and decisive leadership. It was also a brilliant use of the most modern of all the media – television news – to counter the plot and rally the forces of democracy. For ranged around the tank were the camera crews of a dozen or more television news services, from all round the world. Yeltsin knew that the coup leaders could censor what was put out over Soviet television, but that they could not prevent pictures of the overseas cameraman being flashed by satellite around the world. Within minutes of his dramatic gesture on the top of the tank, pictures of it were being viewed worldwide, particularly on the round the clock service of CNN, the American Cable News Network. CNN carried this vivid proof of Yeltsin's survival, and of his defiance, into No. 10 Downing Street, and into President Bush's holiday home at Kennebunkport in Maine. Mr Major was soon telling the cameras, on the pavement outside Downing Street, that Britain opposed the coup and supported Yeltsin. Rapidly similar messages and images were filling the world's screens, as President Bush and other world leaders ranged themselves on the side of President Gorbachev and President Yeltsin and the endangered democracy of the Soviet Union.

This took the plotters by surprise. They realized abruptly that it was no longer possible for repression to be mounted within Russia, unseen by the outside world, and disguised to the Soviet people themselves. These first pictures of Yeltsin's defiance were followed by a stream of further proofs of resistance to the coup – young and old building barricades, huge crowds filling the square before the Winter Palace in Leningrad, a Red Army armoured vehicle engulfed in flames from petrol bombs hurled from a Moscow flyover. Even if the pictures themselves could be kept off Soviet screens by the coup's censors, the events they portrayed were reported by radio messages which flooded into the Soviet Union. The resistance stiffened to a point at which it could be overcome only by heavy bloodshed. Faced with these facts, the plotters' nerve failed, and they threw in their hands. It was a great victory for democracy, and striking evidence of the power of the newest of all forms of journalism, television news. Little wonder that Eduard Schevardnedze, the former Soviet Foreign Minister who had warned of the plot, and who sat at Yeltsin's side in those tense early moments, acclaimed television's role. 'Praise be to information technology!' he wrote. 'Praise be to the reporters and announcers of CNN! Those who had parabolic antennae and could receive this station's broadcasts were getting a full picture of the developments, while the obedient TV of Leonid Kravchenko was pouring forth the murky waves of disinformation and lies'.[1]

This hugely potent force of television journalism was less than half a century old when it played this key role not only in reporting events, but in shaping them. Television news had come into effective being in the United States only in the early 1950s, and in Britain from the middle of that decade. Yet its growth had been so swift that within two decades it was to provide a proof of its power in a form as dramatic as that shown in the streets of Moscow and Leningrad.

This first demonstration came in Vietnam, when the Vietnamese war was at its peak. In the early hours of Tuesday 30 January 1968 the Vietcong and the North Vietnamese for the first time carried the war into the heart of the major cities and towns of South Vietnam. In the darkness they moved out of their hiding places in the forests and villages and rice paddies, and struck into the streets of more than a hundred areas which until then had suffered at most random rocket fire. The attackers gained almost complete surprise. It was the time of Tet, the Vietnamese New Year, which in previous years had been marked by a truce. In Saigon in particular the Vietcong got right to the heart of the city, and even seized for a time the ground floor of the American Embassy.

The next night the American public saw on their television screens exceptionally vivid filmed reports from the streets of Saigon, Da Nang and Hue, newsfilm reeking with authenticity. The fighting had broken out in areas where the camera teams of the American television networks were based: cameramen, recordists and reporters were in the thick of the battles from the outset. Into the homes of television viewers throughout the world, but particularly into the homes of people in every corner of the United States, was to pour for the next six weeks a stream of reports of frontline fighting which had almost the impact of live broadcasts.

For those who viewed this film night after night in the cutting rooms of television news, some of these scenes remain in the mind like personal recollections – American boys,

1   *The Observer,* 1 September 1991.

Fig. 1. American marines landing in Vietnam, 1965, filmed by ITN.

their faces taut under their steel helmets, crouched behind a sandbag barricade in a suburban street in Da Nang before going into an attack; unshaven young Marines, ammunition belts looped over their shoulders, stalking like movie cowboys through the shattered temple gardens of Hue; Vietnamese refugee children hunched amid American troops taking shelter from mortar fire on a road verge. Though the fighting in the jungles and open country had been extensively covered throughout the previous three or four years nothing had the impact of these reports of the Tet fighting as they came through, in colour, evening after evening.

The Tet offensive was, in strictly military terms of casualties inflicted and ground held or gained, a severe defeat for the North Vietnamese and the Vietcong. They were rapidly ousted from Saigon and most of the other urban areas. Only in a few places, most particularly in the ancient capital of Hue, did the heavy fighting last for some time. At the end of six weeks the American and South Vietnamese forces had regained control of all the attacked towns and cities, and the war had reverted to its former pattern of frontal attacks by the North Vietnamese in the North, and continual guerrilla harassment elsewhere. The Vietcong and Northern losses had been heavy, for at last they had appeared in groups large enough to provide a real target for American fire power. It was to be a matter of many months before they could mount another major offensive. Significantly, too, the people in the invaded areas had not risen to help the attackers. On the ground, in Vietnam, the American commanders had reason to claim that in this bitter New Year fighting the victory had been theirs.

But the wider reality was very different. Despite their losses, for the North Vietnamese and the Vietcong the Tet offensive was to prove a spectacular success, was in fact to be the decisive battle of the Vietnam war. For it struck a deadly blow at America's will to win. And it struck that blow through television. Though the invaders may have been forced to withdraw, though their losses were high, this was not the picture which lingered in the American mind. What stayed was the image of their first successes, and the image of the high cost to young Americans of countering these attacks.

The Tet offensive came at a moment when the American public had regained confidence that the war, terrible though it was, was grinding slowly towards an American victory. Two months earlier the American commander, General Westmoreland, had spoken of the low morale of the Vietcong. Now these guerrillas had appeared in the safest of the non-Communist areas, in the innermost parts of Saigon itself. Suddenly, powerfully, there was evidence before the eyes of the public that victory was far from certain. For the first time the American public faced the prospect that their suffering might be crowned by defeat. When Walter Cronkite, watching the first film of the attack in the newsroom of CBS in New York, exclaimed, 'I thought we were supposed to be winning this goddam war', he spoke for tens of millions of Americans.

These were war pictures which were, until then, without parallel, and they were to show that television had become a news medium without parallel. For the first time in the world's history a people at war saw, in the peace of their own homes, the visage of front-line fighting. No censor had intervened here, as in the coverage of World War II, to ensure that only a few glimpses, if any at all, were seen of our troops being killed and wounded. No constraints of distance, or of logistics, or of official policy were to operate, as during the fighting in the Falklands, to inhibit the flow of these pictures to the screen. No patriotic commentary underlined the necessity of it all. Only the laconic voices of the reporters and the shouts of orders and the cries of the wounded were to be heard against the crunch of mortars and the crackle of automatic arms fire. The experience the American people underwent was unique, and suddenly became more than was bearable – or at least more than their leaders judged they could bear. Within six weeks of the first television pictures of the Tet offensive reaching the screen President Johnson swung American policy in Vietnam on to a new course. He announced he no longer intended to stand for re-election as President, and began the process which would lead to America's ultimate withdrawal from Vietnam. Television had shown itself to be not only a major source of information, but a power in the land – a power whose role has widened and deepened year after year.

2

Radio ancestor

Television news did not win its power easily. In both Britain and the United States broadcast news had, from the earliest days of radio, a hard struggle to assert itself against the dominant medium of the time, the press. In Britain the newspapers had used their formidable power to curb the use of the air waves for the provision of news. When the British Broadcasting Company, under the young John Reith, first began broadcasting in 1922, the newspaper proprietors could not prevent news from being broadcast, but were able to ensure that this would happen only at a time, and in a way which would do least damage to newspaper sales. The BBC was forced to agree not to broadcast any news before 7 o'clock in the evening, and was not to gather its own news. It had to rely on a summary of the day's news prepared by the news agencies, a practice which led all BBC News, up to the outbreak of war in 1939, being preceded by the incantation that the news was 'Copyright of Reuters, the Press Association, Exchange Telegraph and Central News'.

Only four years into this strict regime, the General Strike of 1926 gave the BBC a chance to break free for one wonderful gallop. With the newspapers strike bound, the wireless suddenly assumed great importance. The BBC put out five bulletins a day, starting at 10 o'clock in the morning; collected much of its own news; and even broadcast a series of editorials. But once the strike was over, it was quickly hustled back into its role of filling the gap between the appearance of the last of the evening papers, and that of the first of the morning papers. In 1927 it made one minor gain, when 6.30 in the evening rather than 7pm was the permitted time for the first news of the day. Three years later this deadline was brought back to 6pm, with a further important concession that the BBC's newsroom would receive the agency tapes direct, so enabling it to prepare its own bulletins, rather than merely adapting them from the 2,500 word daily agency summary. But despite the flow of highly dramatic news throughout the 1930s, the BBC news bulletins were still confined to the evening hours. Only for a brief period, during the Munich crisis in September 1938, were these restrictions limited. Once that crisis was over, the clamp came back until war in 1939 swept it away for ever.

The parallel ban on the BBC doing its own reporting was another great limitation on the development of broadcast news in Britain. Live commentaries were permitted on sporting events, and on grand occasions such as the Coronation of 1937, but otherwise the BBC was required to confine itself to what were termed 'eye-witness accounts' of non-news events. The Corporation's eye-witnesses might ride in the cabs of express trains, or go down the Thames on tug boats, or mingle with the holiday crowds at Blackpool, but they must not cover the news.

In 1934 BBC News became a Department in its own right, instead of a sub-branch of Talks, and bit by bit enterprising spirits within the BBC Newsroom began to devise ways around these restrictions. Ralph Murray and Vernon Bartlett provided, in the guise of Talks – which were permitted – reporting from Geneva of the activities of the League of Nations.

Kenneth Adam had interpreted his function as Home News Editor as permitting him to describe the lying-in state of George V, of a speech of Lloyd George at the Trades Union Club, and of the opening of a new Shaw play at the Malvern Festival. But it was the young Richard Dimbleby who first saw, and seized the opportunity to widen his role as Topical Talks Assistant into that of a reporter. His live coverage of the Crystal Place fire in 1936, and of the Fenland floods in the spring of 1937 showed what could be done. By 1938 he was covering the return of Neville Chamberlain from his first meeting with Hitler at Berchtesgarten, and from the Munich crisis. In March of the next year Dimbleby was allowed abroad, covering with great ability the retreat of the defeated Spanish Republican Army across the Pyrenees into France, speaking live into the 10 o'clock bulletin 'with one foot in France and one in Spain'. Even so by the time war came the BBC had only two reporters, Dimbleby and Charles Gardner.

This restrictive practice imposed by Fleet Street had denied to British broadcasting the chance to add those extra dimensions of immediacy and authenticity, which are the strength of radio news, to the great stories which unfolded on Britain's doorstep as the 1930s moved remorselessly towards war. The rise of Hitler, the shelling of the workers' flats in Vienna, the Saar plebiscite, the rise of the Popular Front in France (with the first sit-in strikes), the Spanish Civil War, the re-occupation of the Rhineland, the Anschlüss, the long tense summer leading up to Munich, the German seizure of Prague, were not only eminently newsworthy but vivid. They had a force which much news today does not have because Britain was then a real power, whose actions could shape events. The listeners and the newspaper readers of the day knew that by their votes and their voices they could help to determine how that power was used. It was a period which cried out for coverage with the microphone, coverage from on the spot.

The Germans, and to a lesser degree the Italians, gave it that coverage. They did so for propaganda purposes, but they did so with skill and subtlety, seeking to make their impact not so much by preaching at their people, as by describing the events with great vividness, so building an impression of a Nazi machine of irresistible force, which was creating a Greater Reich of equally irresistible force. It was a coverage carried far beyond national frontiers. If you searched around the dial in those days you could hear, through the crackling static, these ominous events unfolding. It was from the big, wooden framed wireless set of the *News Chronicle* – housed with due formality in the top floor Board Room in Bouverie Street – that Vernon Bartlett and I heard on a lovely spring evening in 1935 Mussolini's words as he announced, against the background chanting of 'Duce, Duce' that Italy had invaded Abyssinia. It was from my own bright yellow bakelite set at home that I listened to the tramp of marching German infantry, the rumble of wheels and the clop, clop of the hooves of the horse-drawn German artillery, as the Reichswehr crossed the Rhine bridges to re-occupy the Rhineland. The marching music of the German military bands, their powerful brass and insistent drums, accompanied by the incongruous tinkling cymbals of the glockenspiele, marked each Einmarsch into the Rhineland, into Austria, into the Sudetenland, into Prague. For hour after hour from the Nuremberg rallies the microphones caught the tramp of the marching columns, the shouted orders, the bellowed 'Heil Hitlers' the strains of the sickly but effective Horst Wessel song. And at the high peak of each of these occasions was the Fuehrer's speech, its involved, sustained, high-pitched sentences merging into the thundered responses of the crowd.

In all this, the Nazis and the Fascists had the air to themselves. No British broadcasters sought to describe or interpret these scenes, or to report the fighting around Madrid or the bombing of Barcelona. The only British voice to be heard from the spot as these dramas unfolded was indeed carried by the German Deutschland Sender in its live broadcast from Linz on 12 March 1938, describing the scene as the Reichswehr moved in to seize Austria under the Anschlüss. The *Daily Mail* correspondent, G. Ward Price, a great admirer of Hitler, stood by the Fuehrer's side on the balcony of the Town Hall in Linz, and expressed into the microphones his delight at what he saw.

It was by its presentation, therefore, and not by its coverage, that the BBC was to build up in pre-war years its reputation for news. At a time when so many newspapers seemed impregnated with the views of their proprietors, the public felt that the BBC was trying to give the news straight. It was this trust which gives validity to the claim by Asa Briggs that 'between 1927 and 1939 the BBC established its reputation as the most honest purveyor of news in the world'.

Once the war had freed its hands, the BBC Newsroom steadily developed its own coverage. Within a day or two of the outbreak of war Charles Gardner, resplendent in khaki uniform from Austin Reed, with 'WC' tabs on his shoulders to show that he was a war correspondent, had joined the resident British correspondents in Paris at our regular meeting place in a bistro off the Champs Elysées. When the Russians invaded Finland a new figure, that of Edward Ward, appeared as a BBC correspondent alongside the newspapermen and newspaperwomen (for in this war Virginia Cowles of the *Sunday Times* and Babro Alving of Sweden were very much in evidence) to describe the early Russian defeats in the forest snows.

The war gave Dimbleby the chance to reveal his remarkable talents as a reporter – for the BBC's first radio reporter was also to be its best – and to bring through many other outstanding correspondents like Chester Wilmot, Wynford Vaughan Thomas, Godfrey Talbot, Stewart MacPherson, Robert Barr and Robert Reid. From bombers over Germany, from frigates in the Western Approaches, from the deserts of Egypt and Libya, Algeria and Tunisia, from the mountain spine of Italy the reportage steadily grew, until from the summer of 1944 till the end of the war it culminated in *War Report*, a masterly nightly special programme. The quality of this reporting, coupled with the trust which the news services, despite all the pressures of war, continued to arouse, made the BBC by 1945 undoubtedly the most prestigious news broadcasting organization in the world, outdistancing even the high professionalism of the American networks.

3

From talks to news

In the United States the newspapers had at first made little effort to clip the wings of this new form of journalism. One reason may have been that the press owned, or shared in the ownership of many of the stations which proliferated after World War I. But it was equally likely that the newspaper magnates shared the view that radio's natural diet was entertainment and sport. In news it seemed to pose no threat, even though it had been a news story – the victory of Warren Harding over James Cox in the Presidential election of 1920 – which gave broadcasting its great initial boost.

Throughout their first decade American radio stations helped themselves freely to news not only from any parent newspapers they might have, but from other papers, and from the news agencies. They did not, however, use much of it. News bulletins were neither numerous nor extensive. In 1928 CBS had only a single teletype machine bringing in news from United Press which they used not for regular bulletins, but to announce any big stories from time to time[1]. Not until live coverage of the inauguration of President Hoover in March 1929 had brought the two networks a total audience of 63 million people, did the value of news on the air become apparent. Later that year CBS now full coast-to-coast network, began its first daily news bulletin, its first programme of political analysis, and its first public affairs show.

Radio also began to develop the first of a breed of commentators who combined analysis with opinion, and who were to characterize American radio journalism in this formative period. H.V. Kaltenborn was the first great exponent of this technique. He had been a lecturer before he became a radio newscaster and commentator, and he continued to interweave highly opinionated appearances on the United States lecture circuit with strongly opinionated broadcasting. It was a trend which, as the slump deepened, was to develop in two directions. In one way it helped to bring forward the first demagogues of the air, like Father Coughlin, the Detroit priest who won a huge audience for his populist views, and Huey Long, whose broadcasting carried him to political power until he was assassinated in the Louisiana legislature. But the other branch of its development was to lead to one of its most glittering achievements of American radio, the

---

1   *As It Happened* by William Paley, Doubleday & Company 1979, p. 118.

blend of reporting and analysis which Kaltenborn, Elmer Davis, Lowell Thomas, and Raymond Gram Swing were to pioneer, and of which Edward R. Murrow, Eric Sevareid, William Shirer, Charles Collingwood and Howard K. Smith were later to become such masters.

By the early 1930s the expansion of network news coverage had reached a point which finally stirred the newspapers to action, not least because in the slump their revenues were being hard hit by this upstart medium. The papers managed after long negotiations in the Biltimore Hotel in New York, to force on the networks, under what was to be termed the 'Biltimore Treaty', conditions very similar to those clamped on the BBC 11 years earlier. In return for allowing the broadcasters continued access to the news agencies the newspapers exacted undertakings that the broadcasters would not gather news themselves and would not put out news before 9.30am to protect the morning papers, or before 9pm to protect the evenings'. But the agreement rapidly collapsed under the pressure of events. Broadcasting in the United States was too big – there were already over 700 stations and they were too quickly responsive to the public appetite to be hemmed in. As the turbulent 30s unfolded, the public appetite for news grew, and with it the willingness of sponsors to back such programmes. News bulletins proliferated, particularly once Esso had decided to put its money in one of the main evening news shows. Another programme, *March of Time*, a weekly radio report which presented the week's news in highly dramatized form, and which had come on to the air in 1931, survived these early storms to become a highly effective, if highly coloured form of broadcast journalism. One of its techniques was to use actors to play the parts of the world's leaders. An Italian American called Ted de Corsia, for instance, voiced the words of Mussolini.

CBS News had, under the Biltmore Agreement, disbanded its own news gathering service within the United States. It was nevertheless to find itself in 1938 drawn abruptly into the business of foreign news coverage. The technical development which made this possible was short wave broadcasting, which enabled radio messages to be carried over much greater distances. It had been first used to span the Atlantic in 1930, when both NBC and CBS did some enterprising reporting of the London Five Power Naval Conference. King George V's speech opening the conference had been broadcast live to America, and for some weeks afterwards the networks had carried regular reports from correspondents they had sent to London.

At that time however, the Talks tradition was as strong among broadcasters in America as it was in London. These carefully prepared, often discursive spoken essays ('by Sermon out of Discourse' as E.R. Thompson has described them) had developed steadily in the 1920s in Britain as a way of portraying the immediate world of affairs despite the limitations imposed on news reporting. In America they had a prototype in the work of the touring lecturer, be he or she an explorer, a writer of best sellers, or a celebrity like the exiled Queen Marie of Romania. The lecture circuit took them from Women's Clubs to Elks' luncheons, from College campuses to learned society dinners across the land. Radio talks seemed a natural first cousin to the lecturer, and for several years the short waves were used, not for the regular coverage of news, but to bring radio talks across the Atlantic. G.B. Shaw helped to start the fashion in 1931 when he assured American listeners that the Russian system was 'so successful she has the laugh on us' a remark which had reception of it been possible in the Ukraine, stricken then by the man-made famine of collectivization, would hardly have made for good listening. Gandhi and the Prince of Wales, the Pope and Trotsky all in due course spoke their pieces across theAtlantic.

So firmly fixed did this habit of using the short waves for general talks rather than news become, that the American networks, like the BBC, left the great European stories of the mid-1930s uncovered – except by agency reports in their bulletins. Only one American broadcaster, H.V. Kaltenborn, tried to utilize the short wave link and the microphone to provide any direct coverage of the Spanish Civil War. He broadcast an eye witness account of the fighting at Irún, speaking into the microphone from a haystack on the French bank of the river which marked the frontier between France and Spain. But he had to do it at his own expense, hiring BBC facilities for the job. No other commentators or reporters followed this lead.

It was indeed a Talks producer sent to Europe with instructions not to broadcast himself but to 'arrange for personalities to give informative talks over the network'[1] who was to change this. He was Edward R. Murrow, then 'a sober, earnest young man at 27 with that elongated, sombre face'[2]. He had hired as his colleague in this task a former newspaperman, William L. Shirer, who had had grave doubts about the wisdom of leaving the mainstream of journalism for this less urgent task of putting other people on the air.

Shirer was indeed busy voicing those doubts when I first met him in Rome in the autumn of 1937. I was in Italy probing a story that Mussolini was about to send substantial further reinforcement of troops to help Franco deliver the *coup de grace* to the Spanish Republicans. Shirer was almost envious of my task, for he had just received confirmation that if any news reports were to be done for CBS from Europe, his task and Murrow's was to arrange for newspaper correspondents to do these, not to do them themselves. 'Hell', he said pointing around the bustling Roman crowds in the Galleria Colonna in Rome, 'I know as much about Europe as most other correspondents. I could do them just as well myself'.

Shirer's frustrations were to be short lived. Six months later, on 12 March 1938, when he was in Yugoslavia and Murrow was in Poland arranging musical broadcasts for the American School of the Air, the news suddenly broke that Hitler had sent the Reichswehr into Austria to enforce the Anschluss, starting the landslide towards World War II. Faced with this sudden challenge – and this sudden chance – Murrow revealed his remarkable qualities. He put aside his talks requirements and set about covering the Anschlüss as a news story. He got Shirer to rush to Vienna, survey the scene there, and then fly on to London to send a report to New York from the BBC, since no facilities were immediately available from the Austrian capital. Normal plane flights into Austria were equally interrupted, so Murrow chartered, at the then prodigious sum of $,1000 Lufthansa plane. With himself as the only passenger he flew from Warsaw to Vienna. At 2.30am European time the next day – 8.30pm in New York – Morrow's first broadcast despatch came out of receivers in homes across the United States. 'Young storm

---

1   Paley, *op cit.*, p. 131.

2   Paley, *op cit.*, p. 131.

troopers are riding about the streets, riding about in trucks and vehicles of all sorts, singing and tossing oranges out into the crowd. Nearly every principal building had its armed guard, including the one from which I am speaking'. The broadcasting of foreign news indeed the whole coverage of foreign news, had entered into a new phase. Those of us who telephoned our accounts to our newspapers that night – my own filled four columns of the *Daily Express* – had no inkling of the revolutionary changes in news techniques which were at that moment being set in train.

Within a matter of months both the main American networks were setting up teams of overseas correspondents. The war rapidly accelerated this process. By the end of 1941 Edward R. Murrow's legendary reporting from London in the Blitz, beginning with the dramatically enunciated words: 'This – is London', had made him a world figure. They had even played a part in the course of the war, by wearing down the spirit of isolationism which hampered Franklin Roosevelt's efforts to help the Allies. During the war years, despite the incongruity of having messages from sponsors interwoven with messages from the battlefield, radio news in the United States developed at such a pace that by the war's end it had ousted the newspapers as the main source of news for the American people.

4

Newsreel days

W hen the BBC launched the world's first regular television service in November 1936, news was not high among its priorities. It confined itself to a news summary, read by an unseen announcer from behind a caption, at the end of the evening's programmes, and bi-weekly newsreels, provided by two cinema newsreel companies. It saw no part of its task being to initiate its own coverage of news, except where the outside broadcast of a predictable event was itself newsworthy. This they did with their coverage of the Coronation procession in 1938, and in their sports coverage of Wimbledon tennis, the Boat Race, the 1938 Cup Final and the 1938 Test against Australia at the Oval.

On one occasion, however, before the service closed down in September 1939 at the outbreak of war, there had been a striking demonstration of what this new force could achieve in the coverage of hard, immediate news. This came at the peak of the Munich crisis in 1938. When Neville Chamberlain flew back to London after the Munich conference which had postponed the war at the price of sacrificing the key strategic areas of Czechoslovakia, BBC Television sent its outside broadcast cameras to Heston Airport. From there they broadcast live the scenes of the Prime Minister stepping from his aircraft to wave aloft the piece of paper upon which Hitler had promised never to use war as a way of settling disputes with Britain. Richard Dimbleby provided a commentary and the microphones relayed Mr. Chamberlain's brief triumphant speech.

In the United States the story which gave American viewers a comparable glimpse of the potential of this new form of journalism was even bigger. On Sunday 7 December 1941, Japanese aircraft attacked Pearl Harbor. The news broke in New York early in the afternoon. WCBW, the CBS experimental television station, was brought on to the air ahead of its scheduled time, and its three-man news team mounted a nine hour newscast, relaying to the viewers each item of news as it came in over the wire. They had no film available, but they could use maps, diagrams and stills to explain what had happened. Military commentators analysed and probed. Using everything they had to hand, the staff of the fledgling station, which was then only 160 days old, rose to the occasion. It was indeed an omen for the future.

Both in Britain and in the United States television services were suspended throughout the war. When BBC Television came back on the air in 1946, its new head, Maurice Gorham, made a strong plea for a start to be made with a service of television news, by illustrating wherever possible the items broadcast in the sound radio news. But the plan foundered on the adamantine opposition of the Director General, Sir William Haley.

Haley was a newspaperman, a former editor of the *Manchester Evening News*, the stable companion of the *Manchester Guardian*, and a former Chairman of Reuters. He was in due course to turn from broadcasting to become Editor of *The Times*. A powerful writer himself, he was an even more powerful believer in the importance of the printed word. Even at the peak of the wartime success of BBC radio news, in November 1944, he had declared 'It is no part of the BBC's function to be another newspaper'.[1] To the suggestion that the Corporation might be not so much a newspaper, but an illustrated newspaper at that, Haley was even more strongly opposed. He wrote back to Maurice Gorham 'I doubt whether the implications of a completely visual news bulletin have been fully comprehended'. He continued:

> There is all the difference between a news bulletin and a newsreel. The first is a vital public service charged with responsibilities of all kinds. The second, in essence, is entertainment ... the necessity would arise to subordinate the primary functions of the news to the needs of visual presentation.

He was prepared to allow the development of filmed newsreels '... if they are thought worth developing, so long as they supplement and do not supplant the primary news bulletin'.[2]

So BBC Television, when it resumed transmissions, confined its hard news reporting to a nightly summary of the news, prepared by the radio news division, and read by an unseen announcer, whilst a clock appeared on the screen. The only area in which news in pictures could make any progress was the one which Haley had rather contemptuously accepted, that of newsreels. Fortunately for the BBC – and for television – the cinema newsreel companies refused to renew their pre-war arrangement to allow their material to be shown on the television screen. This led the Corporation to bring into being their own Television Newsreel unit, providing a channel through which that major tributary, film, could flow into the mainstream of television news.

As a news medium, film could claim an ancestry stretching back to pre-wireless days. Newsreels were a key element in the earliest kinematographic shows. Queen Victoria's funeral was filmed, as was the early sequence of Piccadilly Circus packed with horse-drawn omnibuses and hansom cabs, and the occasional motor car, which has been used countless times in later documentaries of the Edwardian era, By 1910 the Parisian Charles Pathé was showing the first regular newsreel in London. It contained among its items a report of a strike, called by factory girls in Camden.

During the next decade a number of small newsreel companies started up and went

---

1   Address to Radio Industries Club, 28 November 1944.
2   Grace Wyndham Goldie, *Facing The Nations – Television and Politics 1936–76*, London: Bodley Head 1977, p. 41.

broke, before in the 1920s the field was left to five main companies which were to endure under highly competitive conditions until television destroyed them one by one.[1]

It has become fashionable among television producers, and even more among media sociologists, to mock the cinema newsreels for their naivety, their strident patriotism, their obeisance to the Royal family, their facetiousness and taste for the banal. Though the commentaries of the reels were often stilted and arch, and their news values narrow, these criticisms are in themselves too narrow. They disregard the aggressive vigour of the coverage, the gusto with which the cameramen undertook their task, the way in which they literally elbowed and shouldered their way into the heart of events to cover the news. No abstract principles of 'news access' then ensured that everyone should be free to film major news events. The most enterprising or the richest newsreel of the moment bought up the big events – and the others set about undermining that exclusivity with enterprise and glee.

The critics too disregard the technical expertise of the newsreel camera teams. Working only with the cumbersome 35mm cameras, which were made doubly cumbersome indoors because they had to be 'bleeped' by great swaddlings to drown the sound of the camera's own motor, they produced again and again material of considerable immediacy and remarkable quality. Few television news pictures have outdone the newsreel coverage of the assassination and of King Alexander of Jugoslavia and the French Premier at Marseilles in 1934, or of the explosion of the airship, *Graf Hindenburg*, in 1936. Nor can coverage, which in due course provided television with *All Our Yesterdays*, a weekly series which ran for years, a series based on the simple but effective formula of looking each week at the newsreels of the same week a decade earlier, have been as scanty or as class-ridden as is claimed. Television news was to owe a great deal to the newsreels. Both the BBC and ITN were to draw into their ranks cameramen, recordists and news organizers from these reels, and their vigour, expertise and cheerful acceptance of the rigours of their craft were to form an invaluable strand in the fabric of television news.

---

1   For an excellent account of this period, see an article by Philip Norman in *The Sunday Times Magazine* of 10 January 1971.

5

Cinema documentaries

The cinema newsreels between the wars came out twice a week and provided the cinema with such hard news as it got. But they were not the only ventures into journalism made by the motion picture industry in the pre-television era. Two other major experiments, one in the United States and the other in Britain, tested the value of the cinema screen as a way of portraying news in depth, as opposed to the smash-and-grab immediacy of the newsreels.

The American experiment grew out of the radio news feature *March of Time* and carried the same title. Henry Luce, the founder of *Time* magazine, set its aim in 1935 as 'pioneering in the possibilities of moving pictures as an instrument of significant journalism'.[1]

March of Time appeared once a month, lasted 20 minutes and usually contained an in-depth report on three or four news stories. Its commentary was declaimed rather than spoken, and concluded with the call 'Time' (pause for effect) Marches On'! It used newsreel material, archive film and, like its radio forbear, an element of re-enactment. Unlike radio, the producers of the film version found it was often better to persuade real people to portray themselves than to engage actors. Producers were soon stage-directing Cabinet members, senators, politicians, labour leaders and hundreds of individuals to repeat for the cameras actions or statements which had made news, to perform as the historian of *Time* magazine has expressed it more effectively than any Hollywood extra'.[2]

> Colonel Francois de la Roque mustered thousands of his fascistic Croix de Feu supporters to a torchlight rally in Chartres for the *March of Time* cameras; Father Coughlin re-enacted the extinguishing of the fiery cross which had once burned on his rectory lawn; Huey Long co-operated in a sequence which turned out to be a devastating satire; General Douglas MacArthur assigned US army units to co-operate with a *March of Time* film unit, and appeared in the same release.[3]

---

1   Robert T. Elson, *Time Inc*, Athanaeum, 1968, p. 230.
2   Elson, *op. cit.*, p. 238.
3   Elson, *op. cit.*, p. 238.

This material was blended with actual newsreel film so that the audience could not, in most cases, distinguish re-enactment from reality – and nor did the producers intend them so to do. The practice was defended on the grounds that 'what mattered was not whether pictorial journalism displayed the facts, but whether, within the conscience of the reporter, it faithfully reflected the facts'.[1] Henry Luce put it more succinctly. When *March of Time* re-enacted events, it must be 'fakery in allegiance to the truth'. Not for him the euphemisms of a later age, with its new jargon of 'dramatized documentaries', or of 'faction, fiction presented as fact'.

March of Time had been regularly shown in cinemas in Britain from 1936 onwards. Unlike *Time* magazine itself, which had at least two British-made imitators on the news stands before the war, the pre-war British cinema did not attempt a home-grown version of the format, and *March of Time* continued to stride its brash way across the screen unchallenged. It was indeed this brashness which was to bring a British rival into the field. Britain's newest film tycoon, J. Arthur Rank, was angered by a *March of Time* report on world shipping which underplayed and distorted the position of the then powerful British merchant fleet. *March of Time* agreed to re-make the film but went ahead with their release of the original version for showing in British cinemas. Rank not only promptly banned it from his two chains of theatres, but also decided then and there to try his hand at establishing a rival series.

The success of British wartime documentaries like *Desert Victory* and *The Road Back*, which portrayed the Western Front from D Day onwards, strengthened this belief in the use of film to portray and examine actuality. Rank's idea took shape in 1946 under the title of *This Modern Age*. After the upheavals usual in any new publishing venture, during which Odhams Press withdrew from participation, it settled down to providing a monthly 20 minute documentary for the screen.

This Modern Age ran for just under five years, until the stringencies of the Korean War killed it. Described as a 'filmic commentary on vital topics', it ranged from compact documentaries on particular countries – part travelogue, part sociological study – to investigations of special problems. Its first issue dealt, for instance, with the post-war housing shortage; the second, entitled Scotland Yard, showed how the Yard tackled a murder case, as part of a discussion about the rising crime wave. It was soon grasping a number of contemporary nettles, with programmes on Palestine (which aroused protests from both Jews and Arabs), education and the future of the arts, under the title 'The British – Are they Artistic'?

It was enthusiastic at the fact that for the first time in history, through the new Arts Council, the State was providing a full £400,000 a year for the arts. Occasionally the programme tackled a news story in depth. The Berlin airlift of 1948, which broke the blockade Stalin had thrown around the city, was one. The East African groundnuts scheme, which was to end the post-war shortage of edible oils, was another – though, alas, the programme did not foresee that the project would be a monumental flop.

This modern age owed nothing in style to *March of Time*, except in one detail. Like the American programme, it finished always with the same phrase – in this case, with the words 'this modern age'. Contriving sentences which ended neatly with these three words, so that the result did not appear contrived, was a minor art. 'This is a programme for us to ponder in *This Modern Age* ...'; 'a choice which faces us all in *This Modern Age* ...'; 'Lancashire time for adventure in *This Modern Age* ...'. They are there in the files to this day, without a single repetition throughout the forty-one issues.

This Modern Age was a quality job. It employed seven camera crews, and was filmed throughout in 35mm. Special music was composed for each edition. There was no question of relying on the gramophone record library. Bruce Belfrage and Bernard Miles were on its panel of commentary speakers. The ratio of film shot to film used was generous, rising in one instance – on the issue of European unity – to some 60,000 feet for a film 18,000 feet in length.

The level of crewing was, by later standards, very economical. On most stories the team consisted only of a cameraman, an assistant cameraman, a sound recordist and a reporter. Directors were seldom used, the cameramen being regarded as a capable of directing themselves. Twenty years later a television company shooting a comparable feature would have had to send a crew of at least seven. Even though they would be working with much smaller 16mm cameras, they would be required, under agreements with the unions, to add an assistant recordist, a director and a production assistant. The likelihood is that they would also take along their own electrician to fix up the lighting, a 'grips' to handle the baggage, and, often, a unit manager to look after the admin. One *This Modern Age* production, dealing with whaling in the in the Antartic, was the work of one lone cameraman. In the heyday of union power such a luxury would have been permitted by the unions – if at all – in areas of high risk, such as the front line in war.

To provide the film expertise for *This Modern Age* J. Arthur Rank, or, to be more exact, John Davis, the Managing Director of the Rank Organization, had appointed as producer Sergei Nolbandov, who had worked in feature films before the war, and had produced documentaries for the Ministry of Information during the war. Nolbandov was a vigorous, warm, concerned and stimulating man whose family had been prominent members of the Jewish community in Odessa before the Bolshevik revolution forced them to emigrate to Britain. He wore the rounded horn rimmed spectacles of the period and combined in this manner a show business flourish with a sudden gravity which suggested the rabbinical scholar. Since 'Sergei' was pronounced 'Sir Gay' this led to frequent misunderstandings by callers on the 'phone, who assumed that he belonged to the ranks of the cinematographical knights, of whom Sir Michael Balcon was the chief examplar.

Flanking Nolbandov as associate producer, with responsibility for the scripts covered by the splendid title of Literary Editor, was the Lancashire novelist and playwright J.L. Hodson. He was a tall, grey, spare man with the gaunt look often left on the faces of those who had survived the trench warfare of Flanders. Jimmy Hodson had done just that, and had come to prominence as author of *Jonathan North*, a novel about that war which had been a best seller on the eve of the Second World War.

This Modern Age had been running for just over two years, and had its 27th programme under way, when I joined to help Hodson with preparing the scripts.

Hodson was a rigid, unhesitating Lancastrian Liberal, in those days when liberalism was synonymous with economic individualism, the archetypal *Manchester Guardian* reader of the C.P. Scott era. The choice of subjects, the treatment of them, and the wording of the commentaries were hammered out between Hodson and Nolbandov with an intensity of argument which I later found equalled only amongst the most temperamental of television producers. Morning after morning we would gather under the Matisse reproductions in Sergei's room in the TMA premises overlooking Savile Row, and the debates about every word of the script would continue as the shadows cast by the big cranes, re-building bombed London, moved like the hand of a sundial across the floor. Yet such was the personal regard and respect that Nolbandov and Hodson had for each other, and so free of rancour was the debate, that they not only sustained this style of production for over four years, but produced admirable programmes into the bargain. They were quite prepared to personalize the argument. 'How can you demand priority for council housing when you have two homes of your own, a flat in London and a cottage in Sussex'? Hodson once declared. Sergei was back so quickly that I suspected that this was a familiar point. 'How many rooms have you got in your house in Wimbledon, James? More than in both my homes put together. Why don't you sub-divide it, and help the housing drive'? Yet these semantics were helpful to me, because often they would resolve their disagreements by leaving me to redraft the script 'in the light of the discussion'. I learnt then that he who writes the final commentary has indeed the last word in every sense in the making of a film.

No reporters appeared in vision. Any interviewing – and not much was included – was done by an unseen questioner. This differentiated the programmes from television news reporting as it developed, where much play was made of showing the man on the spot. But Granada, when they launched *World in Action* in 1963, reverted to the TMA style, and has almost always kept its reporters off the screen.

Nolbandov was a master of the art of catching and holding the audience by swift cutting, and by daring and imaginative juxtaposition of shots. It is a tragedy that he died before he could bring these gifts to bear on the making of television documentaries. His opening shot for 'The British, Are They Artistic'? has lessons for film makers to this day. After the words of the title, set against a background of the National Gallery, in London, had prepared the audience for a highbrow dissertation, up came a sequence showing a celebrated one man busker of the time, who played simultaneously a drum, a cymbal and a mouth organ, to which he added occasional contributions from a cornet. Filmed in a shot which panned down from the facade of the National Gallery to the busker's pitch on the pavement outside, it would have caught the attention of the most indifferent member of a cinema audience.

J. Arthur Rank himself took an interest in the choice of subjects for the programme. Once every three or four months Hodson, Nolbandov and I would walk across from Saville Row to the elegant house in South Street where the great man – and those days he was the great man of the British film industry – had his headquarters. Around a big polished table in a corner of what had been the house's stately drawing room, Rank would discuss past programmes and future plans. At the other end, John Davis, Rank's chief lieutenant and, in due course, his successor, his face gleaming with health after a weekend spent driving a tractor on his Sussex farm, a red carnation invariably in his button-hole, would listen intently, counting the cost. Only a few subjects we were steered away from. One was the British Press. Another, it is interesting to note, was Eire's relations with Britain over Ulster.

Without any prompting from legislators or statutory authorities, the producers of *This Modern Age* from the outset opted for a policy of strict impartiality. 'Impartiality – and again impartiality – that was the aim' said Hodson. This view no doubt owed much to Hodson's own journalistic attitude. But Nolbandov held it equally firmly. I suspect that he knew instinctively what so many Channel 4 producers have since been learning, that one sided programmes tend to be one dimensional – and boring.

This Modern Age could not withstand the slump which hit the cinemas during the early 1950s. Though both the Odeon and Gaumont circuits had shown all editions of it, and though for four successive years it had won both the main British documentary film awards, which in the previous decade had gone exclusively to Walt Disney or *March of Time*, J. Arthur Rank in 1950 decided he must close the programme down. So this bold experiment in film journalism came to an end, and its talented staff dispersed. James Bredin, one of its researchers, went to BBC Television, becoming in due course producer of Aidan Crawley's pioneer current affairs series, *Viewfinder*, and a founder producer-director of ITN. Another researcher, Gerald Hanley, went back to writing best sellers. The chief film editor, Robert Verrall, moved to Alexandra Palace to be chief film editor for BBC News, before also coming to ITN as Bredin's co-producer-director. One of its best cameramen, Ian Grant, was in due course also to join ITN.

This Modern Age would inevitably have gone to the wall once television became established. But during its brief life it met a need. *Persuasion*, a journal of the time, recognized this. 'Applause in the cinema is rare' it wrote in 1948. 'The hypnotized audience comes out of its enchantment without that positive feeling of relief or purification which prompts itself to express its appreciation of stage drama. Nor is it easy to clap a mechanism ... But audiences do, desultorily and briefly, clap *This Modern Age*. These films do not merely 'take them out of themselves', but make them feel *more* themselves'. It was not until television could carry the cinema into every sitting room that film journalism could really come into its own. When that took place it had had a remarkable trail blazer in *This Modern Age*.

6

TV News under way

Television news had not stood still during these years. In the United States a major change had occurred in 1948. When television had got back into its stride after the war, it had been seen primarily as a portrayer of sport. In 1946, 87 per cent of the material broadcast on the two CBS television stations was made up of live transmissions of sport. But in the conventions of the Democratic and Republican parties, held in the summer of 1948 to select the candidates for that autumn's Presidential Election, the broadcasters found an event which lent itself to television as naturally as a game of baseball or of football. That year, too, both parties held their conventions in Philadelphia, readily accessible to the Eastern states, in which the television stations had just been linked by co-axial cable. Though no such link existed with Chicago and Los Angeles, and though there were only 400,000 receivers in the whole of the United States, both NBC and CBS covered the scenes in the convention hall by the hour. The impact of this direct reporting of a news event was remarkable. 'Television that steaming summer brought political conventions to the American people. The conferences on the convention floor, the wild surge of a demonstration, the smoke-filled rooms, the big men and the little men all came alive'.[1] The case for regular news bulletins on television was established. CBS, which had confined their news to a once-weekly broadcast by Douglas Edwards on Sunday evenings, introduced a regular 15 minute news at 7.30pm on weekdays, winning for Edward's immediate fame as television's first regular newscaster. NBC were equally quick into the field.

In 1950 the Korean War added its terrible stimulus to this process. The networks devoted more than 100 hours to live coverage of the United Nations debates on the war – coverage which made the British representative on the Security Council, Sir Gladwyn Jebb, into a star overnight. Filmed coverage of the fighting in Korea added drama and urgency to the nightly news reports, even if these were at first little regarded by those in power.

Yet it remained a minority form of broadcasting. When I went to Washington in December 1950 to report on Mr. Attlee's hasty visit to urge President Truman not to bomb

---

1   CBS: *Television News Reporting*, New York: McGraw Hill Book Company, p. 8.

the bridges over the Yalu River, and so carry the war into China, television had not yet become an essential part of the furniture of the homes of foreign correspondents or even of American newsmen. To watch it you had to peer at a screen placed amid the bottle-lined shelves behind the bar in dimly lit saloons.

The Korean War also brought about one of the most important technical changes ever to occur in television news coverage. The television screen being much smaller than those in the cinema could make use of film which provided less detail, and was of coarser grain than that provided by the 35mm cameras, whose product was magnified many times on the cinema screen. The networks therefore equipped their camera teams for Korea with smaller, more readily handled 16mm cameras. These had come into use by front line cameramen in World War II, and had indeed given the Americans, in colour, two superb pieces of battle coverage. One was of the sea battle of Midway in 1942, which blunted the main Japanese attempt to exploit their opening success at Pearl Harbor, and of which John Ford made a magnificent short film; the other was of the attack of American marines on Tarawa Island in 1943 with vivid close-up shots of the marines charging up the beach. Winston Churchill was so moved by this film that he wanted to make a gift of this British Pacific island then and there to the Americans. But the Australians, and a canny British Foreign Office, stopped him.

Although the Bell and Howell and Auricon 16mm cameras used in Korea had originally been made for amateur photographers, they proved so useful that they quickly became the basic tool of the television news cameraman. In Britain, no less than in the States, they were to play a major role in the establishment of television as a major news source.

Another technical development in 1951 speeded up television news in America. In 1951 links were established from coast to coast across the States, providing a nation-wide hook-up for television news. The development of news in depth and document-aries on the screen was also given a formidable boost in the same year when Edward R. Morrow turned his remarkable talents from radio to television. Together with his producer Fred Friendly he adapted his radio current affairs show, *Hear It Now*, into a television programme, *See It Now*, which rapidly won him even greater prestige in this new field.

In Britain any such swift development was held up by Sir William Haley's continued suspicion of this newcomer to journalism. His insistence upon the news of the day being confined to spoken news, read behind a caption card by an unseen observer, was to endure throughout the first eight years of British television's post-war life. But powerful forces, both technological and personal, steadily mounted to undermine this stance.

Technology found its way forward in the filmed newsreels, whose showing Haley had disdainfully permitted. Under the leadership of Philip Dorte, who came back to the BBC after wartime service with the RAF, and had worked on outside broadcasts and on filming at Alexandra Palace before the war, *Television Newsreel* steadily expanded in scope and in quality. It was 15 minutes in length, approximately double the duration of the average cinema newsreel. On big occasions it was even longer. It had from the outset had a high standard of camera work and of film editing. Dorte saw that the small home screen could allow more intimate coverage than was practicable on the cinema screen. He told his cameramen 'Establish one long shot: get into close-up as soon as possible and stay there'. To this Dorte added commentary writing very different in style to the strident or sentimental tones of the cinema reels. He brought through new young writers, like Richard Cawston and Paul Fox, who took a quieter, more mature, more newsworthy approach to their task. He increased the amount of interviewing carried in the programmes. Where possible this was done on location, in an effort to break away from the embarrassingly stiff pattern of Ministers speaking from behind a desk in an office, their eyes wandering as they tried to pick up words written on a blackboard placed, out of range of the lens, to the side of the camera. He experimented with new techniques. The commentary on the marriage of the Earl of Harewood to Miss Marion Steen was spoken live as the picture was filmed, not added later in the dubbing theatre.[1] *Television Newsreel* was also soon using its nightly showings to scoop the cinema newsreels, flying film in from Doncaster, for instance, to show the St. Leger on the evening of the day on which it was run.

By the end of 1950, BBC Television was showing three newsreel editions a week. In June 1952 this rose to five editions a week, plus a week-end edition which comprised the main stories shown earlier and which had Richard Dimbleby as compere. As in America, the Korean War had stimulated this growth. The war was covered for the BBC by a seasoned cameraman, Ronnie Noble, and a bright newcomer, Cyril Page. Though they worked with the cumbersome 35mm cameras, they managed to secure some natural sound coverage, and made a specialty of interviews with British troops. For these they used a young reporter from the *Exchange Telegraph* called Alan Whicker.

These developments on film in time began to impinge on the area of hard news which Haley had put out of bounds to television. In 1951 Philip Dorte, backed strongly by Cecil McGivern, the adventurous head of BBC television programmes, came back from America convinced that *Television Newsreel* should cover much more hard immediate news. This brought the BBC News Division into the field to protect its rights. Its formidable head, the New Zealander Tahu Hole, sought and got a ruling that the news content of *Television Newsreel* should be the responsibility of the News Division. Michael Balkwill, one of the first recruits to be taken into the radio Newsroom in the 30s, was stationed at Alexandra Palace to execute this task. He quickly showed himself sympathetic to film journalism, but his scope remained very limited. Hole held firmly to the Haley doctrine that the proper place for the day's news was in the spoken bulletin, still read each night from behind a caption card, and set well away from the *Newsreel*.

In the field of current affairs, however, BBC Television was able to make some significant experiments in pictorial journalism. Their enterprising Talks producer, Grace Wyndham Goldie set in train in 1949 a series called *Foreign Correspondent*, which examined issues and surveyed conditions in countries overseas. It was very much on the lines of *This Modern Age*, though less technically sophisticated. They consisted only of silent film coverage, with the commentary read by the reporter as he watched the film on the studio monitor. But when a highly skilled cameraman, Charles de Laeger, teamed up with Chester Wilmot, the brilliant Australian broadcaster who had been a member of the *War Report* team on radio, it soon moved into the sphere of

---

1   John Swift, *Adventure in Vision*, John Lehman 1950, p. 189.

visual reporting, occupying a good deal of news in depth territory which might otherwise have been claimed by the News Division.

With the General Election of 1950, Grace Wyndham Goldie boldly took on a role which was news through and through – the reporting and analysis on television of the results on Election night. Though the actual results were relayed on radio from the News Division, an outside broadcast showed the scenes in Trafalgar Square, then the traditional rally ground on Election Night. There were charts and diagrams, and two Oxford dons analysed and interpreted the results from the studio. For one of them, David Butler, it was to be the beginning of a long career as a television political pundit. The programme was an unmistakable success. 'After 1950 no one was ever to say again that the presentation of the results of General Election had better be left to sound.'[1] In practice on that night of 23 February 1950, the Talks division of BBC Television had taken over one of the key tasks of the News Division – for if ever there is a hard news story, it is the announcement of the decision as to who is going to rule us for the next five years.

These internal rivalries between the BBC News Division, with its deep rooted attachment to sound broadcasting, and the Talks (rapidly being termed 'Current Affairs') department of the BBC Television Service, were a reminder that the technology of broadcasting has its own momentum, helping to bring about change even in the face of resistance. But it was pressure from the outside which was to bring the big leap forward in the use of television for daily journalism, the pressure of the rival television system which was unexpectedly to come into being in the early 1950s.

---

1   Grace Wyndham Goldie *op.cit.* p. 66.

7

Towards competition

It is not often possible to pinpoint a date at which a major change in society gets under way, but in the case of the development of British competitive broadcasting, it is reasonable to take 13 October 1950 as such a day. At two meetings, one public, one private, the scene was set for the breaking of the BBC monopoly, and for the principal actor to cast himself for the part.

The public meeting was the Annual Conference of the Conservative Party at Blackpool, at which a ground floor revolt secured a commitment from a reluctant leadership that the Party would expand housing to a level of 300,000 homes a year. This was to provide a clear aim and a clear slogan for the General Election which came a year later, and was to prove a major factor in carrying the Tories back to power. It was to be this next Conservative Government which, quite unexpectedly, brought into being the commercially financed competitive Independent Television system.

The demand for a figure of 300,000 houses a year took the Party leadership that October morning by surprise. It had been a subdued, indeed sluggish meeting which had debated in the Tower ballroom at Blackpool a motion calling for a 'high priority' for housing. The Korean War was then only four months old and its shadow, bringing the prospect of renewed shortages at home and renewed fighting abroad, seemed to have darkened all hopes of a brighter future. Only one delegate had called for a specific figure to be given as a housing target, and the figure he gave 300,000 a year – seemed quite unrealistic. After all, even Aneurin Bevan, then Labour's Minister responsible for housing, had set a target of only 200,000 houses a year. Yet when Madam Chairman – the Tories in those days made a speciality of having their Conferences presided over by a woman – put the motion there were murmurs from different parts of the hall, and then shouts of 'Three hundred thousand, three hundred thousand'.

From my seat at the Press table I could see clearly the faces of the Tory Shadow Cabinet on the platform. This unexpected demand was clearly not to their liking. Many of them had been Ministers in the war-time Coalition. They knew the strain this new war was throwing on our weary post-war economy. But the Party Chairman, Lord Woolton, left them no escape. He had worked for the past five years to rebuild the Conservatives after their shattering defeat in the 1945 Election. Now, rashly or not, he gave the floor its way. 'This is magnificent!' he exclaimed, once he sensed that the meeting had the bit between its teeth. 'You want the figure of 300,000 put in?'. 'Yes' came back the cries from all over the hall, offset by only an occasional 'No'. One super-optimist called out 'Four hundred thousand'. A few moments later, the building of three hundred thousand homes a year had become Tory policy, and the Party had dealt itself a winning card for the next election. Their victory, though none of us saw it at the time, was to provide the political conditions necessary for the emergence of a rival to the BBC.

But conditions need individuals to exploit them. The other meeting that morning was to produce just the man for that purpose. In London the BBC Board of Governors had met to consider the future of the television service. The outcome of their deliberations was carried on the newspaper placards which faced us as we emerged from the Conference into the garish, pin-tabled corridors of the Blackpool Winter Gardens. 'BBC Chief Resigns' they proclaimed. The columns of the evening papers carried reports that the BBC Governors had passed over the present head of television, Mr. Norman Collins, for a new and more senior post, that of Director of Television, established to reflect the growing role of television. They had opted instead for a radio man, Mr. George Barnes, with the most mandarin of all BBC titles 'The Director of the Spoken Word'.

Norman Collins had promptly resigned, stressing that he did so for policy and not for personal reasons. Equally promptly he had issued a statement protesting against television 'being merged into the colossus of sound broadcasting' and prophesying that 'the future of television does not rest solely with the BBC'. At once he set about the long, and what at that time seemed quite unrealistic task of ending the BBC's sole rights to put out a television service. Other people, other organizations were to join him in that campaign. But Norman Collins, with a decade of successful BBC broadcasting behind him, with his high reputation as a novelist, had a standing and an authority essential for such a campaign to get off the ground. Someone of his stature was needed to counter the charges that those who wanted commercial broadcasting were in it solely for gain. Lord Simon, who was Chairman of the BBC Board which took these decisions, had no doubt on this point. He was later to write 'If we hadn't fired Collins there would be no commercial television now'. And if 'fired' is an inexact word for what happened that morning, the rest of the sentence is surely true.

There was still time, in the 12 months which were to ensue before the General Election, for the BBC's Charter to have been renewed on a basis which confirmed it as the sole broadcasting body in the country. Patrick Gordon Walker, the Minister responsible for broadcasting, pressed for this to be done. But the Prime Minister Clement Attlee had other problems to grapple with. The Korean War in the winter of 1950–51 nearly became a full-scale war with China, and continued to exact its steady toll of British casualities and heavy toll of British resources. At Westminster Labour, with only a majority of six, was kept in power only by ambulances bringing sick members in to vote in 'No Confidence' motions. The Cabinet had been torn apart by the resignations of Aneurin Bevan, Harold Wilson and John Freeman. So when the Election was suddenly called in October 1951 the future of the BBC was still well down the list on the agenda of a harassed Government.

Meanwhile, television was a steadily growing power. Just before the election another two million potential viewers were added to the BBC audience, when a new transmitter at Holme Moss joined Lancashire, Yorkshire, Lincolnshire and parts of North Wales to a transmission area which till then had comprised only London and the Midlands. In the election campaign the real power of the medium became manifest for the first time. To the previous pattern of radio Party political broadcasts was now added the experiment of a series of similar broadcasts on television. It was on a modest scale – one broadcast apiece for the Liberal, Labour and Conservative parties. Yet these attracted much press attention; one incident which arose from them may indeed have been of considerable significance in the consequent struggle about competitive broadcasting.

The Liberals opted for a straightforward television version of the type of broadcast they gave on radio, and had the cameras trained on their elder statesman, Lord Samuel, as he sat at a desk looking directly into the lens. Since Samuel was a good speaker, it was effective enough of its kind, even though at the end he was cut off in mid-sentence. He had at the last moment changed the pattern of words which were to have indicated to the director in the control room that he was near his close.

For the Conservatives, Sir Winston Churchill would have nothing to do with such stunts. He confined himself to the radio, of which he was such a master. Sir Anthony Eden appeared in his stead, wearing a light grey suit and sitting behind a desk across which he was interviewed by Leslie Mitchell. At the time Mitchell was best known for his deep, supple voice, which week after week spoke the commentaries on the *Movietone News* newsreel. He had however introduced the first BBC television programme from Alexandra Palace in 1936, and was to do the same for Independent Television in 1955.

Though this was manifestly a staged interview, with the questions and answers well prepared in advance, the fact that it was live gave it a certain excitement. In the course of it Eden's producers had made use of another visual aid, a graph which illustrated with a steeply rising black line, the way prices had risen in the past five years of Labour rule.

Labour spokesman attacked this device in their broadcast a few nights later in a manner which may well have fuelled, in ways then unforeseen, the drive for commercial television. Christopher Mayhew, who appeared in the Labour programme with Sir Hartley Shawcross, was the one contributor to these election broadcasts very much at home on the screen. He was well-known to the viewers as the anchor man of BBC Television's main current affairs programme, *International Commentary*, on which he had appeared regularly during the 18 months since, at the last election, he had lost his marginal seat. Mayhew proceeded to use the skills and confidence he had acquired to tear to pieces Sir Anthony Eden's use of these graphs. They had, Mayhew said '...been deliberately faked by the Conservative Central Office. They had been distorted, to show the rise to be steeper than was true, by squeezing together the top and bottom of the graph and lengthening out the sides'. Had Mayhew been content to leave matters at that, this might have been brushed aside as a routine piece of electioneering. But he could not resist rubbing in his point in a way which underlined his television background. 'So much for this Conservative chart', he concluded.

It's a fake ... and hats off to television, incidentally the only medium in the world which could have exposed this fake, a medium which I'm sure is going to contribute a lot towards honester policies in this country in the future. And indeed haven't we seen a bit of history tonight. Crippen, you remember, was the first criminal to be caught by wireless; the Conservative Central Office are the first criminals to be caught by television.

To Lord Woolton, Chairman of the Conservative Party, part of whose political stock-in-trade was his utter and obvious probity, these were highly offensive words. Brandished on the screen by a politician turned broadcaster who had been given the chance to gain this expertise by the BBC, they were not likely to commend that institution to this powerful Tory chieftain, who within three months was to be in charge of formulating broadcasting policy for the new Government. Only a few months earlier he had made clear, in a debate in the Lords, his support for a commercial rival to the Corporation. It is not surprising that Lord Woolton was to prove, within the Cabinet, the most forceful – indeed at one stage almost the only – advocate of breaching the BBC monopoly.

The 1951 General Election also marked another advance in television news coverage, but an advance once again chalked up by the Television Service at its new studios in Lime Grove, and not by BBC TV News. As in previous elections, coverage of the campaign was rigorously eschewed by both BBC radio and BBC television, their reporting being confined to information about the movements, but not the words, of party leaders. But on Election Night, Grace Wyndham Goldie's current affairs service once again not only gave the results on the air, but illustrated them with captions on the screen. Three pundits, David Butler, H.G. Nicholas of New College and the economist, Graham Hutton, analysed and discussed the outcome. Outside broadcasts came from four places this time, not just Trafalgar Square. The programme lasted until four in the morning on Election Night, and throughout the next day. Unlike BBC radio, which interspersed its information with 'light music from Jack Sainsbury and his Salon Orchestra and Bernhard Minshin and his Rio Tango Band', television stuck firmly to its task of presenting and analysing the results. Its impact was, however, difficult to evaluate. Even the *News Chronicle*, which had pioneered intelligent film criticism, as distinct from publicity puffs, and which took a keen interest in what was not yet termed 'the media', found no space in which to write about the television coverage of the Election. Nor did *The Times*, *The Daily Telegraph* or the *Manchester Guardian*, which was a pity, as the outcome of the poll was to have a fundamental influence on the future shape of British broadcasting.

Broadcasting policy had played no part in the election campaign, and it came therefore as a surprise when, within a few weeks of the new Parliament assembling, a group of Conservative backbenchers began to press for an end to the BBC monopoly, and for the establishment of a competitive television service, financed by advertising. This set in train two and a half years of passionate debate, in Parliament and throughout the country, which resulted in the Television Act of 1954. This set up the Independent Television Authority, with power to license commercial companies to provide an alternative television service to that offered by the BBC. When Independent Television came on the air in September 1955, the greatest of all stimulants, to news coverage, that of competition, was brought to bear on the development of television news in Britain.

8

The first
TV demagogue

<hr>

Whilst this debate about the future of television was taking place in Britain, across the Atlantic the new medium was giving a formidable example of its power. Day after day in 1953 and in the spring of 1954 it was conveying the spectacle of Senator McCarthy using – and mis-using – his role as Chairman of a Senate Committee to hunt for Communists, and Communist sympathizers, among the ranks of Government employees. It was television news of an immediacy and of high drama, of a kind which has seldom since been equalled. Though the televised public hearings at the time of Watergate provided comparable drama, with the huge added factor that the survival in office of the President of the United States was at stake, they lacked two elements which gave an extraordinary tension to the McCarthy hearings. The Watergate inquiry was conducted fairly, on a basis of scrupulously interpreted law, with the rights of witnesses fully upheld. No such constraints operated with McCarthy. His Committee was a kangaroo court, determined to find its victims guilty. And, guilty or innocent, anyone called to appear before McCarthy was a victim from the moment he or she took the stand. For in the hysteria of the time, to be accused by McCarthy was in itself often enough for someone thereafter to be spurned or isolated or – as often as not – sacked.

Throughout the summer of 1953 the doings of Joseph Raymond McCarthy, the junior Senator from Wisconsin, dominated the headlines and obsessed the dinner tables of the American capital. His use of post of Chairman of the Senate Investigations Sub-Committee to probe, harry and bully those he suspected of Communist sympathies was already making his name a synonym for character assassination and for the use of privileged defamation as a form of terror within a democratic society. Wariness of him, indeed fear of him, permeated Washington like a deadly virus. No one in Government service, no one with any links with Government service, however tenuous, was free of the thought that he might be the next to be affected, the next to be called to the witness stand in the big, high-windowed Committee Room of the New Senate Office Building. There he could be called to account for actions, friendships, thoughts dating back a decade or more, when he might have had contact, however slight or unwitting, with organizations in which Communists were active. Other Committees in Congress had previously sought to identify Communists and their fellow travellers, and in doing so had provided the element of truth upon which McCarthy's fabrications were based. But McCarthy's hearings were the first to be televised. He became the first demagogue of the television age, the first to be made and the first to be broken on the screen.

Through one sultry, humid Washington morning after another I sat in my bedroom at the Mayflower Hotel and watched the cameras depict the hunched, swarthy figure of McCarthy, with deep-set eyes and thinning hair, now in whispered consultations with his young counsel, Cohn and Schine, now swinging round to put a question to the witness in either deceptively soft tones, or with a whipcrack of hostility. Facing him, separated by only a few yards of floor space, would be the man or woman accused of links with Communism, links with the force which the United States was not only up against in the Cold War, but also with whom its troops were then battling in the mountains of Korea. For McCarthy was above all a phenomenon of the Korean War. His wildest accusations found an echo in the minds of people who might otherwise have spurned them, but who listened because they had sons or brothers or husbands risking death or disablement on those bleak, arid Korean mountainsides. McCarthy rose in power with that war. Once it had moved to stalemate and then armistice his power was to be undermined and abruptly destroyed.

But at this stage he seemed invulnerable. Relentlessly the cameras swung from the intent, sneering, grimacing face of the Senator to the tense, sad faces of the accused who, by their very appearance on this stand, were also his victims. Relentlessly the cameras pulled in to peer into eyes strained with sleeplessness or fear or agony of soul, or to the whispering lawyers or the swiftly-writing reporters, or the dark-shirted police guards. A terrible incongruity was added by the summer heat, which gave a festive air as the Senators took off their jackets and sat in their white shirts, whilst sightseers in brightly-patterned summer frocks or seersucker suits came and went from the rows of public seats. Amidst this the accused fought to preserve some shreds of reputation, knowing that their jobs, their careers, were all at risk. They knew that if the Senator succeeded in pinning on them the label of Communist, or Communist sympathiser, they might lose all opportunity of worthwhile employment; they would be shunned by their neighbours, either out of conviction or of fear, and would be lucky if they ended up with the anonymity of filling station attendants, or with a chance to slip abroad to Britain or to Mexico.

All of this was conveyed pitilessly by television into the homes of the friends and neighbours and acquaintances of those being interrogated. On television screens in the corner of rooms where housewives were dusting or preparing the children's lunch the spectacle flickered hour after hour. McCarthy, cool, unhurried, deliberate, his eyes never resting on the witness, but seeming to focus on a point just above his head, was portrayed facing a man who from time to time passed a hand over his sweating face, as if seeking to wake from some fantastic dream. Then the session would end, perhaps with McCarthy refusing – as I heard him once do – to provide information about the charges which would be brought the next day. 'I think we have the right to get information without the witness knowing what to lie about', was his final retort. The image would fade from the screen; the commercials would come up; and the housewife would remember it was time to collect the children from school. It was a drama at once garish and ghoulish.

Television was in the end to destroy this monster which it had helped to create, partly through two *See It Now* programmes by Edward R. Murrow on CBS, partly through the 36 days of televised hearings between the Senator and the Army, in which McCarthy was at last seen for what he was. Yet it must be said that it was not television which led the first fight against Joseph McCarthy, in the days when he was so powerful that even Eisenhower dodged around the issue of whether to support or condemn the Senator. The first early battles were fought by writers like Joseph Wechsler of the *New York Post* and Theodore L. White and by radio commentators like Eric Sevareid. Sevareid had used his nightly news analysis spot on radio to probe and expose the falsity of the Senator's wild claims about subversion, from the time of McCarthy's first outbursts in 1950. By a blend of thorough research, irony and cracker-barrel humour, Sevareid pointed out again and again the Senator's inaccuracies, falsehoods and inconsistencies. It was a very brave act, for few men in broadcasting, or indeed in the press, wanted in those days to tangle too closely with McCarthy.

9

Coronation booster

None of this reached British television screens until in 1954, Aidan Crawley, the BBC's new current affairs commentator, was to reproduce and explain Ed Murrow's celebrated *See It Now* exposé of the Senator. What influenced British television in 1953 was the major event of the year at home – the Coronation of Queen Elizabeth II. This was to stimulate enormously the sale of television sets and to usher in the true television era in Britain. It was also to prove a major television event in the United States, where the three networks each embarked upon elaborate plans to be first on the air with pictures of the crowning and of the state procession through the streets of London. For the two giants who then dominated American network news, CBS and NBC, it was the most important head-on competitive clash since television news had taken pride of place over radio. Each was determined to be first on the air with film of the Coronation ceremony in Westminster Abbey, and each had spent lavish sums on its preparations.

These were the days before satellites, or of wired picture links across the Atlantic; they were also the days before jet passenger aircraft. It was to be a fascinating contest, the outcome of which I watched on the afternoon of Coronation Day with Tor Gjesdal, the Norwegian resistance fighter who had become Head of Information for the United Nations. His splendid office high up in the United Nations skyscraper overlooking the East River was crowded with members of his staff switching from channel to channel on his television set to see who won this extraordinary race.

Video-taping did not then exist. The networks had to rely on tele-recordings, which were filmed versions of the pictures shown on the television screen. CBS set up their own tele-recording cameras in a hut alongside the tarmac at Heathrow. The minute the last can of film had been whipped out of the cameras, it was rushed to a specially chartered Constellation aircraft standing by. Most of its seats had been removed to make room for a film laboratory and cutting room. On the flight across the Atlantic the film was processed and cut, and a commentary added by Ed Murrow. NBC mounted a comparable operation at Shannon Airport in Ireland.

In the event, both networks were scooped by a combined operation of the BBC and the RAF. The BBC had a cameraman, George Rottner, who had a genius for making high quality tele-recordings – a skill he was later to deploy for ITN. Working with Bob Verrall, the film editor who had been at *This Modern Age*, he produced a full length version of the whole Coronation ceremony with Richard Dimbleby's commentary. This was then carried across the Atlantic by an RAF Canberra jet bomber, via Iceland, to Goose Bay in Labrador. There a Canadian fighter plane was ready to take it on to Quebec. It was then ferried to a studio in the heart of Montreal by helicopter. At 4.12pm the pictures were relayed from Montreal, and carried by NBC and by ABC, then much the smallest of the networks.

A quarter of an hour later, CBS was on the air from Boston with its own version, the impact of which was greatly strengthened for American viewers by having Ed Murrow's commentary. The CBS Constellation had also flown to Labrador, where the film had been transhipped on to a Mustang fighter for the final leg to Boston. They were half an hour ahead of NBC's own version. NBC had hoped to outdo all its rivals by flying a copy of the BBC film direct from London by Canberra bomber to Gandar in New-foundland. They had arranged to hitch a ride for this copy on a Canberra due to be flown out for delivery to the Venezuelan air force. But to the immense relief of CBS, this plane had to turn back two hours after leaving London, because of a defective fuel tank.

None of this drama was known to us as we watched in the United Nations skyscraper that summer afternoon in New York. Overshadowing even the excitement of the race between the networks was the magic of this great event appearing on American screens within a few hours of its having happened. At the time, that seemed such a miracle that none of us posed the question as to whether, in our lifetime, it might be possible for a Coronation, or the inauguration of a President, to be viewed simultaneously, as it happened, on both sides of the Atlantic. Yet before another decade had passed, this was to come about, and soon to become commonplace.

Later that day I watched, from the CBS News Studio, the main news bulletin of the evening being transmitted. Formally entitled 'CBS News, with Douglas Edwards', it was known, both in the trade and by the general public, as the Doug Edwards show – the embodiment of that personalization of the news which the BBC so abhorred and dreaded. It represented the most advanced state of the art of television news at that time. Its format, simple enough by later standards of news presentation, was a world away from the BBC's rigid pattern of the news being read by an unseen announcer from behind a caption, and with the day's newsreel carefully segregated at another point in the evening's programming. Even the weatherman at that time was not allowed to appear in vision on the BBC screen. Here Douglas Edwards not merely appeared in vision, but after reading the headlines proceeded to read a commercial for Viceroy ci-garettes, as a picture of their new pack came up on the screen. That jarred, for it seemed to me liable to undermine the authority of the newscaster in delivering the news.

Yet the bulletin which followed had pace and vividness and indeed authority. Though Edwards lacked the presence of a Murrow or a Sevareid, or the quiet authority which was to enable Walter Cronkite, a few years later, to elevate this programme into a national institution, he was a pleasant man, conventionally good looking, with a firm clear voice, and considerable technical skill. He pulled together the small, exactly timed stories and film excerpts and commercials in a way which seemed to me, watching a television news programme from behind the scenes for the first time, nothing short of miraculous. Filmed news reports and interviews were interspersed with the spoken material to illustrate and emphasize the news, with visual material presented because it was news rather than because it was visual. There were interviews with people in the streets of London waiting by their sleeping bags on the pavements along the Royal route, and a recording of a Hyde Park Corner orator denouncing the Monarchy to a barrage of good natured counter arguments. Other film showed French Foreign Legionaires in action in North Vietnam, street interviews about a new Brooklyn roadway, a preview of the night's baseball, and of damage caused by a tornado in the Midwest – an instance of those tornados and whirlwinds and floods were to be such a staple diet of US film coverage for years to come. Stills and diagrams helped out the spoken word where no film was available. It was a pattern of news coverage which was in due course to develop in Britain and Europe, a pattern dictated by the prevailing levels of technological development. It lasted until the development of video recording, and of magnetic stripe sound recording on film carried techniques a stage further.

The setting of this CBS news studio was a reminder of the way in which a commercially financed television service was prepared to devote its resources primarily to what went on to the screen, rather than to the convenience or comfort of the programme makers. The Edwards show went out from a drab, converted former beer hall just off Park Avenue. The next premises of CBS News were not much better. They were on the upper floors of a Manhattan railway station, leading one American media historian to comment that early news production was 'a furtive business, carried out in the recesses of the Grand Central Terminal building, with its Kafka-like corridors, Wagnerian caverns of scenic props, and stories of lost people wandering for years in the gloom'. NBC had grander premises, in its building near Rockefeller Plaza. But it was not until the 1960s that the US networks were all finally housed in glittering skyscrapers which demonstrated their role as major powers in the land.

The Coronation of 1953 was, in the words of the offical historians of the BBC, the time when British television came of age.[1] Fifty six per cent of the population of the United Kingdom – over 20 million people – viewed the ceremony in the Abbey. Since there were at that time only just over two million television sets in people's homes, it was clear that vast numbers of people had watched the broadcast either in the homes of their friends, or in public places like cinemas, public halls and pubs. The outcome was that many people who until then had not owned a set had now tasted what television had to offer, and hurried to get one for themselves. At the same time an appetite was whetted for a second service to flank the BBC – an appetite which powerful forces were only too eager to assuage, as the campaign for a competitive service of commercial television got under way.

---

1   Asa Briggs. *The BBC. The First Fifty Years.* Oxford University Press, 1985, p. 274

10

A clash
of personalities –
and policies

W hilst the battles about the shape of broadcasting were under way, a parallel
struggle had been taking place within the BBC about the handling of news on
television. The ruling late in 1951 that *Television Newsreel* should be seen
as a supply unit, providing the BBC News Division with filmed newsreels, in the way
BBC radio correspondents supplied News Talks with material, left the situation blurred.
Operationally, *Television Newsreel* remained part of the Television Service, not that
of the News Division. Sir William Haley's ruling in 1946 that the news of the day should
not be presented in visual terms, though newsreels could be permitted ('if they are
thought developing') had not been able to dam up the natural force of television as a
form of daily journalism. It had merely diverted some of the hard news covered into the
newsreel, whilst at the same time bringing into being, in the Film Unit, an internal BBC
body which could, and did, resist being taken over by the News Division.

Nor did BBC News at this stage have any clear desire to move fully into television news.
One important reason for this was the attitude of the head of the News Division, Tahu
Hole, a powerful character filling a powerful position. He embodied one aspect of the
Corporation's approach to this revolutionary new form of journalism, just as Grace
Wyndham Goldie embodied another. The clash between the policies, and even more
the practices of these two remarkable figures was to exercise a profound influence on
the development of news and current affairs within the BBC, a development which was
in due course to be carried into the new independent television system and which en-
dures to this day. In this clash the boundary lines between what is news, properly to be
covered by professional journalists, and what is current affairs, a field open to other
talents, were not only to be drawn but were to set like concrete.

Though born in New Zealand, it was in Australia that Hole's career as a newspaperman had been chiefly set. At the outbreak of war he was correspondent in London for newspapers in Sydney and Melbourne, and he came into broadcasting as a member of the BBC's wartime panel of news analysts, interpreting and explaining the news to overseas audiences. (Robert Fraser, then a high official in the Ministry of Information, was another.) These broadcasts won Hole a considerable following, particularly in Australia and New Zealand, where his deep voice and unhurried delivery conveyed authority and reassurance. His entry in *Who's Who* notes, with some pride, that he was regularly attacked by the Nazi propaganda department for his wartime broadcasts and cards listing his activities were found in Gestapo headquarters after the fall of Berlin. This work led him to administrative posts in the Overseas Service, and when in 1948 BBC News was reorganized, he became Editor with authority over all BBC news services except that of the External Service from Bush House.

A very tall man with a long, deeply-lined, bloodhound face, Hole bore himself with an aloof dignity. He had in those days an air of standing apart, as if from his great height he could see dangers and possible disasters which were not apparent to lesser men but which, given the power, he could in his own inscrutable way deal with successfully. He combined charm with an air of brooding gravity, a gravity emphasized by the black Homburg hat which he wore – we all wore hats in those days – a hat favoured not only by statesmen like Anthony Eden, but by pall bearers also.

In his news policy Tahu Hole held rigidly to what he deemed were the basic principles for BBC news – and indeed for all broadcast journalism. Scrupulous accuracy, with facts checked and double checked, should go hand in hand with equally scrupulous impartiality and objectivity. He saw himself as the custodian of the great reputation which the BBC had acquired during the War. Not all his staff, however, agreed with the way he executed this task. 'Determined that this reputation should remain inviolate, he followed a line of hyper-caution', wrote one man who worked in Egton House in those days. 'The bulletins under his direction became colourless, long-winded and dull. Editors seethed with frustration'.[1]

Tahu Hole's determination to conserve that reputation was reflected in his attitude towards the development of television as a news medium, about which he seems to have shared many of Haley's doubts. To one critical eye within the BBC television service it seemed that Hole 'did not understand the technique of television production and appeared reluctant to venture into the presentation of television news, or to welcome the attempts being made in television to produce current affairs programmes'.[2] Haley had sought to reconcile the conflicts between the News Division and Television Services by calling Hole and Collins to a meeting, and telling them that he was sure they could work the problems out together. Had Collins remained head of Television they might well have done so, for the two men were, and remained, close personal friends.[3] But once Collins had departed the demarcation dispute between *Television Newsreel* and the News Division rumbled on, until towards the end of 1953 Tom Hopkinson, the cel-

1   Robert Dougall, *In and Out of the Box*, Collins Harvill. 1973.
2   Grace Wyndham Goldie, p. 145.
3   Norman Collins, in conversation with the author.

ebrated editor of *Picture Post*, was brought in to advise as to how the Corporation should proceed in this field.

But Dorte's Film Unit was not the only part of the Television Service which was competing with the News Division. Chance had thrown up, in the person of Grace Wyndham Goldie, a character quite as strong as Tahu Hole, and one who not only saw the wide horizons stretching ahead of television journalism, but had the drive and talent to move towards them. In her role as Talks Producer she moved swiftly and confidently into the No Man's Land between current affairs and news which the BBC News Division was leaving unoccupied, until she had gathered for the Television Service areas of analysis and interpretation that in radio as well as in the newspapers, were seen as the province of those engaged in the daily coverage of hard news.

Mrs. Goldie followed up her early programme series of *Foreign Correspondent* with a discussion programme on politics, called *In the News*, the original impetus for which had come from Norman Collins. It established a formidable quartet of trenchant debaters in Robert Boothby, Michael Foot, W.J. Brown and A.J.P. Taylor, and soon had the Whips' dovecots at Westminster fluttering madly, since none of the four stemmed from the mainstream of his party. This was followed in July 1952 by the first edition of the interview programme, *Press Conference*. But the most important development came as a result of the defeat, in the 1951 General Election, of the sitting Labour MP for the marginal seat of Buckingham, Aidan Crawley. This was to bring into British current affairs television one of the most effective of screen figures it has ever produced.

Aidan Crawley had had some experience of documentary film making before the war. An old Harrovian, an outstanding cricketer who played for Kent and for the MCC, he became a fighter pilot in the war, was shot down over North Africa, and spent the remaining years of the war in prison camps. He escaped a a number of times, but was recaptured on each occasion. Chamberlain's appeasement policies had turned his thoughts leftwards before the war, and in 1945 he won Buckingham as a Labour candidate, rising to the post of Under Secretary for Aviation in the Attlee Government. He was married to Virginia Cowles, an American who had come to prominence as a foreign correspondent in the 1930s and who had been one of the few women war correspondents during the war. After his defeat in 1951 Crawley and his wife set out on a film making tour of India. He offered a series to BBC Television. With considerable courage – for the Tories were restive at seeing another Labour man come through alongside Mayhew in this new medium – George Barnes, the Director of Television, backed Grace Wyndham Goldie's recommendation that the series be used. Called *India's Challenge*, it was a success and opened the way for a further series from America, in which Crawley brought to British viewers for the first time the spectacle of McCarthy in action. He did this by showing the CBS programme in which Ed Murrow had attacked the Senator, and in interviews of his own.

This cleared the way for Aidan Crawley to present a regular fortnightly series called *Viewfinder*, which had James Bredin as producer. Billed in the *Radio Times* as 'illustrated reports on world affairs', *Viewfinder* did indeed report as well as analyse the news, so carrying the Television Talks department well into the field of foreign reporting. Other regular current affairs programmes were also by now under way. *Panorama* began at the end of 1953 as a topical magazine, but was to move in due course into being a news in depth programme, with as its anchor man Richard Dimbleby, a news man if ever there was one. And *Highlight*, a ten minute nightly studio programme which took a quick glance at some of the issues and people of the day, became a regular feature of early evening viewing. Produced by Donald Baverstock, it was to be one element out of which the famed *Tonight* was later to develop.

This flowering of current affairs on television – for there were other programmes as well, like the highly telegenic *Asian Club*, presented by a dazzling Indian woman journalist – was the outcome not only of Mrs. Goldie's eye for a good programme format, but also for good people both on the screen and behind the screen. Four of her early stars – Mayhew, Crawley, Woodrow Wyatt and John Freeman – were by chance all ex-Labour MP's., but they were also first class television performers. At the same time she recruited a team of young producers, all destined for major roles in the development of television. Michael Peacock came straight into the BBC from the London School of Economics. Geoffrey Johnson Smith was another graduate taken in as a trainee. James Bredin brought his film experience to the role of producer. Donald Baverstock came across from BBC radio. With this team Mrs. Goldie was able not only to make much good television, but to secure for television Talks the task of presenting news in depth which, with radio, had fallen largely to the News Division, in *Radio Newsreel*.

Radio Newsreel had run steadily since July 1940, amplifying and analysing the news of the day. (As chance would have it, I had contributed an item on the French collaborationist Premier, Pierre Laval, to its first edition.) *The Reel*, as it was known within the News Division, provided an important extra outlet for the talents of BBC reporters and specialists. It not only ensured that the news room thought in terms of explaining as well as reporting the news, but also applied the disciplines of daily news coverage to this closely allied field.

The News Division had certainly shown no signs of seeking to occupy this middle ground in television. Its time had been fully taken up, in the early months of 1954, in assuming at last the responsibility for providing a daily service of news in vision. One major obstacle to this had gone with the departure of Sir William Haley to be Editor of *The Times*. The new Director General, Sir Ian Jacob, swiftly made plain that he considered Haley's 1946 directive to be out of date. He had only been in office a few months when he ruled that the daily news summary and the newsreel should be brought together into a single programme, in which the spoken news would be illustrated, where practicable, by still pictures and maps and diagrams, followed by that day's newsreel. Dorte's Film Unit was to pass from the control of the Television Service to that of the News Division, which would move into the Alexandra Palace studios and cutting rooms made available now that the main television output came from Lime Grove.

It was a traumatic moment for those who had built up the *Newsreel*. Two of their best writers, Paul Fox and Richard Cawston, refused to work under the new regime, and remained within the Television Service, each in due course to scale some of its most eminent peaks. Others were later to recall the moment of the take over, when on a spring morning, the huge figure of Tahu Hole led what seemed to be a small army of newsmen from Egton House up the long drive of Alexandra Palace.

The first edition of *News and Newsreel* came on the air on 5 July 1953, a fortnight before the Television Act setting up Independent Television received the Royal assent.

The programme met with a dusty reception. The BBC's own journal, *The Listener*, was in those days, the one periodical which took television criticism seriously. Its critics were of one mind. Margaret Lane on 15 July wrote:

> I suppose the keenest disappointment of the week has been the news service, to which most of us had looked forward, and for which nobody I encountered had a good word. The most it can do in its present stage is to improve our geography, since it does at least offer, in magic lantern style a series of little maps, a pointer and a voice ... The more I see of television news in fact the more I like my newspaper.

A fortnight later Reginald Pound was even more severe. He expressed himself,

> Not surprised to hear of the deprecating clamour which has assailed the ears of Tahu Hole, head of BBC News Service, since he took charge of *News and Newsreel*. I refrain from adding to it in the hope that he is engaged in a process of improvement as well as repentance.

Pound soon returned to the attack.

> *News and Newsreel* evidently will not improve under its present auspices because it cannot. Better return to *Television Newsreel*. The BBC News people have let us down. As Sam Weller said 'Ain't nobody to be whopped for taking this 'ere liberty'.

News and Newsreel had one central flaw. It held to the old principle of having the news read by off-screen voices, from readers who were never seen. The interviewing too, came under *The Listener*'s lash. 'Its interviewers are apt to behave like footmen in the presence of public personages. As for the sharp edged awareness which makes American television news, at its worst as well as at its best, that does not exist'. An interview with Ernest Hemingway was 'a feeble affair, hardly worth mentioning'.

Television therefore moved into 1955, the year which was to see competition on the screen, with BBC Television wide open to attack on its news, the one area in which, given its great radio tradition, it should have been invulnerable.

Setting up ITN

T he Independent Television Authority, which was set up by Parliament to run the
new, commercially funded television service, had as its first Chairman Sir Kenneth Clark, who was then Chairman of the Arts Council and a former Director
of the National Gallery. In later years he was, somewhat reluctantly, to accept a peerage
for his spectacularly successful BBC Television series, *Civilization.* Clark was flanked,
as Director General of the Authority, by Sir Robert Fraser. The son of an Australian
judge, Fraser had been a journalist and potential Labour candidate for Parliament who
had turned administrator during the war, and had become head of the Central Office
of Information.

Fraser devised a regional structure for the new commercial television system, with different programme companies operating in separate regions of the country, with the
four major companies in London, the Midlands and the North each contributing a share
of programmes for a fully networked service. To provide a service of national and international news to this network, the Authority and the main programme companies
agreed that one specialist news company should be set up. This had the advantage for
the companies that the cost of news, which they rightly anticipated could be high, would
be shared amongst them all. For the Authority the plan brought the advantage that the
task imposed on them by the Television Act, of ensuring that all news was presented
with due accuracy and impartiality, could be more effectively discharged if they had only
one news service to scrutinize, instead of several run by the separate companies.

Independent Television News was therefore established in February 1955, as a subsidiary company of the four main networking companies, each of whom would appoint
two directors to the Company's Board. The Director General of the IBA was em-
powered to attend its Board meetings. The executive head and Editor of the Company,
which quickly became known by its initials as ITN, was to be appointed only after consultation with the IBA, and with its prior approval. If that approval was withdrawn, the
Editor would lose his post, and a new Editor would have to be found. The programme
companies were to meet all the costs of the service.

The ITA had no hesitation in approving the first choice of the new News Company for

Fig. 2. Aidan Crawley.

the post of Editor. He was Aidan Crawley, then unquestionably the leading figure in television current affairs, who had had newspaper experience working for Lord Rother-mere's Associated Press Group in the pre-war years.

Crawley was such a valuable catch for the new system that he was able to dictate his terms on two cardinal points. He secured complete editorial freedom in the selection and presentation of the news. Had there been only one proprietor, this might have been more difficult to ensure, but with four companies each was keen to ensure that none or the others should control the news. The second important principle Crawley estab-lished was that the editor should also be the chief executive of the News Company. This was a different pattern from that which applied – and always has applied – in the programme companies, where the man responsible for making the programmes comes under the control of a Managing Director. Since the chief executive of ITN was freed of the heavy burden of selling advertising time, it was practicable for one man to be responsible not only for producing the news programmes, but also for supervising the running of the company as a whole, carrying overall responsibility not only for the editorial staff but also for the engineering, technical, accounting and administrative departments. This gave the company a clear-cut administrative structure, and prevented two power bases developing within it, which could occur in Fleet Street papers if the Editor and Managing Director did not see eye to eye. These two decisions gave the Editor of ITN a degree of editorial and administrative freedom possessed by very few editors in Fleet Street at that time.

From this base Crawley set about revolutionizing television news on the British screen. His central policy was to introduce the newscaster system. Drawing on his experience of American broadcasting, he proposed to replace the BBC's impersonal announcers and news readers with men and women of standing and distinctive personality. To underline the change, he proposed to call them newscasters rather than news readers. They would moreover, not only present the news, but also help to get and prepare it, would share in its selection and evaluation. They would 'go out and work on their own stories and be allowed a considerable say in the formation of the news bulletins'.

For such figures Crawley looked first to Fleet Street. I was then an Assistant Editor on the News Chronicle, but I had done a good deal of freelance work before the cameras for BBC current affairs. Early in the summer of 1955 Crawley invited me to become a newscaster. But I wanted to come into television as an executive, not as a figure before the cameras, and so turned down the offer.

Crawley had no lack of other applicants for the role of newscaster. Actors, journalists, news readers and commentators from BBC radio and television came forward in considerable numbers. Notices put up in the Inns of Court had brought a good crop of barristers. Each group had its drawbacks. Crawley discovered that though the voices of the actors were often melodious and their appearance agreeable, somehow their rendering of the bulletins was hollow. They could not make the news their own. This was in time to be my own experience. Though I tested dozens of actors across the years, Gordon Honeycombe was the only one who had the stuff of newscasting in him – and he had been an actor for only a short time. Lawyers on the other hand Crawley found to be surprisingly good, with a direct incisive approach. Several of them were short-listed. Journalists tended to be nervous and mistrustful of the camera. Some of the applicants from within the BBC might have made the transition from newsreader to newscaster, but ruled themselves out because Crawley sought new faces.

When Crawley announced his team it did not contain any major journalistic figure who seemed fitted to discharge the role of newscaster as Crawley had envisaged. The key man was the Olympic long distance runner, Christopher Chataway, who was then a transport officer for a brewery. Another was an unknown young barrister, Robin Day. A third, interesting figure was Barbara Mandell, a South African engaged to news cast an afternoon bulletin – the first woman to present news on the British screen. The two experienced broadcasters who made up the quartet, David Lloyd James and Ken Keating, were able radio men of little news experience. Faced with the difficulty of recruiting experienced writing or radio journalists, and turning them into television figures, Crawley had, it seemed at the time, resorted to a straight publicity stunt. Chataway had appeared a couple of times on sporting programmes on BBC Television, and had come across there as a figure of charm and force. But how could he, or a barrister with merely limited experience as a radio producer, plus two freelances who had never made it to the top in the BBC, provide the underpinning of true journalistic professionalism which was the secret of Ed Murrow or Eric Sevareid or Charles Collingwood or of the other American giants? What was not then apparent was that both Chataway and Day were instinctive journalists who were, in the intense forcing ground of those early competitive days, rapidly to acquire a true professionalism.

Robin Day's name was there only after a fight. With the heavy horn-rimmed spectacles he wore at the time and with his sharp, aggressive manner, he seemed to some of the companies too great a departure from the element of conventional good looks and matey charm which were associated with the word 'personality'. They could not see Day winning the audience the new system needed. But Crawley was ready if necessary to put his job on the line to have Day in the team. It was not only that he recognized Day's potential. He also wanted to establish that the choice of screen figures was as much part of his editorial prerogative as the selection of news items. He got his way.

Steadily Crawley built up the rest of his team. He had brought across from the BBC James Bredin, who had worked with him on *Viewfinder* and Robert Verrall, who had been in *This Modern Age*. Both became studio directors. Norman Collins made available Philip Dorte as Head of Operations, to organize the technical side. Crawley chose Richard Gould Adams as his Deputy, an Assistant Editor of *The Economist*, an excellent writer with a quiet, scholarly manner. To offset this world of the intellectual weekly, Max Caufield, a former *Daily Express* man, was appointed News Editor. Other sub-editors and reporters were drawn from the BBC newsroom and from Fleet Street. To these more seasoned figures, Crawley, acting on the hunch which marks a good editor, added three comparative unknowns. One was a young actress turned magazine writer, Lynne Reid Banks, who had come to interview him and had taken the opportunity to seek a job. Another was a young researcher at the London School of Economics, George Ffitch. The third was entirely without journalistic experience; he was an Oxford undergraduate, who explained that his ambition was to be a television personality. 'I can't offer you that, but I can make you a television tea-boy', was Crawley's reply, and so Reginald Bosanquet was given the chance to his first steps in broadcasting. They were freer days then. Few editors today have such freedom to gamble on such untested talent.

12

Revolution

A idan Crawley had only six months from the time of taking up his appointment to get his team together, train it, and get on the air. The opening night for Independent Television had been set for 22 September. By the end of August Crawley had gathered most of his editorial staff and Philip Dorte had recruited the film makers and the engineers. Dorte knew the field and was able to secure some of the best men from the BBC and to take his pick of those in the cinema newsreels, where cameramen and film editors alike saw the writing on the wall for their older, slower form of filmed news. For foreign coverage a deal was made with CBS, and a network of freelance string cameramen established in many other countries.

Delays in the delivery of equipment meant that rehearsals could not take place in a studio. Instead mock bulletins were presented in a corner of the newsroom, with the film being projected on to the wall, whilst music and effects were supplied from a gramaphone. The newscaster talked to a wooden stand which represented the camera.

For the four weeks before the opening night the day's news was covered and prepared as if the station was already on the air. Editorial conferences were held, stories selected, camera teams and reporters assigned, and the film shot, cut and scripted as if this were the real thing. On one side of the large newsroom the sub-editors selected and summarized the main news from the agency material coming in over the tape machines, preparing it not for printers but for this strange further element in the news process, the newscasters. Amid this turmoil the newscasters, of whom the chief pair, Chataway and Day, were new, not only to television, but also to journalism, had to find their feet.

'To give some sense of reality, Aidan Crawley assembled the whole of the ITN staff – about a hundred and fifty people – to be an audience. Editorial and production staff, cameramen, technicians, secretaries, dispatch riders, office boys – everybody came crowding in to watch those trial newscasts at fixed times. Five minutes before time all these people would pack the newsroom standing on tables and chairs, waiting for the newscaster to begin. It was a far more unnerving audience than ever the unseen millions were to be'.[1]

---

1   Robin Day, *Television – A Personal Report*. Hutchinson, London, 1961, p. 47.

Fig. 3. Christopher Chataway.

By 8 September, a fortnight before transmission, the first dummy run at 10pm was put out. The format of the bulletins, with film stories interwoven with spoken material for two thirds of the time, followed by a five minute newsreel composed entirely of film, followed the pattern of the *BBC News and Newsreel.*

The components of these early television news programmes still reflected their different origins, with radio techniques dominating the spoken word, with film being seen not only, or even primarily, as a visual expression of the news of the day, but having an added pictorial element in its own right, an element which reflected not only the techniques but the news values of the cinema newsreels. Events whose newsworthiness was nebulous indeed, such as the Jersey Carnival of the Battle of the Flowers, or pancake races on Shrove Tuesday, had won a place in the cinema newsreels not only because of their pictorial value, but because they were predictable, and therefore could be sure of providing a story in a thin news week. Somewhat similar news values had operated in the picture pages of the national press, a technique under which news pictures of the day were not merely scattered throughout the news pages of newspapers, but often brought together on a single page, often the last page of the paper. Even *The Times* followed this practice, thereby enabling it to contain a pictorial element without taking up its sacred space on the news pages with photographs. Indeed *The Times* had a reminder of the power of the visual image when a survey of its readers showed that the picture page was the one to which most readers turned first. These influences were to affect the choice of material for television news for the next two or three years, with such soft pictorial material finding a place until the coverage of hard news in pictures became plentiful, and news values rather than picture values could finally dominate the scene.

The programme companies had opened their schedules with reasonable generosity to the news. There would be an 8½ minute bulletin at midday, except on Saturdays and Sundays. This would be delivered by Barbara Mandell. Another bulletin of similar length would follow at 7.05pm, which Robin Day would put out. The main bulletin would be at 10pm and would last 13½ min, of which the final five minutes would be a newsreel. It was to be Christopher Chataway's programme. At the week-ends the bulletins, broadcast by David Lloyd James and Ken Keating, were shorter, but with the main bulletin still at 10pm.

The threat of this competition had produced changes within the BBC. In June 1955 the title of their main news was changed from *News and Newsreel* to *Television News Bulletin*, which reflected an intention to integrate more closely the different elements of film, words and stills. On 4 September – 18 days before ITN came on the air – the BBC made one further significant change. They brought their newsreaders out from behind the caption cards and placed them before the cameras. For the first time the public were able to attach faces to the voices with which they had so long been familiar. But not names. For though the readers now appeared, they were not identified. That would have smacked too much of personalizing the news. So a series of figures to whom the public were not introduced, appeared night after night in the viewers' sitting rooms, read their pieces and departed un-named. The impact of their reading was also lessened by the refusal of the BBC to allow them to use a teleprompter, so that for much of the time the reader's eyes were on his script rather than on the viewers.

It was to be another fifteen months before the BBC took the further step of naming its newsreaders. This passion for anonymity, which in retrospect seems sheer folly, had at the time quite sensible origins. In radio the BBC had been well served by a practice which stressed that the news was the voice of the Corporation rather than of an individual, however distinguished he might be. During the war, though, the news readers had been named, but this had to be done for reasons of national security rather than of showmanship. 'Here is the news, and this is Alvar Liddell reading it', was a formula adopted to ensure that the public would not be deceived if an enemy penetrated Broadcasting House and used the microphone to send out false messages. But as soon as the war ended the BBC reverted to its old style, ceasing to name the readers, even though their voices were by now as familiar as those of one's own family. But as a journalistic technique in radio this method had advantages not to be sneered at. The measured, strong, warm, yet dispassionate voices conveyed a powerful sense that what you were hearing was true, was a fair and accurate version of the day's events, evaluated and prepared by newsmen who were all the more to be trusted because they too remained anonymous, and because it was presented by someone interested not in influencing you, but in informing you. The technique conveyed a subtle sense that the bulletins were the work of the high priests of a sacred order devoted to assessing, analysing and then finally determining The News, which was then brought forth from the inner recesses of the temple to be proclaimed in its purest form, unsullied on the way by contact with vulgar minds. Even if one were to regard it as a gimmick, it was a highly effective gimmick.

It was also, for radio, a highly efficient method. There were advantages in having a division of labour between those who prepared news bulletins and those who read them. Changes could be debated and made up to the last moment. The reader could concentrate on getting his emphasis right, on getting his timing exact, on having his energies free to give a clear imprint to the bulletin. The method may have obliterated the personality of the individual news reader, but it reinforced the personality of the BBC itself. BBC radio news never lacked personality, but the personality it expressed was the powerful, confident, avuncular, and to a degree, inescapably condescending personality of the Corporation.

Yet this approach could not be transplanted into the new medium. In the glaring light of the studio, under the scrutiny of the camera, the element of mystery which had attached to radio news disappeared. The news came not from a disembodied voice, but from a rather plump or a rather tall man in a dark suit, perhaps with horn-rimmed spectacles on a lined, worried and very human face. Whether news readers were permitted to be personalities or not, they were unmistakably persons. Curiosity was aroused about them, which could only be satisfied when they were not only seen, but named. Willy nilly the BBC, once it was in television, was in the personality game in news as in every other aspect of the medium.

At 10pm on 22 September 1955, the first ITN bulletin went on the air. The last pieces of equipment had been installed only minutes before, and the film went out unrehearsed on the telecine machines which transmitted it. Yet the programme went without a hitch, taking the first step towards establishing the high technical standards which were to be the pride of ITN across the years. A fast moving title sequence which showed film being shot and rushed to the studio, behind a jaunty signature tune, set a note of professionalism allied to informality. Christopher Chataway's newscasting appealed to all but the most cautious critics. His opening words, leading in to a filmed report of the ITV ceremony at the Guildhall, set the tone. 'I hope you don't think we are blowing our own trumpet when we say that today's biggest news is the opening of ITV'. Aidan Crawley promised ITN would 'report the idiosyncrasies – harmful or harmless – of individuals as well as the great news of nations'.

The bulletin which followed covered many of the same stories as did the BBC. Harold Macmillan was filmed addressing a Foreign Press luncheon; the United National General Assembly in New York were seen and heard on CBS film; Marciano and Moore weighed in before their title fight; Eden and Churchill were glimpsed in film underlay to stories of their doings. But in two stories the difference showed through. One was Chataway's presentation of the lightest item of the night, some glamorous shots of the 15 year old Italian Princess Ira von Furstenburg marrying a car magnate in Paris. One critic perceived a twinkle in Chataway's eye which implied 'it is a bit silly for intelligent people like you and me to be interested in the nuptials of a fifteen year old foreign princess. But it is rather absurd fun, isn't it'? The other story was a report from the Old Bailey of the trial of a leading Soho figure accused of stabbing an associate. This was the first time in British broadcasting history that the proceedings – as against the outcome – of a criminal trial had been broadcast.

Peter Black in the *Daily Mail* saw this first ITN bulletin as emphasizing 'as strongly as the commercials the break with the traditional methods of broadcasting set up by the BBC. Christopher Chataway, the four-minute-miler, as composed as though he had been doing the job for years, presented a bulletin which, except for one particular (the Old Bailey report) was much the same as that put out by the BBC ... The style echoed the kind of reporting that journalism has similarly perfected. Chataway was personal, friendly, interested. The news was noticeably quick. But then the whole evening was noticeably quick'. In the *News Chronicle* James Thomas noted that the news was 'sandwiched between an electric razor and a lemon pie. Considering that some of the news department's equipment was installed only during the day the job was slick and professional'.

To get away to a good start in any television series is very important. To have made a successful beginning in charting new routes across the sacred ground of news was doubly important. Over at Broadcasting House, as Sir Hugh Greene was later to recall, the verdict of the BBC news chiefs watching the competition was that they had not much to worry about from such competition. To Greene the reverse was the case. He saw in that first ITN bulletin the beginning of a revolution in news on television which the BBC must match if it was to hold its own.

At seven o'clock the next day it was Robin Day's turn to present his first newscast. Bernard Levin, the television critic of the *Manchester Guardian*, took him severely to task. 'Mr. Day was, to put it mildly, far too eager to please. You cannot sell people the news, as sound radio learnt many years ago, when it banned "tendentious inflection"'. That must have made painful reading for Day, but the striking success of Chataway and the unswerving backing of Crawley were to win for him the breathing space to show what he could do.

13

A change of editors

From the first the ITN service was acclaimed by the critics and liked by the public. It was a bitter blow, therefore, for Crawley when, within a few weeks of the service going on the air, the programme companies, faced by acute financial difficulties, not only limited the funds for ITN but also cut back drastically the time allocated for bulletins. When in December 1955 these pressures reached the form of demands, made in particular by Howard Thomas, the Managing Director of ABC Television, the contractor for weekend programmes in the North and the Midlands, for bulletins to be shortened to a form which would have made them little more than radio in vision, Crawley put in his resignation. Only three months after the new service had come on the air it faced the loss of its first Editor.

This goaded the ITA into action, and they ruled that there must be a minimum of twenty minutes of news a day, and that this must contain a reasonable amount of film. The figure of twenty minutes seems to have emerged in a stormy interview which Aidan Crawley had with Sir Kenneth Clark, and Sir Robert Fraser. In this Crawley, who was unaware of moves which the Director-General had been making behind the scenes to restrain ABC, accused Fraser of never intervening to support ITN. Clark countered by saying that he would insist upon there being a daily minimum of twenty minutes of news. When I asked him some years later what he had based that figure on, he said, 'I plucked it out of the air'. This ruling was to be the Magna Carta of ITN, giving it a secure foundation upon which to build.

Crawley withdrew his resignation, but the companies, finding that the Editor had won this battle, moved against him in the area where they were absolute masters, that of finance. They refused to accept his budget for the required twenty minutes of news, demanding drastic cuts (Crawley's clear recollection is that they wanted the expenditure reduced from £350,000 a year to £200,000 a year) and setting up a sub-committee of the Board to examine the operation and make recommendations about its cost. Crawley saw this as an unwarranted interference with his management, and he and his Deputy, Richard Gould-Adams, resigned. There was uproar in the press, questions in Parliament and demands that the ITA should take over ITN and produce the news itself.

Six weeks later I was appointed Editor and Chief Executive of ITN. I was 45 years old, and was Assistant Editor of the *News Chronicle*, the Liberal broadsheet daily, which in 1960 was to be absorbed by the *Daily Mail*. Though I was a newspaperman, I had done a considerable amount of radio work, and had some experience in both television and film making – both rare qualities among writing journalists in those days.

I approached television as a newspaper man with 15 years of national newspaper work behind me, but also with experience of braodcasting and of filmmaking. I had gained a footing in Fleet Street in 1935 as a reporter on the *News Chronicle*, immediately after I came down from Oxford, where I had been a New Zealand Rhodes Scholar. Eighteen months later the Spanish Civil War provided me with a lucky break. In October 1936 Franco's forces were advancing on Madrid in what seemed an unstoppable fashion. The *News Chronicle* was Franco's least favourite British paper. One of its reporters, Arthur Koestler, had already done a stint in a Burgos jail. It seemed probable that any *News Chronicle* reporter whom the nationalists found in Madrid would at the very least be held under arrest for some time. The paper was reluctant to have one of its stars, like Vernon Bartlett or Philip Jordan, wasted in this way. So they looked around the newsroom for someone more expendable, and their eye fell on me. But Madrid did not fall, and I found myself one of only two Fleet Street men left in the capital, the rest of the press having withdrawn with the Government of Valencia. My reports led the paper day after day, particularly when Franco turned his Italian bombers against its streets, a foretaste of what a second world war might bring.

I returned to find myself with something of a reputation and the material for a book, which was published by Gollancz early in 1937 under the title of *The Defence of Madrid* – books were published in a matter of weeks in those days. This caught the eye of Arthur Christiansen, then at the peak of his fame as Editor of the *Daily Express*. He offered me the post of *Express* correspondent in Vienna, one of the most pleasant newspaper jobs at that period, for your bailiwick covered the varied and lively Balkan countries. I covered the 1938 Anschluss between Austria and Germany, and the Munich crisis from Prague. By 1938 I was promoted to the top *Daily Express* foreign post, that of correspondent in Paris. From there, I covered the start of World War II, moved on to Holland for the invasion scares of the winter of 1939–40 – scares which were more real than we knew at the time – and to Finland for the Russo–Finnish Winter War. From Brussels in 1940 I reported the German invasion of Belgium, spending in the process an uncomfortable half-hour in the company of Hugh Greene, the future Director-General of the BBC, as part of Tournai was bombed to pieces around us. I moved on to Paris to report the fall of France, escaping finally from Bordeaux.

When I got back to an England awaiting invasion, I decided I had had enough of writing about wars, and that it was time to try fighting in them instead. I joined the New Zealand 5th Infantry Brigade, which had been diverted to Britain from the Middle East. My luck held, and I came unscathed through the campaigns of Greece and Crete and the Libyan offensive in 1941, which culminated in the battles of Sidi Resegh.

New Zealand is a small country and one of the advantages of smallness is that it can offer a variety of experience. This certainly came to me in 1942, when the New Zealand Government, having to build its first Diplomatic Service from scratch, took me from the desert, put me back into civilian clothes, and made me First Secretary at their newly-established Legation in Washington. Since the Minister in Washington, Walter Nash, was also the Minister of Finance in New Zealand, the Legation was entrusted to me as Chargéd'Affaires for surprisingly long periods. So it was that I found myself in my early thirties sitting as the representative of a sovereign nation at meetings of the Pacific War Council, headed by President Roosevelt, and at meetings of British Heads of Mission, on occasion chaired by Winston Churchill. I even signed a treaty on behalf of my country, appending my name to the document establishing UNRRA the United Nations Relief and Rehabilitation Agency. We signed in alphabetical order, so I found myself signing for New Zealand just ahead of a young Mr Gromyko of the Soviet Union.

But it seemed right, since I decided I did not wish to remain a diplomat after the war, to see out the remainder of the war as a soldier. In 1944 I went back to the 2nd New Zealand Division at Cassino. In due course I was lucky enough to get back my old job as Chief Intelligence Officer to General Freyberg, under whom i served until VE Day found us in Trieste, one war one but another, the Cold War with Stalin's Russia, only too apparent on the horizon.

When I was demobilised I went back to the *News Chronicle*. I had been promised a post as a senior executive but, in the *Chronicle*'s exasperating way, I was asked to do a stint as a Lobby Correspondent in the interim. It was an interim which lasted eight years, but which brought me something invaluable for my ITN Editorship – a firsthand knowledge not only of British politics, but of British politicians. I came into Westminster with the wave of new men who entered after the 1945 Election, worked with them, grew to know them well, so that when they came to maturity and power in the 1960s and 70s, they were familiar, and mostly friendly figures.

The Lobby had also brought another unforeseen advantage. The firsthand knowledge of politics it gave made me welcome at the BBC as a news analyst – the word 'commentator', with its implication of being an opinionated observer, being rigorously shunned. I quickly realised that one of the basic rules for broadcasting success is that you must not only be able, but available. So I stretched my working day at both ends to do early-morning analyses for Australia and New Zealand, and late-night ones for North America and Canada. I saw more dawns break over Portland Place on more wintry mornings than I like to recall.

In 1949 came my chance to gain experience as a scriptwriter on documentary films. In many long sessions in the *Modern Age* preview theatre I served a concentrated apprenticeship in filmmaking.

In 1954 I moved from the lobby to the post of Assistant Editor. This involved me in supervising the production of the paper at night. I learnt then the hard task not only of deciding the values and significance of stories and pictures, but of carrying your colleagues with you in those decisions. There is an art in guiding the minds of other men and women with strong views of their own, in winning the allegiance and tapping the skills and talents of people who, as often as not, have become journalists because they like doing things their way. There is an added art in doing all this against the clock, with an impatient head printer demanding that the page be closed. It was exhausting work, done into the small hours on a diet of sausage and mash and tea, carried out at unsocial hours, so that you saw your children only at weekends, when you were likely to be half stupefied by fatigue. But it was rewarding work. I came to know the pleasure of holding in your hand a paper fresh from the press with a front page of which you were truly proud, with a clean layout, eye-catching pictures, clear, well-phrased headlines above well-written stories. There was the added pleasure of watching the other papers in later editions switch to your lead story – provided your nerve held, and you had not meanwhile switched to theirs.

Even more importantly, I was able to offer in my application to ITN an ingredient then in very short supply – experience in front of the television cameras. I got my first chance to appear on screen during the tumultuous Labour Party Conference at Morecambe in September 1952, the first since the Bevanites had emerged as a force to be reckoned with. Like virtually all my colleagues in Fleet Street I did not then possess a television set. In the austere post-war years it seemed no more than a luxury gadget, a toy of the rich, the kind of thing which went with the chromium-plated cocktail cabinets in lush sitting rooms in outer suburbia. But on a neighbour's set I had glimpsed an interview programme called *Press Conference*, which the BBC had recently launched, in which three or four journalists questioned someone in the news. When at Morecambe I got a telephone call from Grace Wyndham Goldie, Talks Producer for BBC Television, asking me to go to Manchester to take part in a *Press Conference* interview with Morgan Phillips, Secretary of the Labour Party, I accepted with alacrity.

I drove across from Morecambe with another journalist making one of his first appearances on television – Malcolm Muggeridge. In the Midland Hotel a corner of the ballroom had been curtained off to make a temporary studio. Lights on tall metal stands shone on a table covered with green baize, and on the chair where, at right angles to us, Morgan Phillips was to sit. In the gloom behind the lights appeared a small host of men and women, the technicians and the studio staff. I was relieved to find that the days of yellow grease-paint were over and that our make-up proved to be no more than a dusting of powder. Then we took our places and the lights were fully switched on, plunging us into a glare like that of a Mediterranean terrace. Small lights on the top of the cameras glowed red; the Floor Manager, lines training from his headphones, swung down an arm dramatically to cue the first question, and we were on the air.

As journalism, the programme was scrappy and inadequate. We seemed to get in each other's way, to press none of our points home, to bring out no really new information. I was yet to learn that these are enduring characteristics of interviews conducted by a panel of journalists, as distinct from those where one interviewer can sustain and guide the pressure. But, inexpert though I was, I was also aware that in some definable way the programme was proving viewable. Much of this stemmed from the manner in which Malcolm Muggeridge and television fitted together instantly. He spent no time on the details of the Bevanite struggle. Instead, his voice ringing with mock earnestness, he put this question: 'Tell me, Mr Phillips, suppose I had all the right qualifications for a Labour candidate, how would I go about getting a constituency? Suppose I had been to a good public school and to Balliol, and had a private income, how could I find a seat to contest?'

Morgan Phillips coped skilfully with this bouncer. 'Mr Muggeridge,' he replied, 'you have the advantage of me. I have not been to a public school, or to Balliol, and I do not have a private income. But I do believe in the principles of Socialism – and that is the test by which Labour candidates are selected.'

Then, with astonishing rapidity, it was all over and we were sipping that most satisfying of drinks, the one which follows a programme which has gone well, enabling us to share a moment of euphoria before beginning the long cold drive back to Morecambe.

Other chances to appear on *Press Conference* followed. Among those we interviewed were Aneurin Bevan, Arthur Deakin, the last of the great right-wing leaders of the Transport and General Workers Union, and Archbishop (later Cardinal) Heenan. The Archbishop started off with a marked psychological advantage by telling us, just before we went on the air, that he had spent much of his time in the train from Liverpool praying for us, his interrogators. Under the guidance of a young producer, Huw Wheldon, I joined an equally young lecturer from the London School of Economics, Robert McKenzie, in tackling Sir Godfrey Huggins, the Prime Minister of Rhodesia. He wore a hearing aid, and countered any awkward questions about the colour bar by carefully failing to hear them.

When the national newspapers were off the streets for three weeks in 1955 the BBC gave Donald Baverstock, with whom I had worked in radio, the task of producing a nightly discussion programme on the air. This gave me the chance to learn how to put my own views forward on the air, as well as to seek those of others. It was followed in the autumn by invitations to help edit and to present the BBC's coverage of the Conservative and Labour Coferecnes – the first time both were covered by television cameras. In October I conducted the Budget interviews with the Chancellor of the Exchequer, R.A. Butler, at No. 11 Downing Street, and with Hugh Gaitskell, Leader of the Opposition.

I was fortunate to serve this apprenticeship before the television cameras under the sharp eye of Grace Wyndham Goldie, whose qualities of editorial leadership I rapidly came to respect. She had come into television from sound radio only four years previously. An alert, confident, slightly-built woman with wide-set eyes and a sharply quizzical look, Mrs Goldie's vitality proclaimed her Scottish origins. So too did her outspokenness. Her manner was forthright and direct, verging on the impatient and the imperious, as if there was not a second to waste in pursuing the opportunities opened up by this marvellous new medium.

This capacity to react quickly and clearly to a programme or performance is an essential quality in a television producer. What a performer beforethe camera, or a writer or designer or organiser behind it, wants above all is an evaluation, then and there, of his work. No audience has been within his sight or his hearing to provide a reaction as to how he has done. It is painful to be told, as you emerge from the studio with your adrenalin still racing like a millstrdam, that you did this or that wrong. It is even more painful, however, to meet no reaction, to be left to drive home through the dark streets, uneasy and uncertain about your work, wondering whether to take that silence as approval or disapproval. Grace Wyndham Goldie never left anyone in that sort of uncertainty. She would assess the show with a directness which was unacceptable because it was so manifestly based on a desire to make good television.

One of these experiences before the cameras was etched sharply in my mind. The report of the last day of the Conservative Conference, a Saturday, was scheduled to go out at the peak time of 7.30pm. There had been an exciting atmosphere of show business about the Lime Grove studios that evening. For this occasion I had even been allotted a dressing room. Father Grove of *The Grove Family*, the soap opera of the day, had the room to one side of me; Glyn Daniel of *Animal, Vegetable and Mineral* was on the other side. There was a healthy flow of adrenalin in my veins when I walked across the wide studio floor to take my place at the desk, ready for transmission.

I needed it. For suddenly, alone under the lights in the centre of this huge studio, I realised as never before how much the effectiveness of the next half-hour depended on me, and on me alone. In the unlit half of the studio I could see the gleaming dresses of the girls and the white evening shirts of the men of the cast of the next programme, *Café Continental*. As I waited for the Studio Manager, earphones on head, to swing down his arm to cue me, I was aware of families settling down in their millions across the country in front of their sets, and I felt very much on my own. But the gods were with me and I found myself suddenly relaxed, alert, authoritative. By the time I had finished – and how short that time seemed – I knew that I had done not only a good, but a very good broadcast. As I hurried off the set a murmur of approval arose from the *Café Continental* extras, and the Floor Manager gave me an enthusiastic thumbs-up sign.

That experience was, for me, irreplaceable. For I had learnt, isolated under those lights, the responsibility which falls on any performer who faces the camera alone. Later when I had to deal, not only with newscasters and interviewers, but with restive backroom journalists impatient with the way the front men were handling their copy or their ideas, I drew on the knowledge I had gained that Saturday evening.

14

Seeds to nurture

Only after I had taken on the Editorship of ITN did I learn that Christopher Chataway had resigned at the same time as Crawley, and was due to join BBC Current Affairs at the end of the month. It was a heavy blow. To the public Chataway was ITN. None of the other newscasters had made any comparable impact. With ITV having just opened in the Midlands, and about to open in the North, we would need every scrap of talent in the fight there for audience. There was also the danger, as I knew from Fleet Street, that when one key figure goes, other lesser but still valuable men and women will take alarm and follow.

The only practical course was to build anew around Robin Day, whilst we sought new talent. We were helped by a decision by ATV, who held the contract for weekdays in the Midlands and weekends in London, to close down an arts programme it had mounted on Sunday afternoons – a closure which brought Lew Grade's name into the headlines for the first time. 'High Grade or Lew Grade?' was the title of an article on this development by Tom Driberg in the *New Statesman*. Ludovic Kennedy had been among the programme's presenters, and when it was axed he walked down a couple of floors from ATV's offices in Television House and literally knocked on ITN's door.

Once I began to study the bulletin closely, as a potential producer rather than as a casual viewer, I realised that newscasting was not the only new element which had emerged. There were at least two other significant trends. One was the robust style of interviewing, a complete change from the deferential tone which had characterised much broadcast interviewing in the past. Robin Day had given a striking example of this on the night of Crawley's resignation, when he had interviewed Sir Kenneth Clark. There was no precedent for the head of a great public enterprise being questioned by an employee of one of the organisations he supervised, but Day '...hammered at Sir Kenneth Clark so hard that at one stage a definitely worried look came into Sir Kenneth's eyes'.[1] During Easter the technique of the probing interview had been carried a stage further by another ITN reporter taking his first steps into television, George Ffitch. He and a camera crew had been sent to cover the Communist Party's annual conference – the

---

1   *Evening News*, 14 January 1956.

Fig. 4. ITN pioneers, 1956. Left to right: John Cotter, Ronnie Read, Geoffrey Cox, Arthur Clifford.

first the Party had held since, six weeks earlier, Kruschev had set the pieties of Communism on their head by denouncing the dead Stalin as a traitor to the faith. In the past, had this conference been deemed worthy of coverage at all, it would have been covered by filmed excerpts of the speeches or, more probably, by a spoken report by a reporter. But Ffitch, microphone in hand, stalked up to the Party members waiting to enter the hall and asked them bluntly, 'What do you think of Stalin now?' Nor did he content himself with merely recording their replies. He pressed those who criticised Stalin to say why they had not done so earlier, and challenged the one man who stood up for the dead dictator to justify himself to his comrades. Today it might seem a routine enough line of questioning, though there are few modern reporters who could match Ffitch's swift and clear supplementary questions. At the time it represented a fundamental change, bringing politics alive in a new way, clarifying the issues by sharp edge of the questioning.

The third strand in this early weave, the use of the camera to bring the news direct to the public, had been well illustrated in a story in October 1955 which, routinely treated, would have been commonplace enough. Norman Dodds MP, the Labour member for Deptford, had watched – from his suburban window – Electricity Board workers laying a cable in the street outside. Their low rate of work, and their high rate of consumption of tea, led him to write a letter of protest to *The Times*. The newspapers and radio had reported the news in an orthodox way, with the interviews with Mr Dodds and with the workmen. But ITN set up a camera and microphone in the men's canvas shelter, and persuaded Norman Dodds to argue out his case there with the workmen. The film story opened with a shot of one of the men making tea in a zinc bucket of water boiling over a primus stove. Then, as Maurice Richardson commented in *The Observer*, 'Dodds confronted the tea makers, led by their foreman, Percy Diamond, for five minutes of furious disputation which made any organised free speech programme seem like kiss-in-the-ring. Everybody forgot all about being televised and gave superbly natural performances. Anger tended to obfuscate argument, but viewers got a slice of life'.

In the *Manchester Guardian*, Bernard Levin wrote 'Here at last was pure television, television as it ought to be and yet might be. The people were real and recognisable; there was an intelligent man and a less- intelligent man and a still less intelligent man and a member of Parliament. And the first three were very angry with the last and let him know it in several ways. They argued. They shouted, they banged on the table; and the camera looked at them and at the tea Mr Dodds had accused them of drinking to excess, and at their workaday clothes, while they for their part looked at each other and did not spend their time gawping into the cameras for Aunt Cissie to see. For five minutes the screen looked in on life and came alive with an immediacy and a degree of reality that for the rest of the week it never even suggested.'

The Easter bulletins had contained another example of the way the cameras could not only bring news directly to the public, but could portray it in human terms – for most news is, after all, about people. One of the hardiest of Fleet Street's hardy annuals had long been the regular crop of spring weddings, as couples sought to gain the tax advantage of marrying before the financial year came to an end. In the papers this tended to produce an array of fashionable brides walking on their bridegroom's arm from St Margaret's at Westminster, or from St George's, Hanover Square, or at least from a pretty church in Esher or Sunningdale. But Arthur Clifford changed the scene to a church in Hackney, where Lynne Reid Banks interviewed a series of newly-married East-enders on the church steps. Cheerfulness and Cockney gusto poured from them in accents which would have made Janet Street Porter sound like an elocution teacher.

One bride's cry, 'Ere, can't you wait even a few minutes', as her husband responded with vigour to the cameraman's suggestion that a kiss would add to the picture, had echoes of the Edwardian music hall in its heyday.

Class barriers were more marked then, and this report brought onto the screen people whose day to day lives had not often in the past been though worth reflecting on the air. It gave a new meaning to the journalistic concept of the human interest story. In Fleet Street the term meant stories which were interesting because they were of the unusual, the abnormal, the exceptional. But here the cameras were making fascinating viewing out of ordinary everyday life, bestriding the gap between the classes – and making compulsive television out of it. Whether the story was hard news or not did not seem to matter. It was life, conveyed by the camera with honesty and without condescension, adding interest and humanity to the bulletins in a way unique to this new journalistic medium.

15

The trail blazers

T he editorial staff of ITN in May 1956 was, to say the least, compact. In addition to Robin Day and Ludovic Kennedy, our total editorial strength was 19 – a total today well over the hundred mark. We had two news editors, three reporters, eight sub-editors and six script writers. This would have been far too small a team to produce three bulletins a day on week-days and two at week-ends, but for two factors. The first was that they were all able men and women, some very able, one or two brilliant. The second was that they were all prepared to do any editorial job which was called for. Script writers would readily turn their hands from writing commentary to subbing stories or to voicing commentaries. On occasion they would rush out from the office to do an emergency interview. The sub-editors, for their part, frequently acted as reporters, whilst reporters would take over as relief news editors or do a stint on the subs desk. And all were prepared to work long hours, forego their days off, even postpone their holidays, to keep the service going. This was possible only because of the attitude of the National Union of Journalists, then under the commonsense leadership of Percy Jarret. He knew that if ITN was to survive, its staff must not stand on demarcation lines, few of which were in any event those days drawn with any sharpness. The later rigidities of union practice would have stifled ITN at birth.

The dominant figure in the newsroom was undoubtedly Arthur Clifford, who had held the post of News Editor since the previous November. He was a big man in every way, well over six feet tall with a massive Viking head, a thick shock of hair, alert eyes and the bearing of a boxer – which indeed he had been in his youth.

Clifford was an East Ender who had come into journalism by the traditional route for those without influence or higher education, as a tea boy and copy messenger for United Press, the American owned news agency. He graduated to sub-editing, and after war service in the Coldstream Guards won a job in the BBC Radio newsroom. He came through quickly to be a chief sub-editor, and was one of the team sent off to Alexandra Palace in 1953 to staff the first television news bulletins.

Clifford saw the great possibilities of this new medium, and chafed at the restraints imposed on its development by the BBC news hierarchy. So he took the gamble of joining this new enterprise. Crawley made him Assistant News Editor. When the News Editor, Max Caufield, parted company with ITN early in 1956, Clifford was given the responsibility for selecting the news to be covered, and devising the ways by which that coverage could be madc to fit this new visual medium. This chance he proceeded to take with both of his large confident hands, wading into the problems of each day's coverage with the same vigour with which he had come out of his corner in his boxing days in Simpson's gymnasium in the Mile End Road.

Arthur Clifford had not only a clear idea of what he wanted to do, but also the force of personality to achieve it – a force all the more remarkable because under his tough exterior he was in fact a highly sensitive man. He wanted to use the cameras to bring the news more directly to the public, to let them hear and see for themselves the events and people who made news. Ideas welled up in him day after day, not just ideas of what to cover, but of fresh and original ways of covering it. He had a gift for approaching news stories not head on, in a way which would give no depth or perspective, but from an angle which could bring out the story's light and shade. When the holders of the VC gathered in London for the first time since the war, Clifford did not take the obvious step of asking them how they won their medals, of looking back to the war. Instead he sought them out and interviewed them at their new peacetime tasks, the farmer VC back at his plough, the sailor VC in his new role as a naval frogman, the shoe salesman VC back in his shop. When the Minister of Transport wanted to appeal on the eve of a Bank Holiday for motorists to drive more slowly, Clifford avoided the hackneyed approach of an appeal from behind the Minister's desk. Instead he had him interviewed on the margin of the North Circular Road, with the holiday traffic thundering behind him. When Churchill's birthday came round he did not seek the birthday tributes of the great. Instead he sent a camera team out into the streets to find people with their own wartime memory of Churchill – the former Home Guard sentry who had been on duty when he visited coastal defences at Brighton; the present day tobacconist who, as an air raid warden, had walked with him through the bombed streets of the East End; the woman factory worker who remembered him in her blacked out munitions factory.

The man who had the task of translating Clifford's ideas into film was the Film Manager, John Cotter, a sturdy, muscular figure, cheerful and indomitable. He had been an army cameraman in World War II, covering the Italian campaign. Son of a famous newsreel cameraman, he was imbued with the belief that nothing should stop a camerateam in search of a story, or a film organiser in paying one on.

On the News Desk, Clifford was flanked by John Hartley, who had given up the post of Chief Reporter on *The Times* to join ITN.

ITN's domains were as compact as its staff. On the first floor they were dominated by the newsroom, a big open-plan room, well lit by day by windows on two sides, and at night by strong but warm strip lighting. From the windows the bustle of Kingsway could be seen, its shoppers and office workers a useful constant reminder of the people by whom our work would ultimately be judged. The film and technical areas had, as a precaution against fire, been set apart on the eighth floor at the top of the building. It was there that one became aware that this was indeed a new form of journalism. The telecine room, where film was transformed from a series of images conveyed by light to images conveyed by electronic impulse was, with its gleaming equipment and its white coated operators, like something out of the as yet unrealized space age. The Debrie film processing machine was equally impressive as hundreds of yards of film and of leaders, looped over spools and bobbins in a big glass tank, ran at top speed in spectacular fashion as material was developed, fixed, washed and dried.

The studio itself, the holy of holies, was disappointingly small, with a low ceiling only twelve feet above floor level, which posed severe problems for the lighting experts. Three cumbersome cameras, their grey lens shafts thrust out like the barrels of small cannon, and an overhead microphone boom like a small crane crowded in on the news-caster. During rehearsals the adjoining control room would be a babble of sound, as voices crackled in from other technical areas with queries, or warnings of late film or of incomplete scripts; as the engineer talked to his fellows up and down the network; as the director gave instructions over his intercom to the floor manager or the cameramen. It seemed impossible that any programme could emerge from such chaos. But as the long second hand on the clock ticked down towards 10.45pm, and the PA began her count down Ten seconds to transmission ... nine ... eight, order would suddenly reign. The director would call 'Take two, cue grams', the ITN title would show on the monitor, and our theme music, *Non Stop*, would begin its quick course, to be followed by yet one more curt order into the intercom 'Take three – cue Robin' and one more bulletin would be on the air.

These were cramped quarters which we were soon to outgrow, but in those early years they served us well – very well. They had the great advantage of being centrally placed, so that our film and reporting teams could move swiftly into the main news producing areas of the City, Westminster, the West End. Political leaders, visitors to London, other people in the news would come readily to a handy spot like Kingsway, whereas they might hesitate before making the journey to the BBC at Alexandra Palace. Denied scope in the studio we had, moreover, to get out into the streets and the factories and the countryside, where the news was happening. We were inoculated against that vice which can beset the makers of television programmes, the belief that reality is what happens within their enclosed studio walls.

16

Opening sequences

My first week at ITN was one in which we were accused of faking the news, suspected of running a blue film show, and in which a cameraman was eaten by a crocodile. Whatever other limitations this new medium might have, monotony was not one of them.

Indeed the first story I had to grapple with on 7 May 1956, when I took over the Editorship, might have been specially designed to embarrass the news service of a commercial broadcasting channel. At the morning editorial conference, when the half-dozen department heads and senior production staff gathered, clipboards on knee, around my desk in a corner of the big first floor room which served as Editor's Office, Board Room and Conference Room, the top story on the news list was a statement the Minister of Health was to make that afternoon about possible links between smoking and cancer. It was the first of such inquiries into an issue which had been highlighted by the death in 1952 of King George VI from lung cancer. Two years earlier, in the Committee stage of the Television Bill, this topic had been cited as the kind of news which a commercially financed broadcasting system could not be trusted to handle fairly. One of the most vociferous opponents of the Bill, Sir Leslie Plummer, the Labour MP for Deptford (later to be a Director of Granada Television) had argued that the programme companies should not be allowed to provide a news service, which should be done by the ITA. He had posed the question of whether an ITV news producer would organise a programme announcing or discussing whether smoking has any direct relation to cancer of the lung. 'Of course not,' was his assessment.

Though cigarette advertisers were amongst the few supporting ITV in those lean days, the Minister's statement posed a less difficult problem than at first appeared. It was unquestionably news, and if we did not give the news ITN would have no future. I knew, too, from my experience in Fleet Street that, quite apart from any question of journalistic ethics, there is no practical point in trying to appease advertisers by trimming your editorial copy. What they want is not nice words in the editorial columns – though they will take any on offer – but large numbers of readers or viewers for their advertisements. Only once had the advertising department of the *News Chronicle* sought to influence my presentation of news. That had come when, after seeing an early edition, they had asked if there might not be another place on the front page for a story about a daring bank robbery than immediately alongside an advertisement for a High Street bank headed 'Safe as a Bank'. So I had no hesitation in ruling that we would carry the Minister's statement, together with any comments the tobacco industry or the doctors might offer.

The film list for the day made clear at a glance on what a tight financial rein ITN was held. Only two sound film units were on duty, and the main sound-on-film story on offer was an interview with the Governor of Kenya, Sir Evelyn Baring, about a visit Princess Margaret was due to make to East Africa, which would be her first major public activity since the breakdown of her romance with Group Captain Townsend. Other items showed only too clearly their cinema newsreel parentage – a trade fair in Paris; the annual blessing of the tulip fields in Lincolnshire as the crop came into bloom; the opening of the tomb of an Egyptian princess outside Cairo. It was hardly a list which offered much promise of turning news into pictures.

This thin diet was, however, to be spiced by a dash of controversy involving ITN itself. The editorial conference had been over only a few minutes when the News Editor, Arthur Clifford, was back in the room, accompanied by a tense-faced young man called Ronald Balaam. He was a free-lance scriptwriter who also worked as a schoolteacher, and had been conveniently available when the newsroom needed to interview a teacher about reports of indiscipline in London schools. Balaam had confirmed that there had been considerable indiscipline at the East London school where he had taught. The interview had been supplemented by shots of children pouring out of the front door and down the steps of the school, and by a tumultuous interview with a bobbing, laughing crowd of them outside, in which they all declared themselves firmly in favour of keeping the cane. Although Balaam had talked with his back to the camera, he had been recognised, and the LCC Education Committee had now informed him that he was struck off their list of relief teachers.

Today a great clanking machinery of industrial tribunals and redundancy laws and union consultants and rights of appeal would come into action. The one thing we could do was allow Balaam to defend himself on the air, and so we arranged for him to be interviewed by Robin Day on the late bulletin. I had little doubt that his story would stand up, for only a few months earlier I had edited for the *News Chronicle* a series of articles about the growing indiscipline in inner London secondary modern schools.

Despite the shortage of film we had adequate early bulletins and a surprisingly strong bulletin for the main evening news, which in those days went out at 10.45pm. The trade fair and the tulip ceremony provided some pleasant if not very newsworthy pictures. The interview with Sir Evelyn Baring about Princess Margaret's tour was on a topic of keen interest. Another interview with the world cruiserweight champion, Archie Moore, rated as news to a public not yet sated with the sight and sound of sporting personalities. We had an action story close at hand, with Waterloo Station packed with commuters held up by a signal failure. A mass meeting of BOAC workers, protesting against the appointment of a part-timer as Chairman of the Corporation, provided first-hand coverage of an industrial dispute, still then a relative rarity on film. A Miners' Gala in Edinburgh was all the more pictorial for being held in driving rain and howling winds. Agency film from Vienna of Soviet and American-made tanks appearing side by side in the newly equipped army of neutral Austria was of interest to a Britain filled with wartime veterans. Motor cycles swerving and skidding in a speedway contest – one of the few sports we were then free to cover – were reasonably exciting to watch.

What made the bulletin, however, was the strength of the newscasting. Robin Day was due to present the programme, having hurried back to Kingsway after hearing in the Commons the statement on smoking and cancer. The draft of the story prepared by the sub-editor had been straightforward. 'The Minister of Health, Mr Turton, told the Commons this afternoon that so far two known cancer-producing agents had been identified in tobacco smoke, but he added that it has not been proved that smoking directly causes lung cancer,' was its opening sentence. I was reading this when there was a knock at the door and Robin Day's intent face peered round at me. Could he discuss a point of presentation? Did I think he would be right to personalise the cancer story so as to make it read 'After lunch today I stubbed out my cigarette and went into the House of Commons Press Gallery to hear – with some apprehension – what the Minister of Health had to say about smoking and cancer.'?

It was for me the best moment of a long day. This was exactly the popular yet informed touch which I saw as the key to the presentation of news. When the bulletin came on the air this opening gave it a directness which at once caught attention. The interview with Ronald Balaam provided a dramatic – indeed a melodramatic – close. His eyes glaring with strain and nervousness, Balaam swung round to the camera and declared, 'I told the truth.' It was news in a direct and personalised form which no other form of journalism could have provided.

We had not heard the last of the Balaam affair. The Chairman of the LCC Education Committee retorted that the film sequences showing 'an unruly mob at a London school' had been 'arranged for the television cameras'. Newspaper placards outside Television House proclaimed 'Mob Scenes Staged by ITV' and 'Teacher Sacked after TV Show was TV Scriptwriter'. The LCC told the press that 'a group of boys were induced, in breach of school rules, to run down a staircase normally reserved for fire escape purposes to give the effect of an undisciplined and unruly mob'. Today such complaints would either be shrugged off by the broadcaster, or would make their way through the series of committees and tribunals established to deal with allegations of media misdoings. For the young news service of ITN in 1956 they were dangerous. We had so far been the one part of Independent Television free from the scorn and antagonism heaped on the system by a hostile press. If our product became suspect it would take weeks to repair the damage. Fortunately I knew the subject, and was sure the ITN report was firmly based. So we stood our ground, but gave the complaints full rein on the air, re-running our film to enable viewers to judge for themselves. We also gave Balaam a further chance to confirm his story, which the film librarian duly recorded as 'Live Spot. Ronald Balaam standing by the truth again'. But we could do no more to protect him for his outspokenness. The LCC stood adamantly by their ban, and we had no post we could offer him. A month later he was working as a night porter at the Royal Free Hospital.

The Balaam case had taken up so much of my time that I was not greatly pleased when the next morning another distraction arose. It came in a telephone call from Captain Brownrigg, the former naval officer who was General Manager of Association Rediffusion and Chairman of ITN. His office was just three floors above mine in Television House. His tone was severe. After a brief enquiry about how I was settling in, he asked, 'Are you aware that your film editors are using your preview theatre at lunch time for blue film shows?' I was not so aware. 'I think you will find it is so,' he continued, 'and I look to you to put a stop to it.'

It was certainly not a problem I relished. I hardly knew where the preview theatre was. Was I to go up quietly at lunchtime, fling open the door and catch them in the act? For all I knew in the film world such activities might be commonplace, might be regarded as a custom and practice to which a blind eye was turned. It was not the kind of issue on which I wanted my first contact with the film editors to be based.

I consulted Norman Dickson, the big Scot who was the General Manager of ITN. He dealt with it promptly. That lunchtime he went up to the theatre and found just such a film show in progress – being run not by our film editors but by a group from Brownrigg's own staff on Associated Rediffusion. Dickson warned them off in no uncertain terms. I had some pleasure in passing that information on to Captain Brownrigg.

The third event, that of the missing cameraman, was so macabre and so extraordinary that at first I simply disbelieved it. Among the few pieces of foreign film expected my first day was a report, due to be filmed by a free-lance stringer cameraman working from Nairobi, of a drive by British troops in Kenya against the Mau Mau rebels. On the first evening the Assistant Film Manager, Freddie Partington, told the conference that there were difficulties with the film and it would not arrive that day. Though Partington had come to ITN from Paramount News, he bore no resemblance to the aggressive, bustling executives one associated with the camera newsreels. He was a quiet, rather diffident man, with prematurely grey hair, who might have been a librarian or a backroom scientist. That this unassuming manner hid great determination and shrewdness was something which I was to learn only over the months ahead. When the next evening the film had still not arrived I showed some impatience. On the third evening Partington met my enquiries with the words, 'Well, there are some difficulties. I don't think we are going to get the film after all.' I sensed inefficiency, and asked with some asperity, 'What sort of difficulties?'

Partington looked disconcerted, and blushed with anxiety, 'Well,' he said nervously, 'great difficulties. Unusual difficulties.' This exasperated me. 'What are they?' I insisted. 'What are you holding back?' Partington took a deep breath. 'Well, the fact is' he said, 'the cameraman has been eaten by a crocodile.'

My first reaction was that I was being subjected to some form of sardonic joke, some test which the film industry applied to newcomers. But indeed Partington was telling no more than the truth. The boat in which the cameraman, an East Indian Kenyan, had been crossing a flooded river had overturned. He had been swept away, and had either been drowned or, more probably, had fallen victim to the crocodiles which infested the river. Certainly his body was never recovered. Of the many strange events which occurred within ITN in those early years, this was amongst the strangest, as well as the most tragic.

17

See it happen

The most important development which television brought to journalism was the use of the motion picture to record and convey daily news. Newscasting, and the power of personality in presenting the news was the element which first attracted public attention, and which ITN had stressed as a way of distinguishing its product from that of the BBC. The probing interview was a further technique which television was to bring about in Britain. But the one development which was unique to television was its ability, by use of the camera, to capture and present a picture of news as it had happened, or indeed sometimes, through live broadcast coverage, at the very moment it was happening. 'See It Happen on ITN' was the slogan with which ITN franked its letters in those early days, and was an effective summation of the most powerful new factor which this new medium was to bring into journalism.

The film camera was the instrument by which this new journalism operated, and film coverage was therefore the area which I was most eager to develop when I took over the editorship of ITN. I quickly found that in that spring of 1956 hard news on film was still relatively scarce. That was particularly the case with ITN, where scarcity of funds had cut film coverage back to a minimum. But it was also the case, for technical reasons, with the American networks, and the richer BBC. On ITN during February 1956 film had been available on only four occasions to illustrate the lead story. Three of these had been no more than brief underlays, silent film brought up as background to the news-caster's words. For many important news stories the cameras had not been on the scene. We had had virtually no film of the mounting guerrilla war in Cyprus, where Britain faced an onslaught from the Eoka forces claiming union with Greece; of the continued search and destroy operations against other guerrillas in the jungles of Malaysia; of operations against the Mau Mau insurgents in Kenya.

It did not take long to discover the reason. We lacked hard news film because we lacked hard cash. Film coverage was where the shortage of funds bore hardest on ITN. The clamp on expenditure meant that the excellent network of freelance stringer camer-amen which the film manager John Cotter had set up at home and overseas went largely unused. The budget for the year until September 1956 had provided only

£20,000 for all stringer film coverage. This permitted the commissioning of only two stringer stories a day – and by May most of it had already been spent.

The bulk of our foreign news coverage had to come from the package of newsfilm which reached us from CBS in New York six days a week. This was not an agency service in the fullest sense, offering coverage of all the main stories, but consisted of copies of those stories CBS had shot for their own programmes. This made it not only American-orientated, but frequently meant that stories were some days behind the news. Coverage from Europe and the Far East had to go to New York, to be processed and edited there, before it could make its way back to us. We were still in the era of piston-engined aircraft, and the Atlantic crossing took at least twelve hours. At best film of events on the Eastern seaboard of the States could reach us for showing the next day. Material from other parts of the American continent and from the rest of the world would not be available in under 48 hours. Nevertheless the CBS package was invaluable, for their television newsroom matched the high standards set by their radio news. And we could do something to supplement their service by gathering in, at low rates, material from the European cinema newsreels and, occasionally, from the newsrooms which the European television stations were in the process of establishing. This material was liable to lag after the event, but with skill it could be freshened up and given an impression of immediacy. A news report that Tito, on his first official visit to France, had visited Lille could sustain film of his cavalcade, escorted by French police on motorcycles, passing down the Champs Elysee in Paris, the day before. A shot of troops on routine patrol on Cyprus could help to illustrate a report of the latest bombing or shooting. Above all we could use our own staff cameramen to fill the gap, particularly within the United Kingdom. We had eleven of them, five equipped with sound cameras, the other six with cameras which could shoot only silent material.

Their key instrument was the Aurican Cine-Voice sound camera, a California built instrument which recorded pictures and sound on 16mm film. It looked amateurishly small for its task, despite its triple lens plate, and had indeed originated as an amateur camera. The American networks, facing the need for a lightweight camera with which to cover the Korean war in 1950, had bought Auricons off the shop shelves, modifying them only with a larger magazine capable of providing ten minutes of running time. Yet the Cine-Voice was to become the great work horse of the first twenty years of television news, as durable and as widely used as, in the field of aviation, the Dakota had been in its time. Indoors, and for set piece occasions, the Cine-Voice was used on a tripod. Outdoors it could be humped on one shoulder by the cameraman, for covering swift moving action. The sound recordist, whose apparatus was linked to the camera by a heavy insulated cable, could move with the cameraman to keep near the heart of the action – and they learnt to make such moves with remarkable swiftness and co-ordination.

For filming without sound we used the German built Arriflex, an improved version of the cameras with which the German Army cameramen had provided Dr Goebbels with so much masterly frontline material. We called the six cameramen who used the Arriflex 'silent cameramen': the BBC and the programme companies called their comparable operators 'mute cameramen' – a nice distinction for linguistic experts to ponder.

The problem with our camera crews in 1956 lay not with their equipment, which was then the best which money could buy, but with their numbers. By the time we had made allowance for holidays and sickness, and by the time we had rostered them to work a long day from early morning until nine at night, across a seven day week, we could count on only two or three sound crews being available each day, plus up to three silent cameramen. To back up our crews only one film agency then existed in the United Kingdom, that of the Brennard brothers who covered, in silent film only, the comings and goings of the newsworthy through London airport. In Manchester one freelance cameraman possessed his own Cine-Voice, and we could call on other silent freelances at points across the British Isles. These included a chemist at Lerwick in the Shetlands who was always ready to hand his shop over to his assistant and dash out to film a shipwreck or a storm – all that those as yet undisturbed islands provided in the way of news.

But home stringer coverage, like that of foreign stringers, cost money. So too did the use of our own crews. We could not roam far on the £6,000 a year which represented our total budget for travel, even if petrol cost only the equivalent of 20p a gallon. I quickly learnt that one of the key decisions of the day was how best to deploy the cameramen, and above all the sound crews. It called not only for flair and decisiveness, but also for a mixture of diplomacy and ruthlessness. Crews and reporters had to be hurried and harried from one story to another. Often after a team had driven many miles, and had arranged an interview or a filming session at considerable inconvenience to all concerned, they would be told, when they checked in from a nearby telephone kiosk, to scrap the whole affair and hurry off to some more urgent story.

Despite all these limitations, we steadily increased the amount of hard news coverage in the bulletins, above all by using the silent cameramen as reporters on action stories, relying on their pictures rather than on a reporter's words. They relished the wider scope this gave them after the confines of cinema newsreels which had appeared only twice a week. It may not have been coverage in depth, but it was coverage in pictures. The bulletins became increasingly pictorial – more indeed than was often to prove the case later.

Shortage of money was only one reason why we could not then fully depict the day's news as moving pictures. Another important reason, which applied to all television news organizations however well endowed they might be, was the state of the art. Technology had not then yet developed to a point at which widespread film coverage was feasible. Video taping had not come into operation. Satellite transmission was unheard of – indeed, outside a few esoteric technical circles – undreamt of. Landline links, within the United Kingdom, and between European broadcasters, were patchy and costly. Aircraft were still the main means for bringing in film. There were few cameramen in Europe, and fewer still outside it (except in the United States) who specialized in television coverage. Most foreign stringer cameramen worked primarily for the cinema newsreels, using the heavy 35mm cameras which made coverage of fast-breaking news difficult. The one news agency providing coverage for television, United Press, was based on the Movietone news network, set up originally to meet the needs of the cinema newsreels. Its service was slowed down by the need to strike several prints from the original negative for distribution to their various customers. Very few of their stories were covered in sound. These were severe limitations on the use of the film camera as a journalistic tool.

Few people at the time detected the gaps in our film coverage of hard news. One reason for this was that the public did not yet look to television to provide a full report of the news of the day. Radio was still the dominant form of broadcast news, and radio and the newspapers the prime source of news for the public. Television was seen as a useful addition, a form of daily illustrated supplement to the other sources. The second reason owed more to our own efforts. Enterprising use of the sound film camera to put chunks of real life on the screen, as had been done with the Norman Dodds story in 1955, could provide viewable material which made our bulletins acceptable as good programmes, regardless of whether we had managed to corral the day's news fully into pictures. When Arthur Clifford learnt that I found coverage like that of the Hackney brides very much to my taste, he set about exploiting this vein of human interest material vigorously.

On Whit Monday he sent George Ffitch and a camera crew to Southend to see if that traditional holiday place for London's East Enders had changed. Outwardly much was the same. The pier – at least up to the point where it had been demolished as a precaution against invasion – was crowded with strollers and fishermen; donkeys plied for hire on sands which so soon became mud; there were fathers in braces and mothers in felt slippers. But the young wanted more than this. Men back from the war recalled in interview the sunny Mediterranean beaches they had fought on and now wanted to camp on. The long columns of cyclists which had been a feature of pre-war holiday roads had shrunk to small groups, many of whom spoke longingly of the day when they might own a car. A parallel story, in which we interviewed people on a day trip to Boulogne, confirmed that a major shift in Britain's holiday habits was on the horizon. What had been a routine news story became a glimpse of social history. Indeed the social historians of the future will not need to look beyond the archives of ITN to illustrate the changing pattern of British life since 1955.

We found also that the sound camera could enable us to put into human terms issues and problems which were otherwise likely to be suffocated in the language of official reports or in the circumlocutions of official spokesmen. When yet one more report was published on the plan to drive a relief road for Oxford traffic through the meadows between the colleges and the Thames, we did not adopt the accepted practice of summarising the findings in words, and mounting a discussion in the studio. John Hartley and a camera crew went off to Oxford and interviewed embattled dons and ambitious town planners under the elm trees of Merton Mall, the quiet avenue which would have been the first casualty of the new road. Today such ombudsman reports are commonplace, even if they have tended of late to be confined to regional news magazines. At that time, if they appeared at all on television they found their place in the weekly news magazines.

Where we could combine social inquiry with human interest, the result could be very viewable. When the local authority in Slough forbade people to take dogs into parks except on a leash, we found a rich crop of individualistic Britons ready to voice their protests. When the education authorities in Hertfordshire decided they must counter the sloppy speech of their school children, and appointed a special teacher for that purpose, we not only collected a wide sample of dialects and phrases, but interviewed the teacher. We tracked him down, not in the classroom, but alongside a milk float in a suburban street, where he was plying his second trade as a milk roundsman. Such human interest stories formed a lode which we mined strenuously, and which we had very much to ourselves until a year later, when the BBC's *Tonight* programme set its prospectors loose in the same territory. In 1956 television had not yet tramped bare the by-paths of British life, nor yet helped to spread uniformity. Varied characters, varied scenes came freshly on to the screen, many of them a revelation to people in other places and other classes. In those early years television served to introduce the British people to one another.

Street interviews played an important part in this process. The technique of seeking the views of a random selection of passers-by had been used on radio from time to time in Radio Newsreel, and very occasionally by the cinema newsreels. ITN had adopted it as a way of sampling public reaction in November 1955 to Princess Margaret's decision not to marry Group Captain Townsend. Half a dozen interviews shot in the street outside Lancaster House had brought the man in the street literally to the screen, well supported by the woman in the street. From the summer of 1956 we increasingly utilized this technique. (Its later name, Vox Pop, had to wait until the classicists of *Tonight* took it up.) It provided a sample, albeit a very random one, of what the public were thinking. We never sought to present this as a fair or accurate sample, but merely as a varied expression of views. We deliberately selected some speakers for, and some against, and made clear in the commentary that the outcome was not to be taken as a measure of public thinking.

Successful and popular though such sound film coverage could be, it was essentially away-page material and did not solve the problem of presenting fully the hard news of the day on television. Moreover, the silent camera, valuable reporting instrument though it was, lacked one important dimension. It captured only the sight of events, not their sound. Only on ceremonial occasions such as Trooping the Colour, where the cameras and the microphones could be placed in position beforehand, did we use the sound cameras to record the natural sound, as well as the picture. This was in accordance with newsreel practice, established in the days of the cumbersome 35mm cameras. Like the newsreels we backed silent action film on the screen either with music or with dubbed effects from the sound library – cheering for football crowds, clapping for cricket, cheering and the rumbling of wheels for processions, indeterminate noise (called 'mush' in the trade) for more general scenes.

This system I took for granted until a CBS report from Cyprus made me aware for the first time of how much the actual sound of an event could add to its impact and authenticity on the screen. Towards the end of May 1956 a riot in Nicosia was captured at considerable length by the sound cameras of CBS. Their film began with shots of a march, headed by Cypriot schoolgirls in their clothes of white blouses and dark skirt, chanting for union with Greece and carrying the banned blue and white striped flag of Greece through the narrow Streets of the old town of Nicosia. The camera had recorded not only the blazing eyes and defiant looks of the girls, but their shrill cries of 'Enosis, Enosis'. The CBS reporter had been on the spot with the camera crew and had spoken his commentary as if at a live outside broadcast. 'Here come the troops' he said urgently as a platoon of the Royal Lancashire Regiment, riot shields in hand, their faces set and tense under their steel helmets, their boots sounding sharp and insistent on the cobbles, mounted the steep roadway. There was a sudden click as they unhooked their batons and broke into a charge. The demonstrators scattered and behind the girls one glimpsed the ranks of the Eoka men who had organized this demonstration. One girl seized back a Greek flag which the police had taken and held on to it as a soldier tried to wrench it from her. Then suddenly there was the crunch of an explosion. 'A grenade', said the commentator, 'a policeman has been wounded'. And in the middle of the street a burly Cypriot gendarme, in shirt and black shorts and flat black cap, was huddled and writhing. A Red Cross jeep raced into the street and two soldiers lifted the policeman on to its tailboard. His knee was a mass of blood, pitch black on the film. Pain struck him as he was lifted, and he gave out a short howl of pain, like a wounded forest animal. The camera zoomed in on his smashed leg and on his face taut with agony.

Here indeed was news as it happened. The natural sound of the chanting crowd, of the marching troops, of the wounded officer, intermingled with the words of the reporter, gave an authenticity and force to the material which I had not known in any film I had ever seen on television. In particular, the shots of the young British National Servicemen made dramatic viewing in the homes from which they were drawn. We ran the whole film, cutting out only the most gory close-up of the shattered knee of the gendarme. I thought it right to precede the story with a warning that some grisly material was coming up on the screen. When I heard the words on transmission, they sounded unnecessary, almost hypocritical. I sensed that the public had given the broadcasters their trust as to what was proper to show, that it was up to us to decide on their behalf, rather than hand that decision on to the audience. We avoided such warnings from then on.

To me that CBS report was a revelation of what the sound camera could achieve. I asked Cotter and Clifford whether we could not shoot all action news in this way. Cotter spelled out to me the technical difficulties. Our sound was recorded optically by a system which transferred sound waves into light waves, which were recorded on the edge of the film. This method worked well only if the microphones were placed close to the source of the sound. CBS, in John's view, must either have had warning of the Cyprus march and have been able to get their cameras and microphones into position, or must have been very lucky. (The answer, it later emerged, was a blend of all these factors.) If we tried to do the same thing in a story where there was a lot of movement, such as a demonstration or a riot, we would have to be very lucky indeed. The reporter would have to rush, microphone in hand, into the heart of the action, hoping that the cameraman and the recordist, both linked to him by the microphone cable, could keep up with him. And the ensuing sound would be pretty ropey. Moreover, if we wanted to cover hard news with sound, then we must hold a sound crew in readiness, in a fire brigade role, ready to dash out when the news broke. At present we confined that function to a cameraman working with a silent camera. If one man spent much of his day kicking his heels in the cameramen's room, with perhaps only an underlay of a traffic jam or a minor rail crash to show for it, that could be justified as a reasonable insurance against a big story breaking. But if we tied up a sound camera team in this way, we could cut back drastically the other stories we might cover. The most we could do at this stage was to note the technique and seek an early chance to apply it.

That chance arose a month later, on Tuesday 24 July 1956. The main item on the film schedule at the morning conference had been the strike at the Austin works at Long-bridge, the first major stoppage in the British motor industry since the war. We had a sound crew on the job, with John Hartley as reporter, Stan Crockett as cameraman, and Bill Best as recordist. They formed a strong, assertive and quick-witted group. Our coverage the day before had been along accepted lines – some silent footage of pickets outside the factory gates, interviews with Union leaders and with the Austin public re-lations officer. But the situation that Tuesday morning looked nastier. The strike was not unanimous and some workers and lorries were forcing their way through the pickets at the main gates. Police, mostly on foot, but with half-a-dozen mounted men in reserve, were present in force. In mid-morning a lorry approached the gates. The strikers formed up to halt it.

Normally such a scene would have been filmed with a silent camera. But at that moment the crew were on the outskirts of the crowd, preparing to use the sound camera to interview strikers. Suddenly the mounted police moved into the midst of scuffles which had broken out around the lorry. Hartley, Crockett and Best, held together by the quar-ter inch insulated cable which linked the microphone to the camera, thrust their way through the crowd towards the scene of action. John Hartley moved in front, holding out the microphone to pick up the sound as the mounted police reached the crowd around the lorry. Struggling to keep up with him, Crockett filmed the scene from the sound camera on his shoulder.

When we viewed the film that evening I knew we had something special. The clatter of horses' hooves, the half bantering, half menacing shouts of the pickets – for we were a long way then from the grim visages of flying squads of secondary pickets – the curt orders of the police, the roar of the lorry engine revving up, the clang as the factory gates shut behind it all gave not only vividness but authority to the story. It gave, too, an added element of truth. 'Mounted Police Charge Strikers' ran the headlines on the evening papers. These words were accurate enough in themselves, but they conveyed an inaccurate impression of a cavalry charge, of horses thundering into the midst of ranks of strikers, whereas the film showed the careful if frightening manoeuvring of the police horses into the midst of the pickets. Cheerfulness as well as anger came across in the shouts of the strikers. It had the ring of real authenticity. We had achieved for ourselves what CBS had done in Cyprus two months earlier. This was truly a case in which we were able to let the public 'see it happen'.

Our coverage was noted within the BBC. Their star newscaster at the time, Robert Dougal has told how 'this fresh visual approach' impressed him and his fellow news readers at Alexandra Palace. He quotes the *TV Mirror*, a popular weekly of the time:

> The BBC treated the subject with scrupulous fairness. A few brief newsreel shots were supplemented by long carefully modified verbal reports of what the people involved had said and what the management and unions were going to do. Factual, but to the great majority of people, dull. The ITN version consisted largely of lively gripping film shots of the picket lines outside the factories (the part which, let's face it, has the greatest appeal for the mass of the public) backed by a simple lucid commentary giving the main facts.[1]

1   Robert Dougal, *In and Out of the Box*. Collins 1973, p. 218.

In those few minutes Hartley, Crockett and Best had carried the coverage of news on television in Britain a major step forward. Though our chances of using the technique were for many months ahead to be limited by a shortage of cameras, the shooting of natural sound to accompany action film was now established as a key element of the new journalism.

We did not, however, put the sound camera to what is today its commonest use – as a means for the reporter to recount into camera, against a background which symbolises or illustrates the story, his report of an event. That came later, when recording techniques improved. For the moment the reporter's task was seen less that of amassing and reporting the facts than of doing one specialized task – interviewing. Facts for stories were, for the most part, taken from agency copy, though extra information might be telephoned through by the reporter or recorded on the cameraman's dope sheet. But reporters were not encouraged to linger on the scene to delve more deeply. Their role was to get back into the car with the camera team and hurry to the next location to provide yet another interview, leaving a despatch rider to rush the film back to Kingsway.

18

Newscasters

Christopher Chataway made his last newscast for ITN four days before I took over as Editor. His going was a severe loss. Yet it was remarkable how soon this breach was repaired. Robin Day soon developed a trenchant authority and – to my surprise – a touch of wit and humour which had hitherto lain unseen. Ludovic Kennedy proved an ideal counterpart to Day. Darkly handsome, with a natural warmth, and an easy clarity of speech, he soon proved himself popular both with the viewers and the critics. He brought to the screen the confidence not only of an Old Etonian but of a man with a good war record in the Navy, in which he had served on the Arctic convoys to Russia. This was particularly apparent in his capacity to take in his stride the technical breakdowns which were a hazard of those days. In his first week with ITN the film suddenly broke half way through a story, leaving the screen blank and flickering. Newscasters wore no hidden earpieces then through which instructions could be relayed. But Kennedy was not troubled. 'It looks as if the film has broken' he told the viewers. 'Oh well, I expect they will want me to read a bit more news'. And he picked up the next story from the desk without any sign of flurry or embarrassment.

Ludovic Kennedy did not parade his very genuine interest in miscarriages of justice, a concern which was to find powerful expression in a book about the Rillington Place murders, a book which did much to prevent a return to capital punishment in Britain, and which was to be followed by inquiries into other questionable judgements. These achievements, which were to bring him a knighthood in 1994, then lay in the future. Indeed in 1956 press stories about Ludovic Kennedy tended to concentrate on his marriage to the glamorous Moira Shearer, then at the peak of her fame as a ballerina and film star. I feared that in those days of more sharply defined class shibboleths Kennedy's unmistakable upper-class bearing might lessen his appeal to our largely working class audience. This might have been the case had he not lacked all sense of class consciousness, and had he not rapidly proved himself to be a clear, authoritative and relaxed presenter of the news, whose impact was all the greater for being in contrast to Robin Day's sharp-edged urgency and emphasis.

When Chataway had first told me in April that he was resigning, he gave as one reason his view that the public could quickly tire of men and women they saw daily on the

Fig. 5. Ludovic Kennedy.

screen. 'People's faces wear out' he said. The reverse in fact was to prove the case. The public have shown a remarkable loyalty to those who become familiar figures on their screens – as witness the anguish caused when Reginald Bosanquet finally left ITN. But the counterpart to this is the speed with which the public forget those who are no longer before them, the eagerness with which they transfer their support to new faces. 'Out of sight, out of mind' is one of the many old adages whose truth has been under- lined by television.

We made much play, in stressing the differences between ITN newscasters and BBC news readers, that the newscasters were men (or women, for Barbara Mandell still broadcast some of the early evening and weekend bulletins) of personality. But the key to the system was that the newscasters wrote the news in their own words, and took as full a part as they could in the shaping and evaluation of the bulletin. They attended the editorial conferences, and could – and did – voice views about the film as well as about the words. This was important, because the effectiveness of newscasting depends above all on the power to communicate – or, to be more exact, the power to communicate news. This power is reinforced if the newscaster is truly interested in the news of the day, and knowledgeable about it. If he has helped to prepare, and above all to gather it, those qualities are the more likely to show through. It was important, therefore, in these formative years to ensure that the newscasters were fully enmeshed in the process of making the bulletins, however many other problems that might give rise to.

One problem which did arise, and to which we had to work out an answer, was the degree to which a newscaster might inject a dash of his own opinions into the news. People of strong personality tend also to be people of strong opinions. How far, therefore, in deploying the element of personality by which we set such store, was the newscaster entitled to express his own opinions on the air? How far into the field of comment should he carry his interpretation of the news? This was a new problem for me. In Fleet Street news and comment were never sharply divided into separate compartments. If it was in the nature of the newspaper correspondent to interweave with the facts of the story some of his personal reactions to those facts, that was accepted and acceptable. It applied not only in the popular papers. The great *Times* reporters of the 1930s – Norman Ebbutt, Douglas Reed, de Caux – and men like G.E.R. Gedye and George Steer of *The Daily Telegraph* – had left no one in any doubt about what they thought were the rights and wrongs of the events they described. C.P. Scott's dictum that comment is free, facts are sacred, was not seen as incompatible with a report which interwove facts and comment, provided the facts were scrupulously accurate.

I was now, however, working under the Television Act, which behoved me to ensure that the news should be presented 'with due accuracy and impartiality'. I saw this as an advantage rather than a constraint. Impartiality, if it was interpreted actively, and not passively, could be a means both of protecting our independence and of strengthening our power to gather and interpret news, to arrive at the truth. It was a safeguard against pressures not only from the Government or other people of power, but also against the views and whims of the programme companies who owned us. When I first read, in the Lobby correspondents' room high above the Thames at Westminster, Clause 3 of the Television Bill of 1954, with its requirements about the accuracy and impartiality of the news, my determination to get into television increased. These few words could free a television news editor from the proprietorial pressures which were then widespread in Fleet Street – much wider than is the case today. They could give him the freedom to create something new in popular journalism.

Impartiality could also strengthen ITN journalistically if we applied the principle actively, if we interpreted it as placing on us the positive responsibility to seek out all sides of an issue, rather than confining our role to making a fair selection of facts and arguments which reached us from other sources. We could not rely just on presenting a fair balance of the news which reached us from the agencies. We had to ensure such fairness by our own coverage as well. My training and instincts were those of Fleet Street, where news was not something which came along on the agency conveyor belt – valuable though the agencies were both as guide and support – but was something you had to hack from the coal face yourself. Within the highly sensitive area of public broadcasting, such direct news gathering was helped rather than hindered by the requirement of impartiality, for the need to give all sides justified asking difficult and probing questions. It afforded a basis upon which we could maintain the right to question public people in the public interest. It also provided a guide line to ensure that we put such questions to secure information, not to grind axes or stage a scene. It took me only a few weeks in Kingsway to realize that not only a strict but a willing application of the principle of impartiality was one key to using to the full the opportunities offered by this new journalism. I became therefore an ardent exponent of the doctrine that news must not only be fair, but must be seen to be fair.

The doctrine had, however, not merely to be expounded, but put into practice on the day to day production of the bulletins. The small size of our editorial staff meant that I was drawn into a direct role in that task. One of the economies which the ITN Board had made was to do away with the post of Deputy Editor. A Deputy Editor was the natural person to carry out the task of Output Editor, of making the final decisions about what should go into the bulletins. Richard Gould-Adams had fulfilled that role for Crawley. I decided to take it on myself on weekdays, even if it involved me in a 12 to 13 hour day. I did so with avidity. I relished every minute of the work, and I was well aware that I, too, had an apprenticeship to serve in this new medium. That was particularly so in the selection and editing of film.

We had carried over from the newsreels the practice of all film being screened, in the first instance, in a viewing theatre. The length and rough shape of the story would be determined there, with the material then being handed over to a film editor and script writer for final shaping. Into the small, fusty viewing theatre on the eighth floor of Television House would gather an expectant audience. The shift leader of the film editors would be there, together with any editors not already at work in a cutting room; the script writer working on the story; when possible the reporter and the cameraman – though as often as not they would be on their way to cover another story. The technician in charge of the processing laboratory might come to check on the quality of his work, and the film librarian to keep track of material. It could have been a difficult atmosphere in which to make borderline editorial decisions, but I found the reverse to be the case. These early ITN pioneers were nothing if not outspoken. If I sought views, they were forthcoming. Indeed on questions of taste I could often sense, from the atmosphere in the theatre as the film was being run, what was their reaction. I valued those views and reactions. For these men and women were not only skilled in the craft, but to a large degree represented our audience. In those days of narrow educational opportunity, none of the film editors had been to a university. Most had served in the war. Many had experience beyond the confines of the media. One film editor ran a stall in Wimbledon market on his days off. The words – and the silences – of the audience in that crowded preview theatre played a valuable role in establishing ITN's standards.

To the film editors the concept of impartiality was new. The cinema newsreels had often been blatantly propagandist, sometimes Tory, sometimes strongly on the side of the welfare state. The concept that controversial issues should be balanced was new to film editing. But the editors learned eagerly.

Within the newsroom the sub-editors and script writers who had come to us from the BBC were already steeped in the Corporation's practice of impartiality. Other journalists who had come from Fleet Street quickly adapted to this line. In this regard, Arthur Clifford, who had been a Chief Sub-Editor at the BBC, was a tower of strength. Unorthodox in his newsgathering, he was orthodoxy itself when it came to fairness of presentation.

At the same time, the heart of the ITN operation was the newscaster system, which calledfor the news to be given in a robust and human form, in adequate depth and perspective. We wanted the newscasters to be men of personality: yet a key element in any personality is the strength of his opinions. It was easy to decide that, in pursuit of impartiality, analysis and interpretation were all right, but expressions of opinion were not. It was another matter to determine, in the constantly changing pattern of daily news, exactly where that line should be drawn. Was it right for a freelance broadcaster (I tried out a number of new faces on the 5.55pm early bulletin we did for the London area) to modify an item which had reported that 'in Cyprus we are continuing to practice stern measures' into one which said 'in Cyprus we are, for bette or worse, continuing to practice stern measures'? I thought so when I read the words in the script, and passed them. But on the air they sounded not only like comment, but like comment we were trying to smuggle in by the back door. Almost every bulletin posed a problem of this kind, as we sought to personalize and clarify the news, and yet keep it fair. One of Napoleon's maxims about war – 'It is a simple art: all lies in the exercise of it' – quickly proved to be true also of television journalism. In exercising it in those early days the newscasters played a cardinal role not only in their work on the screen, but in the discussions and debates off screen in which we built up our own case law in the new visual journalism.

19

The probing interview

One of the new techniques of this new journalism, the probing interview, was to revolutionize not only political journalism, but politics itself. Until this time people had been largely dependent for their information about the political scene on the impressions of others – of Gallery and Lobby correspondents, of political columnists, of cartoonists and still photographers. It was through their eyes, their pens, their lenses, that the public gained their knowledge of the people who ruled them – or sought to rule them. Few people, even those ardently interested in politics, had a chance to meet or study at close quarters the leaders of political parties, or of the trades unions, or of the Church. They saw at most a distant figure striding through crowds, or glimpsed on a public platform. Still photographs, or shots in a cinema newsreel could provide an outward impression of a man or woman in the news. But these did not convey a first hand impression. To learn what the great, or the would-be great were really like you had to rely on what an inner circle of writers and reporters vouchsafed to you.

Radio had added one further highly significant dimension to this study of politics and of politicians. It had provided a directness of spoken, if unseen contact between the leaders and the public. It was through the radio that the British people felt that they knew Churchill not only well, but very well, because his words had conveyed not only his ideas but the man himself. Television now offered a further major step forward in the political process. It could bring the politicians into every sitting room in the land, could provide for the first time a chance for the citizen and the voter to scrutinize closely those who would be their leaders. People could now not only look at politicians, they could stare at them in close-up, could have the means of forming their own opinions about them on the evidence of their own eyes and ears. So long as the television cameras were not admitted to Parliament, the interview was the best way in which television could bring this new sharper view to bear. It had, however, to be an informed, questing, challenging interview, capable of testing and portraying the politician's personality as well as his policies. Otherwise this powerful new medium would merely be a passive platform, a way of enabling you to see people better, but not necessarily to know them better. A new style of questioning was needed to complement the electronic picture, if television was to convey to the public a fully rounded view of people in the public eye. The rigorous interviewing style of ITN met that need.

To utilize it, we had, however, to gain acceptance among those who were interviewed. Not all of them by any means favoured this new approach. How new it was can be seen from an article by George Scott in the *Manchester Guardian*. He began with the text of an imaginary interview from pre-ITN days.

'Sir, would you say that your visit to Timbuktu was worth while'?

'Oh yes, I would definitely say my visit had been worth while. Yes, definitely'.

'Ah, good. Could you say what topics you discussed, sir'?

'No, I'm afraid I couldn't do that. These talks were of a highly confidential nature, you understand, and you wouldn't expect me to reveal anything which might prejudice our future relations'.

'No, of course not, sir. Well, sir, you must be very tired after your talks and your journey – may I ask, sir, if you are going to take it easy for a while now – a holiday perhaps'?

'Ah, if only one could. But you know a Minister in Her Majesty's Government can never take it easy, never rest, not really you know. *They're* waiting for me now'.

'Well, thank you very much, sir'.

'Thank *you* very much'.

That Scott concluded, 'in essential caricature, is the kind of BBC airport interview we used to see on our television screens not so many years ago. I for one say thank goodness things are not what they used to be'.

This is indeed a caricature, but it was the over-statement of a true fact. Before competition existed, broadcast interviews were not only very much rarer than they are now, but they tended to take place on the terms of the man or woman interviewed, not on those of the interviewer. Ministers and other public figures claimed the right to decide in advance what questions they would be prepared to answer, and were often able to establish this right. They frequently regarded themselves as conferring a favour on the broadcasters by agreeing to be interviewed at all. The view that the broadcaster, since he represented the general public, had the right to put any question which might be in the public mind, was not one which found favour in Whitehall.

Such rigidities, and the pat-ball style of interviewing which George Scott parodied were now being eroded by the advent of competition and by the inherent nature of television, a more candid medium than radio or print. Under the candid eye of the camera artificiality and reticence were much more readily apparent. Within BBC Television, in programmes like *Press Conference* and *Viewfinder*, a more vigorous style of questioning was encouraged. This trend had been stimulated by the recruitment in the early 1950s of three former MPs as BBC interviewers – Aidan Crawley, Christopher Mayhew and Woodrow Wyatt. They were accustomed to the cut and thrust of Parliamentary debate, and instinctively applied a more rigorous approach to the questioning of public figures. This style Grace Wyndham-Goldie continued when in 1955 she took over *Panorama*, and Aidan Crawley brought into ITN. When I took over the Editorship I readily confirmed the rules he had laid down. Foremost amongst these was the insistence that a list of questions should not be submitted or agreed in advance, and that the interview should not be rehearsed. This change made it an interview on the broadcaster's terms, not those of the person questioned. It affirmed the principle that within our democracy the broadcasters were probing issues on behalf of the public at large. It also had advantages as a technique.

An interview in which the questions were not known or rehearsed in advance tended to be much fresher and have more immediacy and impact, indeed more truth, than one where the answers had been worn flat with repetition. Above all, it made possible the use of supplementary questions, which arose out of the answers give by the person interviewed. Above all, it made possible the use of supplementary questions, which arose out of the answers given by the person interviewed. Experience was to show that it was in answer to supplementary questions that very often the most important information emerged. Devising such supplementaries, with the split-second evaluation of the primary answer, became the greatest of the interviewer's skills.

It was a technique which had to be fought for. Many politicians disliked it; all public relations officers detested it. Its acceptance had certainly not been acknowledged by the spring of 1956. Again and again throughout the ensuing months Arthur Clifford and I would have to argue the issue out with yet one more Ministry, one more firm, one more trade union, all of whom wanted questions to be submitted in advance.

The law and Parliamentary practice also hampered the development of the political interview. The Fourteen Day rule still appertained, under which broadcasters were forbidden from discussing on the air any issue which was due to come up in Parliament in the next fourteen days. It was a time, too, when Ministers observed punctiliously their duty to report their decisions, and indeed their views, to Parliament before they talked to the press or the broadcasters.

Offsetting these constraints was the fact that the television age was also the air age. We were still a couple of years away from jet travel, but even in that era of piston-engined aircraft London Airport had become the gateway through which Ministers and diplomats passed, as they increasingly used aircraft to supervise and exercise Britain's power, then still widespread and strong. From 1956 onwards the VIP lounge at Heathrow, with its improbable background of patterned curtains, which gave it the look of the sitting room of a pretentious seaside boarding house, became a setting in which public men (for there were then few women in posts of prominence) expounded their policies, and in which television interviewing stretched its fledgling muscles. Gradually, too, Ministers came to appreciate, or at least to accept, the value of the short interview which was all that television, by contrast with radio, had space for. R.A. Butler, that master of the cryptic utterance, was one of the first to do so. 'Anyone with anything worth saying can say it in three minutes' was his response when I told him that that was all we could allocate to him when we interviewed him during Suez.

In June 1956 one interview confirmed my faith in the probing television interview, not only as a revolution in political journalism, but as excellent viewing. It was conducted by Robin Day with ex-President Harry S. Truman, then on his first visit to Europe since giving up the Presidency. For a man who prided himself on not being an intellectual,

Fig. 6. Robin Day, 1955.

the ex-President had taken what in those days was an unusual step and had written a book about his days in the White House. Oxford University had invited him to accept an honorary degree and Mr. Truman was combining his journey to receive that degree with publicizing his book in Britain. The only minor cloud on this otherwise clear horizon was that a Sommerville don, Miss Anscombe, was seeking signature to a petition opposing the conferring of the degree. She argued that since it had been on President Truman's orders in 1945 that the atomic bombs had been dropped on Hiroshima and Nagasaki, he was no man for Oxford honour. This was one of the first stirrings of protest in Britain against the bomb. The Americans had tested their second H-bomb Bikini, only a couple of weeks before Truman arrived, without the explosion arousing much interest, let alone protest.

Robin Day told me he proposed to raise, in his opening question, the issue of the Oxford protest. In the broadcasting climate of the time, this was an iconoclastic move. It might be thought discourteous both to the man and to the office he had held. Tradition demanded that such a question – if it were to be put al all – should come later, after the ex-President had been able to play himself in with some less provocative questions, on, for instance, Korea, where the war had been followed only by an armistice, not by a peace treaty. That was the type of issue the BBC and the press were likely to raise when they interviewed Truman – and they did. Were we not just indulging in stunt journalism by putting the Oxford protest first?

Perhaps. But there were good arguments for doing so. It was a new issue, which might produce new information – and that was what we were in the business of providing. It was an issue which the viewer could readily take in, whilst these other wider questions might well pass him by; and it was issue which could be put simply and shortly and which might evoke simple and short answers, ideally suited to a news bulletin. So I agreed to Day's plan.

Once he settled down in his turn to face Mr. Truman in a corner of Claridge's ballroom, Robin came swiftly to the point. 'Mr. President', he began, 'I understand that one reason for your visit is to receive an honorary degree at the University of Oxford'.

'That is so'. Truman looked pleased by the question.

'Are you aware, Mr. President, that a lady at Oxford is campaigning against your receiving that degree because you authorized the dropping of the first atom bomb?'

Truman looked, for a brief moment, disconcerted. No, he was not aware of that.

The next question was nothing if not succinct. 'Mr. President, do you regret having authorized the dropping of the atom bomb'?

The President's concentration seemed almost visibly to tighten. There was no delay in his answer. 'No, I do not. I made the decision on the information available to me at the time and I would make the same decision on the same information again.' He paused, and then with a smile. 'But you can read all about it in my memoirs'.

Day was back immediately. 'Mr. President, this programme is going out to people who cannot afford thirty shillings even for the memoirs of a former President of the United States. Won't you explain your reasons a bit further'? Truman did, clearly and forcibly. It was marvellous television. Even today the copy in the ITN archives, drab though the picture quality is, in the black and white filming of the time, radiates vigour and interest. In the bulletin that evening it provided several minutes of sharp drama, demonstrating the qualities which were to establish Robin Day as the screen's best political interviewer. It produced something not only eminently viewable, but also provided information both about a key issue and about the character of this small, bespectacled man who had been such a truly big figure of our time. This had been accomplished by questions which went to the point and by an interviewer who listened to the answers, and based his supplementary questions on them, not just on further questions written out on his clipboard.

The Truman story firmly established the probing interview as an integral part of ITN's technique. I used to have it run through for later recruits as a model. Not only Day but George Ffitch and Reginald Bosanquet quickly became masters of the technique. It was something which politicians expected when they faced an ITN camera – and something which most of them valued as a step in the right direction for the democratic process.

20

Sport makes news

Sport, that essential element in popular news, posed from the earliest days of television news complex issues of access for news organizations to sporting events, issues which were three decades later to reach the High Court. In television sport is not only the raw material for news; it is programme material in its own right, highly viewable action capable of pulling in huge audiences. The sports promoters and the sports producers were in no mood to allow television news, in the name of freedom of reporting, to pick the plums out of their cake by showing the key goals, the close finishes, the winning hits. Their approach to television news was the same as that which the promoters had adopted towards the cinema newsreels – if newsmen wanted to cover sport, they could pay for it.

The issue first forced itself to my attention not because of a sports story, but because of a general news event placed within a sporting setting. The drive of the Royal family in their landaus along the course at Ascot before the day's racing has been for decades one of the most durable perennials of the newspapers and the newsreels. When early in the afternoon of 19 June 1956, I watched, on BBC Television's outside broadcast, the Queen and Prince Philip make their way up the course of the opening day of Ascot, a day of glittering sunshine, the scene seemed to me ideal for television. Then I recollected that coverage of this drive had not been on the film list we had discussed at that morning's conference. I checked with the newsroom. We were not covering the Royal drive because the Ascot authorities were adamant that their agreement with the BBC ruled out any filming by ITN on any part of the course. Though this was designed to protect the exclusivity of the racing coverage, in the view of the authorities it included any other news at Ascot. We had a camera crew and a reporter covering the Ascot fashions, but they were doing so outside the gates, not within the ground.

This seemed to me absurd. The Royal drive was a news story, and my first reaction was to help ourselves by telerecording it off the BBC's outside broadcast. But this proved technically impractical, and legally dubious. All we could do was, the next day, to station our cameras on the Heath which stretched opposite the stands, and which was theoretically open to the public. But the cameraman was spotted, and within minutes the

Ascot authorities were on to John Cotter, threatening to sue if we used the material, and even more ominously, to ban us from every racecourse in the country.

It proved to be an empty threat. We ran the material that evening, and no action followed. We had won that immediate battle. But the wider question of news access to sporting events remained. How could we win for our cameras the same freedom to report sport as was open to the newspaper reporter and the newspaper cameraman?

The cinema newsreels had dealt with this problem either by paying for the coverage rights – or by pirating them. When a rival newsreel bought the rights to a Wembley Cup Final, Movietone's star cameraman got on to the field disguised as the West Ham mascot, and filmed the game through the end of the big mock hammer which he carried. When Paramount pirated a Test Match at the Oval by building a scaffolding tower overlooking the ground, the companies who had bought the rights tethered a big gas-filled balloon in front of the tower. Paramount riposted by trying to shoot down the balloon, and when that failed, managed to cut the cable holding it. Bill Hodgson, who was to become ITN's General Manager, recalled being sent down as a boy with the sandwiches for his cameraman father, who was lodged in a plane tree overlooking the Oval, helping himself to a share of another newsreel's exclusive. It was a contest which had its own rules – the most important of which was that no newsreel, however much its costly rights were impaired, sought to invoke the law – for indeed next week they might well be the contract breakers.

I could see only one answer to this problem. Television organizations would have to be given access to sporting events as of right, though the length of their coverage could be restricted so as to protect the programme interests both of sports promoters and of programme departments. This right should be written into the contracts made by the broadcasters with the sporting bodies. I put this idea to the programme companies, to the ITN Board, and through them to my opposite number on the BBC, Pat Smithers, Editor of BBC Television News. Smithers sensibly took the long view. He foresaw that the day might come when ITV had money enough to buy up exclusive rights to sporting fixtures. Nor did he, as a seasoned journalist, need any convincing on the principle of free access, He therefore won over the BBC hierarchy to allowing us to show two minutes of coverage in each bulletin of play in the remaining Test matches against Australia, provided we acknowledged that this came 'with the co-operation of the BBC Outside Broadcasting Department'. We secured similar access to the tennis at Wimbledon.

This was an important breakthrough which enabled us from then on to give regular coverage to the main events in the sporting calendar, instead of the haphazard reporting of any odds and ends of sport which might be accessible. We still faced considerable technical problems in covering with film cameras games which stretched over days, as with cricket, or over several hours, as with tennis. If you tried to film everything not only would it be outrageously costly, but you would expose much more film than you could process or cut in time for use. Estimating when the high spots in these games were likely to occur, and concentrating your filming on them became a fine art.

Our informal agreement with the BBC was strengthened by the mutual battle we fought in the autumn of 1956 about coverage of the Olympic Games, which were due to be held later that year in Melbourne. All visual coverage would have to be on film. The Australian Olympic Committee were very foolishly holding out for high sums of money not only for the full filmed reports of the Games, but for any excerpts to be used in cinema newsreels or on television. Throughout the summer and autumn the British cinema newsreels, the BBC News and ITN negotiated with the Australians on this point. Afternoon after afternoon we met in offices overlooking Soho Square to discuss the latest message from Melbourne. I saw then how formidable Tahu Hole, then Editor of BBC News, could be in a committee. He was unwavering in his refusal to pay for news access to the Games, even if this meant that they went uncovered on the British screen. It was not a stance which commended itself to the BBC Sports Department, but it carried the day. The Australians proved equally stubborn and in the end the 1956 Olympic Games took place without a foot of film of its events being shown on British television.

Discussion of the broader issue of news access continued to rumble on between the programme companies and the BBC until, in the winter of 1959–60, the problem came to a head during the MCC tour of the West Indies. The West Indies Cricket Board sold exclusive rights in coverage of the tour to Eddie Carroll, a West Indian calypso singer, who was certainly not going to allow any news organization to have access without paying. The BBC stood admirably firm and refused to buy any of Carroll's longer reports of the matches for showing in their sports programmes until BBC News and ITN were allowed to film short excerpts for their bulletins. They won the day, and Carroll gave us news access. This speeded up a final agreement between the companies and the Corporation. In January 1960 what amounted to a treaty was signed between the two broadcasters. Each agreed, in negotiating television rights for sporting events, to include a clause along the lines I had proposed to the ITN Board in 1956, to offer free access for news organizations to secure film coverage. Such coverage was to be brief, and to be shown only in regularly scheduled news programmes, not in longer sporting programmes. There was a great deal of haggling about what should be the proper length of such news items. In the end this came down to two minutes per bulletin for most events. For some the limits were shorter. On the Grand National only the finish and another 15 seconds of the racing could be shown. For boxing matches, where the knock out was by definition not likely to last, even with its preliminaries and aftermath, more than fifteen or twenty seconds, the scheme proved unworkable. No promoter was prepared to let those few seconds go for free. But by and large the agreement opened up sport to coverage by television news on much the same basis as by radio and newspapers. The battle which began on the day of that Ascot meeting in 1956 had proved worth fighting.

21

News values

Our news values in 1956 were pitched between those of the popular and those of the quality papers. I set our goal as that of carrying the main stories which made the front page of the *Daily Telegraph* and the back page of the *Daily Mirror* – then a model of clear, sharp sub-editing together with a dash of the flair and style of the *Manchester Guardian*, I believed people could take somewhat harder intellectual tack than they were being offered in the popular dailies, provided it was presented with clarity, gusto and a human touch, and provided serious and significant news was interwoven with lighter material. There was a didactic element in my approach. I saw the task of the journalist as being not merely to inform, but to widen and sharpen public interest in the big issues of the day, not by preaching at them or trying to guide their views, but by setting out the facts clearly and comprehensibly, breaking complex matters down into terms which could be readily understood. 'Say simple things to simple people' A.J.P. Taylor was urged by his mentor at Oxford. I would have put this a little differently, if less elegantly, as 'Say things simply to ordinary people'. But the aim was the same. And in television we had now the great new instrument of film to help do this.

ITN had widened broadcast news values significantly from the moment when, in its first bulletin, it had reported on the progress of a crime trial at the Old Bailey. I extended this still further, for I set myself the goal of making a daily newspaper of the air, with its sport, show business, fashion and feature pages, its crime and human interest stories, as well as the hard news of the front page. It was to prove an overambitious scheme, for no bulletin lasting just under fourteen minutes a night could encompass all that. To provide a newspaper of the air needs a whole television channel, not just a news bulletin, and as the months went past we found ourselves forced more and more into the mould of a front page, with at best a glimpse of what the other pages might carry. But it was not a bad goal to set, for it broadened our ideas and our horizons.

We took fashion seriously, regularly reporting the London and Paris collections, engaging artists to sketch those models we were not allowed to film, avoiding the arch and condescending commentaries of the newsreels, treating these shows as news events which set changes of style for High Streets up and down the country. We widened

Fig. 7. George Ffitch.

coverage of the arts from the newsreels traditional quick look at preview days at the Royal Academy to include interviews with Maria Callas and with Margot Fonteyn, and with some reporting on the theatre, the ballet (of which Lynne Reid Banks was a devotee) and on books. When Colin Wilson sprang to fame as author of *The Outsider* we interviewed him outside the bivouac tent in which he slept on Hampstead Heath. When we got a free ride to the Cannes Festival for Lynne, she interviewed not only starlets on the beach, but Jean Cocteau in his home. We even tried our hands at theatrical criticism. On the London first night of *The Caine Mutiny Courtmartial*, a dinner-jacketed Ludovic Kennedy appeared in the late bulletin to give his appraisal. The newspapers warmed to the idea. One said we were 'leaping along with a string of ideas the BBC should have thought up years ago'. But the item scared the programme companies (particularly those with theatrical interests) and the ITN Board insisted that such reviewing, if it was to be done at all, belonged within the magazine format of *This Week*. Our experiment was to prove the only attempt to review plays on television until BBC2's *Late Night Line Up* did so a decade later.

We treated film stars as news, as they undoubtedly were in those days when the star system operated not only in Hollywood but in the minds of the public. Cinema going was not yet undermined by television; film stars were glittering and remote figures, a world away from their counterparts of a generation later, leading anti-war demonstrations in duffle coats and jeans. But we sought to treat the system with candour and humour, and to avoid being enmeshed in public relations fantasies. When Marilyn Monroe paid her first visit to London in the summer of 1956 we detached Robin Day from his duties as our Political Correspondent to interview her. Our cameraman at Heathrow had already added his own further dimension to the traditional coverage of a star's arrival. He had not waited until she stepped out on to the aircraft gangway, but had caught the moment as she paused inside the doorway to pull her already skintight dress just a shade tighter, and as she composed her mouth into her celebrated pouting smile, before she swayed down the steps.

Clifford had rightly detected that Robin Day had not a little of the showman in him, and would be able to cope with Miss Monroe as effectively as he had done with Truman. But he had to do so without words. Sir Laurence Olivier, with whom Marilyn Monroe was due to co-star in the film *The Prince and the Showgirl* ruled that she should give no interviews. The most he would permit was a shot of Robin seated beside the goddess on a striped silk divan in a suite in the Savoy Hotel. It would have appeared like a stiffly artificial reversion to film in the days before the talkies had Robin not had a bright idea – and the nerve to carry it out. On his way to the interview, he bought a red rose from the florist in the lobby of the Savoy. This rose he presented to Miss Monroe as the silenced cameras began to roll, to the delight of the photographers, producing a sequence which added a marvellous touch of slightly mischievous glamour to the ITN bulletin that evening.

One important element of the ITN bulletin formula was not designed. It just grew. This was the tailpiece, the quip or brief light-hearted story with which the newscasters rounded off the bulletins. It was to become as much the trade mark of the early ITN programmes as was the hard hitting interview. The tailpiece developed from the interplay of the minds of three men – Robin Day and Ludovic Kennedy before the cameras, and the Chief Sub, Desmond Grealey, behind them. Day had the relish of a former President of the Oxford Union for a neatly turned and pointed phrase; Kennedy had an instinct for doing things with a flourish; Grealey an Irishman's sense of the droll. Since the best tailpieces owed their impact to their aptness in highlighting or off-setting some point on the major news of the day, it is difficult to convey their effectiveness. So many words are needed now to describe the setting the viewer at the time took for granted that the items can seem laboured. But some survive the strain of the years.

In the spring of 1956 the Dockers were an inescapable element in every gossip column and, often enough, on the front pages of the popular papers. Sir Bernard Docker, a prominent Midland businessman with a peculiarly woebegone expression, was married to a petite blonde with a skill for backing into the limelight. They practised ostentatious spending in times grey with austerity, travelling in a gold-plated Daimler (the cost justified as publicity for the car), or moving about the Mediterranean in their yacht, their doings watched with apparent fascination by the mass public, perhaps because they were a reminder that hard times need not always be with us.

In April 1956 Lady Docker let it be known that she was dissatisfied with the seats allocated to her and her husband in the Cathedral at Monaco for the wedding of Grace Kelly and Prince Rainier. She threatened to leave before the ceremony. 'It remains to be seen', Ludovic Kennedy added, 'whether anyone will stop them'.

Peter Black of the *Daily Mail*, a man who could see television in its social setting, wrote the next day:

> I imagine that a gasp and then a shout of laughter ran round the whole of ITV's network. This healthy irreverence for the gods of the mob is something new in TV journalism (the BBC ignored the story). It is very much worth having.

Sometimes the touchés had a more specialist appeal. All journalists are familiar with the expression commonly used to avoid contempt of court when an arrest is made. It runs – 'Later, a man was detained and is helping police with their inquiries'. When an Alsatian dog went beserk, broke away from its owner on the top deck of a London bus and terrorized the conductor and the other passengers, the bus driver coped with the problem by driving to the nearest police station, where a professional dog handler got matters under control. 'Later, a dog was detained' the report concluded.

Robin Day's tailpieces tended to be more tightly integrated with the story of the day, to have a rare quality of sharing a joke with the audience. When the Grenadier Guards celebrated the three hundredth anniversary of their founding, Reginald Bosanquet rounded off an ITN report of their parade by interviewing the adjutant of one of the battalions. It was clearly not a process to the officer's liking, and a cold disdain impregnated his answers. One factor may have been Reggie's hairstyle. The camera, filming over his shoulder, emphasized the fact that, horror of horrors, his hair was long enough to overlap the top of his collar. It was a detail likely to catch the eye of every male viewer in those days of soldierly short back and sides. Robin summed up their probable reaction neatly. 'That's the news from ITN' he said at the end of the bulletin, 'and' he added in tones as incisive as that of the adjutant 'a haircut for that ITN reporter'.

The tailpiece was a technique which had to be handled with care, to ensure that it did not degenerate into that widespread sin of the broadcaster, facetiousness. It depended too on the earlier part of the bulletin being packed with hard news and strong film, to set this final shaft in perspective. Yet night after night for our first three or four years we were able to find an item or a quip which ended the day on a touch of humour. The tailpiece became an important element in establishing and sustaining our link with the public. By the time it died away, as such things will, that bond was strong enough to endure.

ITN's signature tune, *Non Stop*, too played an important part in establishing its individuality. It struck exactly the right note for those pioneering days, with its lack of pomp and pretension, with its implication that something exciting and yet stimulating was about to be reported. It was a musical statement of the proposition that news is too serious to be taken too seriously, expressing the jaunty confidence not only of a news medium, but of a country at last emerging from war and austerity.

Non Stop was not the work of a professional musician. It had been written by a Wimbledon solicitor, John Batt, based on a tone poem he had composed whilst still at school, in response to a challenge from his music master that dance music could never be as good as classical music. Needing money as a law student, Batt had hawked his compositions around the London music publishers, finally selling the copyright to Frances Day and Hunter for one shilling and half the royalties for ever. That half must have made a pleasant addition over the years to John Batt's other professional fees, though with the coming of *News at Ten* it was to be ousted.

We had to set our own standards day by day. Few signposts hadyet been established for this pictorial journalism, carried directly into family sitting rooms. One event which guided us resulted from a coincidence which, had it occurred in fiction, would have seemed impossible. When Arthur Miller married Marilyn Monroe, a woman reporter working for *Paris Match* was killed in a car crash on her way to cover the wedding. A freelance cameraman filmed her body by the roadside. In the picture her face was clearly visible. The film was used in a week-end bulletin which I had not seen on rehearsal. Watching in my home I recognized the dead girl as Princess Mara Scherbatov, a White Russian who had been our secretary in the *Daily Express* Paris office before the war. I had not seen her for some years, but even so the shock of the picture was considerable. I realized that to a relative or very close friend the impact would have been severe, quite unjustified by any legitimate news demands. We established then and there the ruling that in an accident the faces of the dead or maimed should not be shown – as later, in reporting funerals, we decided that close-up shots of grief were seldom if ever permissible.

Another story presented me for the first time with a problem which is with television to this day. How far is a story which is undoubtedly news invalidated by the fact that it is also propaganda – and intended as such? A freelance cameraman had spent some time behind the lines with the Algerian guerrilla forces, then in the early stages of their long and grisly struggle with the French. He had filmed the ambushing of a French paratroopers' jeep. The film showed the guerrillas lying in wait by a dusty road, opening fire on the jeep and gunning down in the open the one man who escaped the first burst of firing. It was an arresting sequence at a time when such scenes on film were rare. The cameraman made no secret, however, of the fact the ambush had been laid on especially for him to cover. This made me pause. We were only t10years away from a war which had cost millions of lives. British troops were still being killed and wounded daily in Cyprus and Malaysia. There was enough death in the world without it being especially organized for television.

The story also seemed to me journalistically invalid. Specially staged as it was, it was propaganda as much as it was news, propaganda which was claiming a place in the bulletins because of its dramatic impact. I resented having my hand forced in this way, resented material forcing its way into the bulletins because it was vivid picture. This was not the only film available of the Algerian war, though it was certainly the most arresting. We were not suppressing the news if we did not show this particular sequence. For these double reasons, human and journalistic, I turned down the story.

Yet the stance I had adopted was soon to prove hard, if not impossible to sustain in the future. The imperatives of the picture asserted themselves, by which the vividness and the violence of the action recorded became of interest in itself, and so became newsworthy, whatever its propaganda content. Indeed much news has, and always has had, inescapably, such a content. The answer lay not in keeping such material off the screen, but in keeping it within limits, and above all in setting it in perspective, and in identifying clearly those elements which were propaganda. Yet this Algerian ambush in the summer of 1956 had demonstrated the dangers as well as the advantages to society which the camera was bringing, and I do not regret halting to consider them before plunging down the road ahead.

These developments within ITN took place against a background of financial crisis within the programme companies. By July 1956 their losses totalled £10 million – a huge sum in those days. It was a period when, as the ITA were later to assert, the system was on the point of collapse. Yet for us in ITN that summer was a time of combined pressure and exhilaration. We knew that our very survival was at stake, but at least we had our hands free to fight for it. Our technical and financial resources might be limited, but our editorial initiative was unfettered. Every day new possibilities as well as new problems opened up, and we could tackle them unhampered by tradition. No hierarchy breathed down our necks, no higher command demanded explanations or laid down guidelines. The companies and the Authority had too many difficulties of their own to be greatly concerned about ITN. We sought no guidance from others. We could not afford to journey to the United States or Europe to study their output. We had no course but to go our own way, which we did with alacrity, as if not only Independent Television but television itself had just been invented.

And there was the nightly reward of seeing our product on the screen. I usually watched the main evening bulletin from the control room, my seat a canvas-backed chair on the grams dais – for we ran to no reserved space for visitors. This was the moment when there came together the results of the day's conferences and discussions, of the filming and interviewing and recording in the field, the processing and evaluating and editing in the cutting room, of stories pondered, stories cut, stories rewritten. All this now faced its unforgiving 13 minutes, 58 seconds on the air. I knew too that elsewhere in the building other were watching equally intently. In the newsroom the journalists would be gathered round the corner set; in the preview theatre the film editors would have switched off the film projector and have turned on the television monitor; from the processing plant the operatives (unless they had some last-minute film to put through the bath) would have come to the preview door, to watch the monitor from there. In the gleaming telecine room the white-coated operators would be ready to set their machines in motion; in the dubbing theatre, dark except for the lights above the reading desk, the 'voice' of the day and the scriptwriters would be ready for their turn; in the racks the engineers would be at their posts. For the moment we were no longer just in journalism. We were in show business, as dependent for the success of our production as is any playwright or any theatrical producer. This gave both an added tension and an added satisfaction to our work which newspaper journalism did not have. All of us in ITN, journalists as well as technicians, shared in the elation of a good bulletin, or in the dismay if one went awry. If I had missed the transmission of a programme I could tell from the faces of the staff, as they poured out of the life afterwards, whether it had been good, bad or indifferent.

It was an exacting way to end the day – but an exhilarating one. It left me – unless disaster struck – curiously refreshed, with fatigue and worry for the moment banished, to drive home through the darkened streets of North London, my batteries already partly recharged for another day on the morrow.

22

Proving ground

A hard proving ground for this new journalism was at hand. On Thursday 26 July 1956 President Nasser of Egypt announced that he intended to nationalize the Suez Canal. We were plunged into a period of news unlike any which post-war Britain was to experience until the Falklands crisis, a period in which interest in the news was dramatically heightened by the possibility of Britain being once again caught up in war.

ITN's records of the weeks which followed Nasser's speech provided a case study of how the technology and the methods of the time were used to cover a major, long-running story. On the fourteen days immediately after the speech, Suez was to provide the lead story in every one of ITN's main news bulletins, and in most of the early evening bulletins as well. Yet for the first two of those days, no film coverage was available from Egypt. CBS, on whose film service ITN relied for its Middle East coverage, had had their cameras at the rally at which Nasser announced his seizure of the Canal. But their film had first to make its way to New York, and 48 hours were to elapse before copies of it reached London. All that ITN could offer its viewers in the meantime were shots of vessels passing through the Suez Canal, obtained from wartime film in the possession of the Central Office of Information, and a glimpse of Nasser speaking into a microphone, from the CBS film library. Only late on the Saturday evening did we have the actual scenes of Nasser telling a wildly cheering crowd that Egypt 'would meet force with force'. It was to be another three days – five days after Nasser's speech – before any further film reached us from Egypt, when CBS came up with a brief sequence of Egyptian troops standing guard outside the seized offices of the Suez Canal Company.

The mind boggles at what would happen on such a story today. Within hours electronic news gathering teams and film crews, commentators, reporters, producers and film editors, traffic managers and news organizers from all over the world would be descending in their hundreds upon Cairo and Ishmalia, pouring out their pictures by satellite or by air freight, filming every inch of the Canal from Port Said to Suez, interviewing every Egyptian spokesman in sight against a background of the waterway, flashing pictures of every public meeting and demonstration on to our screens within minutes of their happening indeed as they were happening. By today's standards our coverage was austere indeed. Yet at the time its impact was remarkable. For this was the first major crisis to hit Britain in the television age, the first which could be seen as well as heard. Any pictures were a bonus gladly received by the viewers, accepted as providing a further dimension to the coverage in the newspapers or on radio in a way which was new and almost magical.

We were helped too by the fact that the centre of the story moved quickly from Egypt to London, where the decisions lay as to what action Britain and the other countries of the West should take. This brought the story within range of our home-based cameras, the only ones we could afford to deploy. On Sunday, 29 July French and American Ministers flew to London for the first of many meetings. Robin Day was newscasting that evening, and his opening story reflected his style, personalized and yet dramatized. 'At this moment, as I am talking to you, the Foreign Secretary, Mr. Selwyn Lloyd, is talking to the French Foreign Minister, Monsieur Pineau, and Mr. Murphy, the American Deputy Under Secretary of State, talking, of course, about what to do next about President Nasser'.

This is a good example of the approach we adopted to our audience at that time. We were conscious we were talking to individual viewers, many of them newcomers to the medium, and that our first task was to engage their interest. We were conscious too that news was something to be spoken, not announced, or proclaimed. It was a style which, as film became more abundant, was to become less intimate, as pictures rather than words provided the link between the viewer and the news.

Three days later the crisis assumed a new and more formidable shape. All countries whose ships made considerable use of the Suez Canal were invited to a further conference in London in a fortnight's time. At the same time the Government announced that the Queen had signed a proclamation calling up a number of reservists. The RAF stated that leave had been curtailed at a number of bomber stations; the Navy were preparing tank landing craft for service (withdrawing for this purpose some tank landing craft from their new civilian role of transporting liquid milk from Ireland). For good measure the Foreign Office was advising British subjects in Egypt to leave as soon as possible.

These were all portents of war – as was to prove the case. That afternoon I had a call from the Prime Minister's official spokesman, William Clark. He had been a wartime information officer in the United States who had joined *The Observer* after the war, and had returned to officialdom to serve Sir Anthony Eden at No. 10. We were old friends and colleagues and had gained our first television experience on the same programme, *Press Conference*. We talked in his ground floor office overlooking Downing Street, where a small crowd of holiday sightseers strolled and stared from the far pavement.

William came straight to the point. The Government meant business. The partial mobilization was not a bluff. Whatever happened in the weeks ahead, it was important to bear in mind that the Government was not going to let Nasser get away with seizing the Canal.

Clark made clear he had taken the decision to tell me this entirely on his own initiative. It was not a statement I could use, or attribute in any way to him. It was intended only as guidance in a situation which was likely to get confused in the weeks ahead. 'However different things may seem from time to time, as events unfold, I think you will find that this is what the policy turns out to be'.

It was chastening information. The risk which I had been concerned about from the outset, that a major crisis might hit the country before ITN was solidly established, was now a reality. The temptation to our audience to quit us for the BBC, which had served them so stoutly in the war which had ended eleven years earlier, would be great. Clark's news had, too, a personal aspect. My older son was about to begin his National Service in the Royal West Kent Regiment. If the fighting spread and lasted, it would be his intake who would have to carry out this policy. There were better places for 18 year olds to gain their baptism of fire than against guns dug in on that bare, drab desert wasteland south of Port Said.

Clark's information was of value to me in a flurry which blew up about our late bulletin that evening. I had had to take a telephone call during the rehearsal, and had failed to check part of the copy. I was taken by surprise, therefore, when Ludovic Kennedy, after film portraying the detailed measures for this partial mobilization, added the words 'whether all this means we are preparing to back our beliefs by force, or is a piece of gigantic bluff for the benefit of Colonel Nasser, your guess is as good as mine'.

This was not mere speculation. Kennedy had maintained the links he had made during his wartime service in the Royal Navy, and had good contacts with senior naval officers. They were aware of the difficulties of mounting an invasion of Egypt, and had good reason to believe that the Prime Minister must be bluffing.

I could not cite Clark as proof to the contrary. Nor was that the heart of the matter. What seemed to be posed here, illuminated by the glare of crisis, were the proper limits of newscasting. This was how the *Daily Telegraph* saw it the next day, when it rapped us over the knuckles in an editorial. 'No one is going to contend that this is a blunder of major importance, out of which Colonel Nasser is likely to make capital' it argued. 'But it offends against a principle which newspaper experience at any rate has established as of permanent value, that of the separation of comment from news'. In fact that was not the issue. Kennedy's words were not so much comment, not a view on the rights and wrongs of the issue, as an interpretation. Our mistake was to have raised a major, basic question about the Government's strategy without exploring or examining it fully. We had in effect said 'Eden may be bluffing' without offering evidence for or against this vast proposition. Today a host of pundits and experts would be on the air in a host of programmes, analysing and probing the issue from *every* angle. But in August 1956, except for *This Week* once a week, the ITN news was the only actuality programme on independent television. We had no scope in a 15 minute bulletin for any analysis in depth that evening. It had been all we could do to pack in the day's news.

Nor did the atmosphere of the time make debating a sensitive issue like this practicable on the air. We were only 11 years away from the end of World War II, and only three years away from the end of the Korean War. The public was not only used to restraint in discussing military possibilities, but approved of such restraint.

I was concerned that our estimate of Eden's intentions might serve to harden Nasser's

Fig. 8. Lynne Reid Banks.

attitude, and so make a settlement less likely, that the newsboys outside the Continental Hotel in Cairo the next morning might be proclaiming 'British TV say Eden is bluffing'. But the Egyptian newspapers did not pick up the story, or if they did we never heard of it. We were able in the next day's bulletins to get back on course by underlining the statements of the British and French Governments that they meant business, and by stressing their words that they were 'prepared to use force if necessary to secure an international Canal authority'. In the bulletins from then on we confined ourselves to proven information. The incident had indeed provided a sudden proof of how sharply words cut in this potent new medium.

Yet if we did not mount in the studio discussion of the Government's policy, the issue did not go undebated. For we carried at considerable length reports of the Parliamentary debates on the issue. Indeed we reported these at greater length than television did of the Commons debates on the Falklands issue, devoting at times seven and eight minutes of time to Robin Day's account of the events in the House. Each night Day had to rush back by taxi from the Commons Press Gallery, and deliver his report live into the bulletin. He spoke from notes, as there was no time to type out a script. Yet the outcome was a series of verbal sketches of which a veteran Gallery sketch writer could have been proud, mingling description with an element of evaluation which was then rare, if not unknown, in political broadcast reporting.

Two days after the reservists had been called up we were into August Bank Holiday, and our cameras caught the strange spectacle of one part of the nation spending its holiday watching the other part get ready for war. Seaside holiday makers crowded quays to see equipment and troops being loaded on to the aircraft carrier Theseus at Portsmouth. Holiday traffic was caught up on roads jammed by convoys of Army lorries. We filmed the wedding of a paratrooper due to leave within hours for the Middle East, and interviewed him and his bride just before they parted. It ran alongside film of the Battle of Flowers in Jersey, and of Derek Ibbotson running the mile in 3 mins 59 secs in drenching rain at the White City Stadium.

The contrast of that Bank Holiday was best caught by cameraman Ronnie Read in a sequence showing *H.M.S. Bulwark* moving down the Solent on her way to the Mediterranean. Sunshine broke through the storm clouds as holiday makers watched from a hillside. No reporter's words could have better conveyed the emotions of the moment than did Read's pictures, as men in white shirts and grey flannel trousers, or wearing army surplus khaki shorts which were the accepted holiday garb of the time, and women in bright print dresses watched the great ship move steadily away, leaving a wide gleaming wake in the sunlight.

We carried that night news that two days later the Prime Minister, Sir Anthony Eden, would speak to the nation on television and on radio at 10pm – the first time there had been a simultaneous Ministerial address on both television channels, and the first time that a Prime Minister had used television to speak to the country during a crisis. We had at the time in Television House a device for measuring the instant reactions of a panel of viewers within the A–R transmission area. A group of homes numbering, I think, 28 in St Pancras and 28 in Hastings was wired to a central point in Television House. Any switching of their sets was reflected instantly on a graph. On the evening of Eden's speech we watched this keenly, to see whether ITV was holding its audience in the crisis.

Within seconds on the Prime Minister starting his broadcast there was a sudden flurry on the graphs, which began to criss cross one another, as if the machine had developed a fault. The viewers were certainly switching channels, but in both directions, from ITV to the BBC, and from the BBC to ITV. The deduction was unavoidable. Many viewers, far from being glued to their sets to hear the Prime Minister's words, had hastily sought an alternative programme on the other channel. Finding no such thing, they had reluctantly settled back to watch – or at any rate to leave theirs sets on. It was a chastening reminder of the public's reaction to a crisis, a reaction you could attribute to the best of British nerve, or to heads in the sand.

23

The party conferences

The autumn of 1956 also saw an important advance made in the television coverage of politics in Britain. For the first time both the main parties, the Conservatives and Labour, agreed to allow television cameras to record fully the proceedings at their annual Party Conferences. These Conferences were, as a result, to become the main political events to come under the close scrutiny of the cameras – apart, of course, from General Election campaigns – until, some three decades later, the cameras were allowed into the House of Lords and then the Commons.

Newsreel cameramen had in the past been allowed in to Party Conferences to record brief excerpts from set piece orations by Party leaders. But any regular or consistent coverage, particularly of contested issues, was denied to the cameras because that would have demanded a level of lighting which those at the Conference were not prepared to accept and, which indeed, the newsreels could not have afforded. But once television's Outside Broadcast cameras had been admitted, the level of lighting provided for them enabled the film cameramen to work at will, so enabling the proceedings to be covered on a basis of their real news value.

The Conservative Party had admitted the television cameras in 1954 and 1955. But the Labour Party, under Clement Attlee, were prepared at the most to allow coverage of one half day of their proceedings in 1955. But with Hugh Gaitskell installed as Labour Leader that was changed. He saw television as a valuable counter balance to predominantly Tory press, and readily allowed full coverage of the Labour Conference.

Precedent suggested that we should recruit at least one strong outside specialist to reinforce our own journalists. This had been the BBC pattern over the previous two years, with William Clark and Robert McKenzie presenting the coverage of the Conservatives in 1954, and with McKenzie and myself doing the same for both parties in 1955. Aidan Crawley had brought in Percy Cudlipp, the former Editor of the *Daily Herald*, to strengthen the ITN team in 1955. I decided to break with this pattern, and to use only our own reporters for the task. If we were to build up a truly professional team, we must give our own staff the chance to gain every bit of experience going. Though neither Day nor Ffitch had previously reported a Party Conference, I decided to gamble on them, the more so since Day's reporting from Parliament had been of such a high standard. Back in Kingsway I could bring my own experience to bear by supervising the cutting of the film and editing the special conference reports.

On Monday, 1 October the Labour Party Conference got under way at Blackpool in the Tower Ballroom, whose ornate setting the cameras were soon to make as familiar to the general public as it already was to political journalists. All our Conference coverage had to be on film, for unlike the BBC, the ITV system had no lines on which live pictures or live interviews could have been carried. The first day was harassing, for the film had to be shipped by train from Blackpool, and rushed from Euston by despatch rider. Coverage of the morning session did not reach us until about six o'clock in the evening, and only the early part of the afternoon's proceedings could reach us in time for the late bulletin. I was thankful for the experience I had gained at Lime Grove the year before in the selection of film excerpts, and thankful too for the swift competence of the ITN film editors with whom I worked in a tiny cutting room, half of it filled by the Steenback editing table. The last segment of the film was still 'green', its emulsion soft from the developing tank when we dealt with it.

The result was encouraging. We had caught well both the atmosphere and the arguments of the main debate on Suez, and of a debate on industrial policy which had brought a fine clash between Sam Watson, the Durham miners' leader who had taken over Ernest Bevin's mantle as leader of the right, and Frank Cousins, newly emerged as a left winger. Robin Day rounded off the proceedings neatly with an interview with a cheerfully stubborn Irishman called O'Reilly, the one lone delegate who had opposed the Party line on Suez. He wanted us to attack Egypt, whether or not the United Nations approved.

The next day the cameras caught the drama of the announcement of the voting for the National Executive, and we followed our report of the debates with contrasting interviews with Aneurin Bevan and George Brown. Once again the camera work from the hall was first class. Like cricket coverage, filming Party Conferences called for skill in anticipating the big moments – for speakers like Aneurin Bevan never dreamt of working from a script – together with swift reaction to interruptions or heckling. Some of the older speakers co-operated with the camera crews by using dodges that stemmed from the days of the cinema newsreel. Manny Shinwell for instance, would pause and mop his forehead with his handkerchief as a sign that he was about to reach the key passage of his speech. But with speakers called to the rostrum from the floor that was not possible.

The third day the techniques of the time, and human fallibility, produced a film sequence which has become part of the folk lore of the early days of television. It arose from the practice of using cut-away shots to portray the reaction of the audience to the speakers. We did not have enough cameras to film both the speaker on the rostrum and the audience in the hall in the way which can readily be done with outside broadcast cameras. So we used a device long practised by the newsreels, under which a sound camera filmed and recorded the speaker, whilst another camera would film shots, termed cut-aways, of the audience in different moods – applauding enthusiastically, or lethargically, or listening in stony silence, or looking interested, or bored. The reporter would note on the film dope sheets which type of audience reaction would be appropriate, and the film editor would seek such a shot from amongst the cut-aways. There was an element of cheating in this, for the audience might have been reacting to a different speaker. But it was a legitimate element, provided we sought to convey accurately the audience's response.

But on this occasion the method came unstuck. Harold Wilson made a powerful speech from the platform. The editor, working as ever against the clock, put in a cut-away shot showing the audience clapping vigorously. It was, however, from another debate, and it showed, well to the fore amongst that audience, none other than Harold Wilson, applauding vigorously. What the viewers made of this I do not know. Perhaps they put it down to the marvels of this new medium.

The Tory Conference a week later at Llandudno proved even more of a logistical nightmare than had Blackpool. To get film of Sir Anthony Eden's main speech on Saturday afternoon back in time for use that evening we had to charter a light aircraft. Watching the report on the Steenbeck screen only 12 months after I had, at Lime Grove, viewed him speaking at Bournemouth, I was struck by the manifest strain in Sir Anthony's voice and manner. Even in the black and white negative the traits of a man feeling great tension were noticeable. To round off this Conference, Robin Day sought out two women prominent in the Tory Party, so giving the public the first chance to study in close up Lady Clarissa Eden and Lady Antonia Fraser.

This extensive political reporting was made the more palatable because there was plenty of other news with which to leaven the bulletins. Princess Margaret went to East Africa on her first major tour since severing her links with Group Captain Townsend. We had no money to cover such an extended journey, but we devised a scheme under which we shot en route some training film for an airline in return for a free passage, a device which enabled Ronnie Read to demonstrate to the full his skill as a portraitist with a film camera. One shot, showing Princess Margaret in a ballgown, and wearing a tiara, coming down a staircase for a ball in Nairobi, dazzlingly symbolized her return to the public stage. Another caught the almost imperceptible tightening of her expression as she came face to face, at a diamond mine in Tanganyika, with Peter Townsend's brother, who was an official in the Colonial service. But it was Read's filming of children along the Princess's route which gave these reports their remarkable quality. A childless man himself, he was a master at picking out in crowds the eager or drowsy, alert or solemn faces of children as they waved their flags or shouted their greetings.

Another story which enlivened that grim autumn concerned the hat-loving lady discus thrower. One outcome of the visit of Bulganin and Khruschev to Britain in April, the first by any Soviet leaders since the war, had been an agreement to increase sporting and cultural links between the Soviet Union and Britain. A Russian athletics team came to compete with Britain at the White City, to be followed by the first post-war tour of the Bolshoi Ballet.

This cosy rapport was disturbed when the Soviet Olympic champion lady discus thrower, Nina Ponomerova, was stopped as she left C & A Modes in Oxford Street, and later charged with stealing five hats to the total value of £1.12s.11d. When she failed to appear to answer the charge a warrant was issued for her arrest. The Russians called off the athletics match, declared Mrs. Ponomerova had been a victim of a 'dirty provocation' and threatened to cancel the visit of the Bolshoi 'for fear they might be exposed to similar provocation'. In the end, however, the Bolshoi's visit took place. At a press conference soon after the arrival of the dancers their director, Mr. Chulaki, was asked a somewhat double-edged question. Would the dancers be allowed to go shopping in London? He replied carefully, 'if they have the money, they will'.

This reply nearly landed us in a legal tangle that could have found its way into the text books. At the last moment, into the script of the story about this press conference, one line of comment found its way. To the report of Mr. Chulaki's reply about shopping were added the words 'Let's hope if they don't have the money, they won't'. Those ten words would make a neat subject for study by students of law and journalism. They contained two libels, one contempt of court, and the makings of a diplomatic incident. Set against the background of the yet uncompleted Nina Ponomerova trial, the words libelled her by implying that she had stolen the hat; they libelled the members of the Bolshoi by implying that they might steal rather than buy; they were in contempt of the court which had not yet completed the proceedings against Miss Ponomerova; and they could well have led the Soviet authorities to take such offence that they might have cancelled the Ballet's tour. When I heard them on rehearsal I leapt from my seat at the back of the control room, heading for the studio. In the doorway I collided with the chief sub-editor, also rushing towards the door. He sent me flying against the wall, nearly knocking me out, but did not stop. He leapt across the studio, seized the copy and struck out the final line. It stands there, hastily pencilled through, in the ITN archives to this day, an interesting reminder of one that did not get away.

24

Suez and Hungary

From mid-October onwards the Suez crisis moved steadily back to the centre of the stage. It became the main issue at the United Nations session in New York, the proceedings of which were well covered by the UN's own television cameras. Telerecordings were available to all TV stations, and though by today's standards these were drab and grainey, they did enable us to reflect directly the debates on a new aspect of the Middle East crisis, that of mounting tension between Israel and her Arab neighbours.

It was on to this scene that there burst suddenly the upheavals in Eastern Europe which were to culminate in the Hungarian rising. The first signs of trouble came from Poland, where mass meetings demanded the return to power of Gomulka, the leader ousted by Russia. Soviet troops stationed in Poland moved on Warsaw, and Soviet political leaders arrived there to impose their will. We had no means of getting a film crew into Poland, but the Polish authorities, intelligently alive to the value of publicity in the West, surprised us by making available excellent 35mm coverage of the Communist Party in session, of Gomulka and the new Politbureau, and, most valuable of all, shots of people at factory meetings and reading news in the papers in the streets. We backed this with first hand impressions from travellers back from Poland. One of these was the former Labour Minister John Strachey, who in the 1930s had been one of the main apologists for the Soviet Union. No reporter was available to interview him when he arrived at London Airport, but the cameraman, Cyril Page, put a series of questions to him which Arthur Clifford had telephoned through. It was an action which cut across at least two of our agreements with unions. But those were other days, and there were no repercussions.

Poland did not hold the public's attention for long. On Wednesday, 24 October the uprising began in Budapest. This time we were determined to get our own cameraman on to the scene. I drew on my experience in the Spanish Civil War and in Finland in 1939. I learnt there that in wars and revolutions there is a period of some days when matters are flexible and uncertain, when one set of red tape has not yet been replaced by a new set, a period when journalists can roam about with surprising freedom. I had been able to report at first hand on the opening battles in the Arctic Circle in Finland by the simple expedient of getting on a train and going to the front, without any special pass.

To cover Budapest we chose Martin Gray, a big, quiet resourceful cameraman from Movietone who had filmed in 1944 one of the war's most spectacular actions, the Allied bombing of the monastery at Monte Cassino. Like all our cameramen, he always carried his passport with him, and in a matter of hours was on a plane to Vienna. There he hired a car and set out for the Hungarian frontier. Around the frontier post milled a crowd of reporters and cameramen held up because they had no visas for Hungary, and could get none. All Gray could do that first day was film these frontier scenes, put his film on a plane from Vienna, and phone us through a report on events in Budapest as told him by a business man who had just got away from there. For Gray, too, there was no *punctilio* about demarcation lines. It was good, on the spot material, but it took second place in that night's main bulletin. We had an even stronger lead to hand, for an hour before we went on air news reached London that the Israelis had invaded Egypt.

That evening, Monday 29 October, the newly founded Guild of Television Producers was holding its second annual dinner and ball at the Savoy Hotel. It was not yet the television spectacular it has since become, but it was important for us because Christopher Chataway had won the award for the outstanding personality, largely because of his work for ITN, and ATV an award for *Sunday Night at the London Palladium*. Hugh Gaitskell was to make the presentations. I was sitting near him at the central table, when a waiter asked me to take a telephone call. It was from Arthur Clifford. 'The Israelis have invaded Egypt', he said. I scribbled a note, and placed it beside Gaitskell's plate. He at once hurried to the telephone in a nearby room, spent several minutes on it, returned to distribute the awards, and then drove back to the Commons.

We had got the news on to the screen within minutes of its reaching us from the agencies. Arthur Clifford had persuaded the Transmission Controller at Rediffusion to the flash the information by a primitive but effective technique. A slide on which was written in crude lettering 'Israel has invaded Egypt' was put on the screen in the midst of *Son of Fred*, the witty, somewhat surrealist satirical comedy show of the time. It was a rough and ready method, but it worked.

In reporting the great events which followed we had, unexpectedly, plenty of time on the air. Since we were the last programme of the night, I discovered it was possible to secure an extension of several minutes to the late bulletin simply by ringing up the Transmission Controller at Rediffusion, who would then notify the other companies of the length of this over-run. These gave us one of the greatest boons a television newsman can have – a flexible length to his programme. It was flexibility we were to utilize fully, until we were putting out bulletins nearly half an hour in length. In the pressures of that extraordinary autumn the half hour news format was tried out some eleven years before it found a permanent form in News at Ten.

Though we had no film of the Israeli invasion of Sinai – the Israeli censors saw to that – we were able to illustrate the story with earlier shots of Israeli troops on patrol in the desert, of Egyptian troops in their trenches, of air raid precautions in Tel Aviv, and of *H.M.S. Theseus* sailing from Southampton with British reinforcements. From Hungary, too, we had Gray's film of the aftermath of fighting just inside the border and more stories of the revolt from eye witnesses who had escaped to Austria. Contrasting with this were pictures of the previous night's Royal Film Performance, all the more vivid for being shot on 35mm cinematographic film, under an arrangement with the news reels. It showed the Queen and Princess Margaret in full evening dress meeting, in the theatre foyer, Marilyn Monroe and Brigitte Bardot, Victor Mature and Michael Powell.

Martin Gray had meanwhile found an unguarded side road on the Austro-Hungarian border and together with John Davies of the *Daily Express* had driven the 200 miles to Budapest. He filmed there for a couple of hours, and then he and Davis started on the long haul back to Vienna, snatching a few hours of sleep there before setting off on the road again. This was to be the pattern of their days for the rest of the week.

Gray's coverage was not only exclusive; it was admirably shot. Here for the first time were the students and workers of the new Militia, their shoulders draped with bandoliers, rifles and machine guns in hand, patrolling the streets of their liberated capital. Huge Soviet metal stars were hauled from the front of Communist headquarters; a statue of Stalin was toppled from its pedestal and smashed. One gripping sequence showed secret police of the old regime, curiously young, with lank, dishevelled hair, their faces white with terror, being escorted at rifle point from their headquarters. In another a frenzied crowd dug away at rubble barring the entrance to a building where other police agents were still holding out. Here indeed was television news fulfilling its role, catching a moment of history in the making.

This coverage from Budapest was all the more dramatic because the war in which Britain was herself engaged had, except for the continued bombing of Egyptian airfields, entered a curious limbo. Time was needed to move the cumbersome invasion forces from Malta, Algiers and Cyprus towards Port Said and the neighbouring Port Fuad, time filled only by reports of the attacks on the airfields and by the fierce debates in Parliament and in the United Nations.

On Saturday evening, 3rd November, Sir Anthony Eden addressed the nation once again on television and radio, to prepare the public mind for the assault which was to be launched onto Egyptian soil in the small hours of Monday. Soon before he was due to speak, I had a call from Hugh Gaitskell's office. He lived only a couple of blocks away from my home in Hampstead. He had no television set. Could he come round and listen to Eden on mine? He did so, and then and there sat down at my dining room table and wrote his reply. Had he stuck to that first script, his broadcast the next night might have been better. As it was he was harried and buffeted by advisers throughout the day, and appeared tense and edgy when he spoke on both channels the next evening, Sunday November 4.

We carried this reply of the Leader of the Opposition in a massive bulletin lasting 26 minutes. For on that Sunday the Suez story moved to our very doorstep, to the streets converging on Trafalgar Square, where the biggest demonstration since the war had been mounted by the Labour Movement against the forthcoming invasion. Even so that demonstration did not lead the bulletin, nor did our reporting that a landing of British and French troops was imminent. What led that Sunday night programme – for 'bulletin' was no word for a report of that length – were the reports from Budapest that Hungary's brief freedom was in its death throes.

By Saturday November 3 it was clear inside Budapest that the Russian forces gathered round the city were about to strike. Martin Gray realised that if he were caught in Budapest, he would have no chance of getting any film back. So, together with Jeffery Blyth of the *Daily Mail*, he set out by car for the frontier early on the Sunday morning. On the road outside the city they suddenly saw, pounding towards them, a long column of Russian T 34 tanks, dark and powerful against the drab winter landscape. Through the windscreen, with the wipers clearing a cone of vision through the rain, Martin Gray filmed these tanks, so securing one of the classic film stories of the crushing of the Hungarian revolution.

Near the frontier the road was closed by a Russian patrol. When Gray put his hand to his pocket to pull out his passport, the guards misunderstood the gesture, and fired a volley of warning shots through the car roof. They turned Gray back to a small town inside the frontier. There he met Noel Barber of the *Daily Mail*, whose head was in bandages, Russian machine gun bullets having grazed both sides of his head. Barber was confident that as a wounded man he would not be searched, and, he therefore took over Gray's film and carried it safely over the frontier to Vienna. Gray and Blyth found their way by detours and side roads into Austria, where Gray collected the film and rushed it by air to London. He had been the only British cameramen to cover events in Budapest, all the other filming being done by crews of the American networks, NBC and CBS, and by the American agency UPI.

25

Into battle

That long Sunday bulletin ushered in one of the most extraordinary weeks in British journalism. One great story pounded on the heels of another, all set against the highly emotive background of a country finding itself yet again at war.

The announcement that the attack had begun, with British and French paratroops dropping on to the Port Said airfield and around Port Fuad, came early the next morning. The first film we could expect would come from the cameramen who had been selected to cover the action on a pooled basis, for BBC, ITN and the newsreels. One cameraman went in with the airborne troops, and another with the main forces following up by sea. Censorship had been imposed, and all coverage would have to come back through Cyprus to the War Office in London. It would be twenty four hours before we could expect to have any film of the landings.

We had, however, good coverage from Cyprus of paratroops boarding planes, of their weapon cannisters being loaded, and of the accompanying bombers being armed. Ludovic Kennedy skilfully wrote his story so that it could be underlaid by this film, conveying the atmosphere, if not the actuality of the event. And if film was scanty from Egypt, there was good material from the Israelis, at long last, of their advance into Sinai; there were Martin Gray's chilling shots of the Soviet tanks on the rainswept road to Budapest; and there was, to finish another long bulletin (it ran some 20 minutes) the first of what was to prove a heart rending series of reports from the Austro-Hungarian border, as refugees began to stream across from reconquered Hungary. Among them were a group of bewildered children, some with labels tied to their clothes by parents who could not accompany them, giving their names, and their families' addresses.

This group came across at the frontier post, just before the Russians closed it. But others were to escape – and to be filmed escaping on subsequent days – at a point where the frontier was marked only by a narrow stream into which men, women and children slithered and floundered their way, clinging to a rope until the arms of the Austrian guards on the near bank could rescue them. To British people, many of whom had seen their own children labelled for evacuation in the early days of the war, and whose minds were filled with film shots of the long calvary of World War II refugees along European roads, these shots had a particular poignancy. They were to provide a highly emotive final item in bulletin after bulletin for nights to come. One sequence in particular struck at the emotions. A Hungarian carrying a large, closely wrapped parcel stepped into the icy river and, holding the parcel carefully above the water, moved with slow care to the Austrian bank. Once there, under the lens of the camera, he unwrapped the bundle carefully, even tenderly, to reveal inside it a baby, its eyes alert and eager, reflecting the joy and thankfulness on the man's face.

Ludovic Kennedy, who did much of the newscasting in these crucial days, to enable Robin Day to report from Westminster, conveyed by his bearing and his tone the emotion this stirred in him, as in any viewer. I agreed one evening that he should read, over that night's film of the refugees, a letter he had received, postmarked Uxbridge. Its words were 'Dear Mr. Kennedy, I hope you will not mind this letter direct to you, but I have been wondering, after seeing last night's late news, if you could find out the name and address I could apply to to take one of those poor bewildered little children who crossed into Austria with labels attached to them. My husband and I adopted a little girl eight years ago, and I think if we could give some of the happiness to one of those little mites that our own little girl has brought to us then perhaps we may be helping a little bit towards the awful problem of those brave people'. Presented with mawkishness or insincerity, this could have struck a false note, but done with the genuine feeling which manifestly animated Kennedy, it gave expression to a deep emotion in the country, and did much to set on foot the schemes for Hungarian relief which were to follow.

As if it were not enough to have the Suez and Hungary stories to report, we had to cope the next day, Tuesday 6 November, with all the panoply of a State Opening of Parliament (the old Parliament had been prorogued the afternoon before, just in time to save Eden from the embarrassment of explaining that his news of a Suez surrender was wrong) and with the American Presidential Elections, which were also held that day. The State drive, with the Queen and Princess Margaret in the State coach, and the escort of Life Guards provided an element of pageantry and glitter in what was otherwise a recital of war and politics – British and French troops embarking on transports for the seaborne landings which had taken place that morning; Israeli troops entering Gaza, Gaitskell and Frank Cousins speaking at a mass 'Law, not War' rally at the Albert Hall. The indefatigable Robin Day, having covered in the late bulletin Eden's announcement in the newly convened Commons that the fighting had ceased, went on to present a special 40 minute report on the American Presidential Election. We had even a live insert from the American Embassy in London, covered by an outside broadcast camera provided by ATV at a specially low price – the first occasion on which ITN had used such electronic coverage of a news story.

Good viewing though all this was, the real test for television that week was the coverage on film of the landings at Port Said. I was confident that Page would serve us well. Very tall, in his early thirties, he had a boyish face and manner which belied his swashbuckling assertiveness in pursuit of news. He was the only ITN cameraman who had not worked with a cinema newsreel, having come to us from BBC *Television Newsreel*.

Page had covered much of the ugliest fighting in the Korean War, and when that quietened down he devised a programme called *Messages for Home*, in which he filmed troops sending a message to their friends or families. His interviewer was a young corre-

Fig. 9. Robin Day interviewing General Stockwell.

spondent for the *Exchange Telegraph* called Alan Whicker, taking his first steps into television.

With Page's assertiveness went considerable artistic skill. Even after he had joined ITN two examples of his work continued to appear on the BBC – *The Potter's Wheel* and *The Swans* – two of the short atmospheric pieces with which the Corporation marked the intermissions between programmes. Page had too, one further quality invaluable for a cameraman – luck. That luck held when, among the score of cameramen waiting in Cyprus, he won the draw to go as the pool cameraman on the invasion fleet. At that stage another future television star was written into the script. For the conducting officer put in charge of the press for this stage of the operation was a young National Service Second Lieutenant named Michael Parkinson.

Page landed at dawn on Monday 5 November, with the first wave of supporting infantry, on a beach alongside the airfield, which the paratroops had captured shortly before. After filming the scenes at the airport, where the paras were dug in around the perimeter, Page got a lift in a jeep into the centre of Port Said. There he made it his task to liberate a large lemon-yellow Chrysler Bel Air convertible touring car, conveniently placed in a showroom window. With this Page rapidly toured the town, filming the bomb damage, the bodies lying in the streets, the troops and tanks moving forward, and one particularly macabre scene of dead bodies being loaded into a Coca-Cola truck. But he knew that film, however good, has little meaning unless it gets back quickly to base. Soon after midday, therefore, he drove back to the airfield, found an officer about to fly to Larnaca and persuaded him to carry the film with him.

Under the pooling arrangements, the film should have gone through Army Headquarters in Cyprus, where all potential users would have been advised of its existence. At Larnaca, however, the officer saw a plane about to take off for London. He gave the film to the pilot, who delivered it to the War Office in Whitehall. The next day the War Office handed the film on to us without any reference to its having been shot for pool use. Along the way the dope sheets on which Page had recorded his coverage had gone astray. Overnight, too, the cease fire had been declared, and the Services had abruptly lifted all censorship. In this sudden change the pooling arrangements were forgotten. When Page's film reached us in Kingsway, we assumed in good faith that it was our own, and used it as such. The BBC, equally in the dark, made no effort to claim a copy. So chance, coupled with Page's swiftness and ingenuity, gave us a scoop on the biggest story of the year.

Except for the one particularly horrific shot of the mangled, fly-encrusted face of a dead civilian, all of it was material which manifestly could and should be shown. We cut it into a story seven minutes long – an epic in those days of scrappy film sequences. Most of the shots were self explanatory, and we could interpret them without the dope sheets. One sequence, however, raised baffling questions. This showed a body, shrouded in a grey army blanket, being buried in a hastily dug grave in a public garden near the water-front. The Army firing party which fired a salute over the grave left the obvious assumption that this was the burial of a British soldier.

It was emotive material, which brought home sharply the human cost of these operations. British casualties had been slight, but in at least a handful of the watching homes this body in its grey blanket shroud might well be that of a husband, son or brother. Yet we had no sure knowledge whose body it was.

I decided we should show it, with a brief commentary that neither posed nor answered the question of identity. 'The dead were buried where they fell' were all the words needed. On the screen it formed a deeply moving conclusion to the report, evoking the realities of this struggle under the drab grey skies of an Egyptian November. It was only when the dope sheets finally escaped from the web of official red tape a week later that we learned that it had, in fact, been the funeral of an Egyptian. He was a lone sniper who had held out so bravely against the paratroops that they had accorded him this final tribute.

As I made these decisions, crouched over the cutting table with minutes ticking away towards transmission, I sensed how powerful was this new force of television in the coverage of war. It was the first time that it had fallen to an editor to make such rulings about scenes of battle on which our own troops were engaged. All previous film of action had been subject to censorship. The military authorities had decided what scenes should or should not be shown. Only the sudden accident of this two day war, which was over before any film had come in from the front, had removed that censorship, and placed this unique responsibility on our shoulders.

Even though the fighting was over, I knew that these scenes would stir deep feelings, political as well as human. The pathetic, crumpled bodies in the streets, the shattered buildings, the burial of this unknown soldier displayed the cost of war, arousing feelings only partially offset by the sense of strength and accomplishment conveyed by the British troops moving cautiously but steadily forward through the streets. This came through most vividly in a spectacular sequence of a Centurion tank racing towards a street corner and then swinging its gun in a 90 degree arc before moving on towards the Canal. The scenes of death and of damage would provide powerful arguments for those who opposed the action, and a stern glimpse of reality for those who supported it. In films of the Second World War few such casualties had been shown. In all the footage of D-Day, used over the years in countless documentaries, you will seldom see a British or American soldier fall as the troops storm ahead – and then only in a distant shot. Moreover, those scenes were at the time viewed only in the cinema, and some days later. These pictures were going into the homes of people throughout Britain almost as soon as the action had taken place. Yet I could see no other guide to their presentation than to present them in full, cut only for the purpose of clarity, except for the one peculiarly grisly shot whose loss detracted nothing from the impact of the whole. I was thankful that I had had to face these decisions only briefly. It was not an editorial task to be relished over a long period.

Excellent though Cyril Page's coverage of Port Said had been, it lacked the added dimension of natural sound. We had not been able to afford the extra fares necessary for a sound crew. But a chance to get a recordist on to the scene arose when the Central Office of Information asked us to film the damage done by Allied bombers in Port Said. They wanted the material to answer allegations that there had been widespread and wanton destruction of civilian areas. We were not caught up here in making propaganda, as our task was a purely contractual one of filming the scenes and handing the material over to the COI. Once this was out of the way, we were able to use the sound crew for our own purposes. Robin Day eagerly took on the task of reporting with them from Port Said, thankful for a break after his long days and nights in the Press Gallery at Westminster.

It produced some noteworthy material, in particular of the historic moment when the Danish troops, as part of the United Nations force, took over from the British troops in their foremost positions along the road towards Cairo. The Allied advance had halted at El Cap, some 10 miles south of Port Said, along the causeway which carried the road and railway between the Suez Canal to the east and wide salt marshes to the west. Here men of the York and Lancaster Regiment were dug in, facing the positions of Nasser's infantry and tanks several hundred yards ahead. And here, in the sunshine of a bright Egyptian December morning, the moment of the turning of the tide of British imperial power was recorded by this new and potent portrayer of history, the television film camera. Danish troops, tall, young, gangling conscripts, wearing the blue painted American helmets which were to become the hallmark of the United Nations, lined up on the roadside, with the waters of the Canal gleaming behind them. The curt commands of the young and very correct subaltern commanding the forward platoon of the Yorks and Lancs were clearly heard on the film, as were the click of rifle slings and the clatter of boots as the riflemen clambered out of their slit trenches, and lined up on the canal bank ready to begin their march northwards, as they – and the British Empire – withdrew.

Robin Day made the most of this, his first foreign assignment. He interviewed General Stockwell, the ebullient and forthcoming commander of the Anglo-French force, against a background of the harbour of Port Said, where the masts of sunken blockships still showed above water. Twenty years later the General was to recall 'the young Robin Day, with his insistent questioning'. Day discovered, too, that a neighbour of his, the Borough Engineer of Chelsea, had been recalled to the Royal Engineers to get the damaged sewage system of Port Said working again. Day began his report by popping up out of a sewer, lifting the manhole cover, and starting his commentary. He ended neatly, 'I return you now from the sewers of Port Said to the ITN studio in London'.

When the newspapers came to assess television at the year's end, they reinforced the approval ITN had won over Suez and Hungary. 'Consistently the news has led not only its BBC rivals, but most of the programmes around it' wrote Bernard Levin the *Manchester Guardian*.[1] *The Spectator* declared 'ITN ... have for the first time presented news to fit the medium, rather than ignoring the camera while reading the news. The considerable improvement in the BBC's standards is largely due to ITN's splendid pioneering work'.[2] They made pleasant reading within an organization not yet two years old.

---

1   *Manchester Guardian*, 22 December 1956.

2   *The Spectator* 28 December 1956.

26

The camera's victory

T he Suez invasion and the Hungarian uprising demonstrated as never before the power of the new element television had brought to journalism – the moving picture. The scenes which the cameras had recorded in Budapest and Port Said, and which were carried night after night into the homes of British viewers, made a powerful impact on the public mind. In watching, in a corner of their living rooms, the sight of young British conscript soldiers, their faces taut under their steel helmets, moving through the drab, shattered streets of Port Said, the British people had a foretaste of the experience which the American public were to undergo a decade later in the Vietnam war. And the sight of Hungarian civilians, rifles in hand, battling against Soviet tanks in the grey streets of the Hungarian capital conveyed an impression of Soviet aggressiveness which was to endure.

The impact of this film was the more remarkable because it was all shot with silent cameras. The pictures had to do all the work without the reinforcement of the natural sound of the events. Neither the BBC News nor ITN sent sound cameras into Egypt or Hungary whilst the fighting was under way. The only use of a sound camera in Hungary was by *Panorama*, who sent a sound camera and a reporter across the Austrian frontier to interview people in an Hungarian frontier town. Robin Day's expedition to Port Said with a sound crew, hard on the heels of the fighting, was the only one of its kind made by any news organization. It says much therefore for the skills of the cameramen who had covered the fighting that their silent pictures made such impact. They were all men of long and hard experience, several of them veteran cameramen from World War II, all trained to ensure that the pictures they recorded told the story in pictures. They argued indeed that they deserved the title of director cameraman, able not merely to record action, but to record it in a way which could be swiftly edited into usable sequences, seeking to compose their shots even when the action was fast moving, and providing a well-judged mix of long and medium shots and of close-ups.

This pictorial element in the television news bulletins attracted the attention and praise of the critics, not least in the BBC's own journal, *The Listener*. It praised the way the BBC had used the radio telephone to bring in spoken reports from capitals all round the world. But it added that BBC News 'did not bring us pictures as graphic or as red

Fig. 10. Huw Thomas. Photo courtesy of ITN.

hot topical as those of the Budapest funerals or the rebels digging up the street with their hands to get at the secret police in their basement hiding place. These were ITN picture scoops'. Suez and Hungary firmly established the camera as the great reporting tool of the television age.

The Suez and Hungary crises had also been an important forcing ground for interviewing, and on-screen reporting. The BBC had made wide use, by telephone reports relayed live into their bulletins, of the Corporation's network of foreign correspondents. For both ITN and the BBC the flow of statesmen and political leaders in and out of London had given reporters a chance to hone their skills in the VIP lounge at Heathrow. The Parliamentary debates were a challenge superbly met by the BBC's experienced correspondents in the Press Gallery, and their work was more than matched by that of Robin Day. Within ITN these long weeks of intensive news coverage had also given an opportunity to Lynne Reid Banks to prove that she could cover all types of news as well as any man.

ITN had from the outset brought women journalists on to the screen, with Barbara Mandell as an early evening newscaster, and Lynne Reid Banks as a reporter. Women now play such a large part in every aspect of television news that it is difficult to recall that this is a development only of the last twenty years. But Aidan Crawley, whose wife, Virginia Cowles, had won fame as a war correspondent in World War II, had been determined to open the way for women in to television journalism. In Lynne Reid Banks he had found an ideal pioneer for this task. With her wideset eyes, good humoured mouth and sharp intelligence, she soon became an important element in ITN's screen persona, coached, encouraged, chided and praised by Arthur Clifford, for whom she would have tackled any task on earth. She had got an early scoop from the Soviet Deputy Premier, Malenkov, by the simple process of pushing through the crowd outside the House of Commons and thrusting a microphone under his nose. Finding this charming girl in front of him, Malenkov made a quick politician's speech, which his interpreter translated, and Lynne Reid Banks had an interview without asking a single question.

The range and style of her work can be seen from an article she wrote at the end of 1956.

> Thanks to the Bolshoi, ballet really hit the headlines in 1956. I spent days in and around Covent Garden interviewing gallery queues, officials and commissionaires.
>
> At last the *corps de ballet* arrived, hundreds of them, shabby, weary and uncomprehending. In the crimson and gilt foyer of the Opera House, Margot Fonteyn greeted Ulanova, and what a contrast they made. Dame Margot, sparkling like a handful of jewels, all diamonds and jet and scarlet silk; Ulanova, unmade-up, her pale gentle eyes circled with tiredness, incongruous amid the plush and crystal in her putty-coloured mac and clumsy shoes.
>
> On the first night when all the glitter and glamour had been swallowed up in the dark breathless auditorium, my secret hope was fulfilled. I was told I might stand at the back of the circle. I watched Ulanova, incredibly transformed from a colourless middle-aged woman into a soaring goddess.

Of another evening's work she wrote

> As I was leaving the office, we learnt that a jet plane had crashed in a Kent village. I drove most of the way, the "meat waggon", as we called the lighting truck, skidding and jolting through the dark. I hated the journey, and feared what we'd find at the end of it.
>
> We arrived at last. The plane had crashed into a store after tearing the tops off some little houses, and they were all still burning. The street was a morass of mud and glass, snaked with firemen's hoses: through the streaming rain and hot flying cinders, the blaze lit up the sky and silhouetted hurrying, shouting figures.
>
> We found a fireman, who had stopped work long enough to have his cut face dressed, to tell us what he had seen and done. Two hours later the film was on the ITN screen.[1]

Lynne Reid Banks was the forerunner of today's generation of women journalists, who are prominent in every aspect of news coverage. She was an admirable forerunner, not only for the quality of her work, but also for her readiness to tackle all types of stories, however difficult or dangerous. She did much to overturn the assumption, widespread in all forms of journalism in the 1950s, that women should confine themselves to covering items deemed to be of special interest to women – education, housekeeping, children, fashion – and not get caught up in the hurly burly of general news coverage.

---

1   *TV Times*, 4 January 1957.

27

The BBC
counter-attacks

N ewscasting, as a technique, had stood up well to the test of Suez and Hungary. Over the long weeks of intense scrutiny, the more personalized style of Day and Kennedy had not cost ITN authority or impact. It had indeed strengthened ITN's contact with the audience. John Beavan, the London Editor of the *Manchester Guardian*, had noted this in reviewing television coverage of the crisis for *The Spectator*. He wrote 'the last item was another moving newsreel from the Hungarian frontier. At the end of it Ludovic Kennedy spoke one simple sentence about this concluding the news for the night. Kennedy did not conceal, as a BBC announcer would instinctively have done, that the film affected him as deeply as it had us. Here I think is the real difference between the BBC and ITV News. The BBC announcer is a real purveyor of information. The ITV newscaster shares the news with the viewers'.[1]

The BBC had, however, in that autumn of 1956 taken some important steps towards reducing the advantages in presentation which this more personalized style had conferred on ITN. They put names to the news readers whose faces had been familiar on the screens for the past fifteen months. The burly man with heavy horn-rimmed spectacles emerged as Wallace Greenslade, already newsworthy as the possessor of a gimmick – he put on his spectacles to mark the start of the bulletin, and took them off as a sign that he had finished. The round faced man with the measured manner of a high court judge was Frank Phillips. He had in fact needed no introduction to many older viewers, because during the war he had been one of the radio news readers who were deliberately named before the bulletins as a safeguard lest some wily German might gain access to the studio, and broadcast false news. The neat, incisive reader with superbly clear diction was Richard Baker. The son of a plasterer, he had been schooled at Kilburn High School, where he had won a scholarship to Cambridge, before becoming a wartime gunnery officer in the Royal Navy – a background very much that which we sought

---

1   *The Spectator*, 8 November 1956.

for recruits to ITN. He was soon to be joined by another wartime sailor, Robert Dougall, and by a youthful Kenneth Kendall. Within a matter of months Greenslade and Phillips were to be phased out, and the more telegenic trio of Baker, Dougall and Kendall were to give the BBC a highly effective and efficient team of news presenters.

Their impact was helped considerably by the Corporation's decision to do away with another self-imposed limitation, and allow the use of a teleprompter. It is remarkable how much more strongly spoken words come over on the screen when they are delivered by a man or woman looking steadily towards the camera, rather than changing their gaze to look down at a script. Further improvements to the BBC News bulletins came as they deployed more effectively the abundant resources at their disposal. Their film camera work had always been good, but had been marred by the poor quality of its film processing. Old fashioned processing equipment at Alexandra Palace had often brought drab and grubby pictures on to the screen, a technical defect which had added considerably to the impression that BBC bulletins were dull. Now a new processing plant was providing pictures as sharp and clear as those which an excellent modern Debrie machine had given ITN from the outset. The BBC also improved markedly their film coverage of news from overseas. They had relied to a considerable extent for foreign news on the material provided by the one international newsfilm agency, United Press International – UPI – an offshoot of the Fox Movietone newsreel service for cinemas. Though this was competent, it was at times inadequate because it was shot not specifically for British viewers, but for the American networks and the emerging news services in European countries. ITN, by sending its own cameramen from London, had produced much better coverage of the tour of the Queen and Prince Philip to Portugal and Sweden in 1956, at a time when Royal tours, particularly those of a young Queen still in the early years of her reign were very newsworthy.

To improve their foreign coverage, BBC News took, early in 1957, the major step of setting up its own international film agency. This venture, in which it was joined by the Canadian, Australian and New Zealand broadcasting services, was at first called BCINA – the British Commonwealth International News Agency. This name was, however, soon changed to Visnews, a title which had not only a more modern ring, but was a better title under which to sell the service to television stations in Europe, and soon throughout the world.

By the early months of 1957 television news in Britain, both on the BBC and ITN, had settled into a common technical pattern. A single newscaster in the studio, almost always a man, presented a programme of between 10 and 12 minutes in length, in which spoken news alternated with film reports. Unlike today's practice, very few, if any, of these film reports showed the reporter in vision, speaking into camera on the spot. Technology was not sufficiently advanced for that technique to be practised, except in rare instances, within the limited time available for daily news coverage. A reporter might occasionally appear in vision, in the studio, introducing a film item, but his main role out in the field was that of interviewer. Even then he would not be responsible for the final shape of the story of which the interview was a part, nor did he write the commentary for it. That was the work of a script writer in the newsroom. He – or she – for there were able women script writers and sub-editors, both on ITN and the BBC from the earliest days of television news – would write an introduction to the story, to be read by the newscaster or newsreader in the studio, and then the commentary which would go with the subsequent film. The film would be usually silent coverage, into which the reporter's interview would be woven. The commentary over such film was, in the case of the BBC, read by the news reader from the studio. In the case of ITN, it was read by an offscreen 'voice' – a commentary reader working from another studio. Each method has its merits and demerits. The BBC's method gave the bulletins unity and smoothness of flow because the filmed news as well as the spoken news was delivered by the same figure. The drawback was that the news reader needed added time for rehearsal, so that problems arose with late stories. The ITN method left the newscaster free to concentrate on his central task, that of presenting the main body of the spoken news from the studio. It also gave a variety and pace to the bulletins, because different voices came in with different pieces of film. At times up to three different voices might be on the job, one dealing with political items, one with sport, and a third – often a woman's – with items like fashion. Still pictures, maps and brief snatches of film, termed underlay, were used to illustrate spoken news from the studio. The commonest form of underlay film was that of Ministers arriving at Downing Street for a Cabinet meeting, and was termed derisorily by some critics as being simply moving wall paper.

On both services a reporter would on occasion come in to the studio to deliver a spoken report, usually on a political, diplomatic or industrial story, and occasionally on a story of high drama, such as a train crash. The one area of news always covered in this way was Parliament. A two to three minute report of the day's debates in Parliament was a regular feature of news bulletins of those days, and indeed the proportion of bulletin time devoted to Parliamentary coverage was greater then than is the case today. Presenting these spoken cameos of Parliamentary events was an art in itself, and produced a number of very skilled practitioners. E.R. Thompson had been the great pioneer of the genre from the BBC, soon to be flanked by Conrad Voss Bark (an ardent fly fisherman who rested his nerves after broadcasting by tying trout flies) and Roland Fox. For ITN, Robin Day set superb standards, followed by Ian Trethowan, George Ffitch, Alastair Burnet and John Whale. The task was in due course taken over first by recordings of the sound, and then of the sound and picture of the Lords and, finally, of the Commons in action.

In its first two to three years ITN often included a live studio interview in its bulletins. This was done partly because such interviews had the added spice and excitement of being live, of providing an element of the unexpected. But they were in part the product of necessity. They were cheaper than filmed reports. With the number of camera crews drastically cut back in the days of financial stringency, ITN could still bring people in the news before the cameras by inviting them to its Kingsway studio. Centrally placed as it was, within a ten minute taxi ride of Westminster or the West End, ITN could use this method with a freedom denied to the BBC, away in the outer North London suburbs.

One editorial problem posed by the state of technology at this time was that of adding artificial sound to news pictures which had in fact been shot with a silent camera. Although we had continued, ever since that morning outside the Austin factory in the summer of 1956, to record wherever possible the actual sound of events, the microphones of the time were not yet sufficiently developed to enable this to be done easily. Nor did we in ITN have enough sound camera teams available for this task. And though the BBC had more crews, they too were reluctant to keep crews standing by for possible hard news coverage when they could be otherwise used for essential interviews. Yet silent film, without any sound backing, looked and sounded artificial.

The answer of the cinema to this problem had been music. Film producers had backed their newsreels with music just as, since the early days of the lone pianist hammering out mood music, the background to feature films had been music. Indeed the movies had become the talkies in the late 1920s as an accidental by-product of the search for a way of transmitting specially recorded music tracks to accompany feature films. The technique by which appropriate music could be matched to picture proved equally efficient for matching the sound of words to the movement of the lips of the actors and actresses, and so the talkies were born. But all this required elaborate sound stages and complicated recording gear which could rarely be used to film news. So for the newsreels, musical backing remained the main way by which film could be made presentable.

This method had been carried over into television from the newsreel, modified only by the use of dubbed sound. The cinema newsreels had, on occasion, added clapping or cheering or even specialized sounds like the crack of bat on ball at a cricket match. We carried this process still further. Both BBC News and ITN steadily built up extensive effects libraries of recorded sound effects with which to give a simulated reproduction of natural sound. Our dubbing editors vied with one another in the skill and speed with which they could match the sound of gunfire to film of fighting, or pick the appropriate level of crowd noises for demonstrations and processions. We both strove to produce a high level of verisimilitude in this work, yet inevitably it involved an element of deception, which troubled the more punctilious journalists. One BBC executive confided to me his concern at being asked to authorize a bonus to a film editor who had skilfully matched artificial sound to pictures of trees being cut down along the Berlin Wall. 'It could have been the real thing' read the commendation. 'I thought we were in the business of providing the real thing' the executive commented to me, as we discussed this problem which had been with picture journalists ever since Luce had told his *March of Time* editors to 'fake the truth'.

The use of music as backing to news programmes and documentaries was to be strongly criticized by the Pilkington Committee in its Report on Television in 1932. But by then it had largely died out. The development of striped magnetic film, and of improved microphones made it easier to record the real thing. Public opinion also played a part in opposing the techniques, once the politically active had hit upon the demonstration as a way of attracting publicity for their causes. The level of clapping at a cricket match, or cheering at a Cup Final, did not have to be exact to meet the needs of reasonable accuracy. But political events were in a different category. Demonstrators scrutinized every foot of coverage of their actions which appeared on the screen, and were quick to protest against anything which they might deem to be distortion. There was no way in which we could accurately simulate the shouts of demonstrators or the voices of the police. Only genuine natural sound coverage would serve. Where that was not available, we had no alternative but to run the film silent, with only commentary to back it up. We had to have regard, too, to the fact that filmed reports were no longer just news. They were also evidence which might be cited in court as to the behaviour of demonstrators or police – and complaints about police methods soon followed demonstrations as night follows day. The conditions which had made both music and dubbed sound acceptable in the 1950s did not survive into the 1960s, when television news secured pride of place as the main source of broadcast news. Fortunately by then technology had provided better film and microphones to meet the needs of this truer actuality.

28

Politics televised

T
he Suez crisis had one immediate effect on the broadcasting of politics. It brought to an end the Fourteen Day Rule, under which broadcasters were forbidden to discuss any issue which was to be debated in Parliament in the coming fortnight, or to invite any MP to discuss on the air any bill before the House. The Rule represented Parliament's last effort to keep some grip on the choice of subjects to be broadcast, as distinct from insisting that public issues should be treated impartially. It had come into being after the war, and had at first rested on a gentleman's agreement between the BBC and the political parties. With the coming of ITV it was, however, made into a formal rule, promulgated by the Postmaster General, Dr. Hill, in July 1955. Winston Churchill had strongly supported the Fourteen Day Rule. He was concerned with protecting the House of Commons against the rise of rival forum, the television studio. With remarkable prescience he sensed the power of this apparatus which could carry pictures in the corner of every sitting room in the land. He believed that democracy could be endangered if access to it was controlled by people chosen not by public vote but by producers not directly answerable to the electorate. 'It would be a shocking thing' Churchill said, 'to have the debates of Parliament forestalled on this new robot organization of television and BBC broadcasting. The rights of Members of Parliament must be protected against the mass and against the machine'.

The Suez crisis was too big to be contained within such rules. Coverage of it soon made a nonsense of any requirement to stifle debate on matters due to be raised in Parliament within the next fortnight. Every interview we did at London Airport, every report on public reaction, every street interview was a breach of the Fourteen Day Rule. The issues of Suez went too deeply into the lives of the public to be inhibited by such formalities. When the Rule came before the Commons for renewal early in December, Eden yielded to the logic of the situation and abandoned it.

In the aftermath of Suez another more fundamental inhibition on political broadcasting also began to be undermined. This was the taboo on the coverage, during Parliamentary elections, of the arguments of the candidates and of the parties. Ever since 1945 the BBC had confined its coverage of the arguments put forward at elections to a summary of the manifesto of each party, and the formal party political broadcasts, carefully allo-

Fig. 11. Ian Trethowan.

cated by agreement amongst those parties with a substantial number of candidates in the field. Apart from these, the only election news was of the movements of Party leaders and candidates and non-contentious information about the number of contestants and the arrangements for polling. Anything which could influence the way people voted was rigorously excluded. This had been sensible enough in the conditions of 1945, when the General Election was conducted whilst we were still at war with Japan, and when opening the air waves to controversy could have had repercussions far beyond our borders. It persisted, however, throughout the General Elections of 1950,

1951 and 1955, surviving even such a manifest absurdity as the banning from BBC news bulletins in 1950 of any reference to a proposal made by Sir Winston Churchill in an election speech at Edinburgh for a Big Three conference on the future of the atom bomb. This decision was described by a leading historian as 'neurtrality carried to the lengths of castration'.[1]

One reason why this ban was continued into the 1950s lay in the Representation of the People Act of 1949. This had set in train a long overdue redrawing of constituency boundaries, and had done away with the historic anomaly of the University seats. It had also cleared up an obscurity about election expenses. There had for many years been legal limits on the amount of money which candidate might spend in pursuing a campaign. But the growth of the newspapers, with their widespread coverage of elections, had produced a grey area. Was newspaper support for a candidate, or news about him and his activities, to be reckoned as a contribution to his expenses? The 1949 Act ruled clearly that it was not. In clearing up one obscurity, the act produced another. For it remained silent on whether broadcast coverage was equally exempt – a point which at the time passed unnoticed not only in Parliament, but in the press. Yet the Act as it stood could be taken by any rigidly-minded lawyer – or broadcasting executive – as implying that any reporting of elections on radio or television was an election expense. If this were so, any broadcaster who covered the arguments of an election campaign risked a fine, or even a year in prison.

Independent Television had not been on the air at the time of the General Election in April 1955, and none of the by-elections during 1955 and the early months of 1956 had been of sufficient interest for us to consider reporting their campaigns. Soon after Suez, however, a key by-election was called at Melton in Leicestershire. Not only did it provide the first gauge of public opinion since Suez, but it was in the seat vacated by Sir Anthony Nutting, who had resigned both from the Foreign Office and from Parliament as a protest against Eden's policy. It was clearly a story we should cover.

In planning its coverage I did not take up time seeking a legal ruling on the Representation of the People Act, in the hope that radio and television might have grown so greatly in the interval that they would now be deemed to be covered by the exemption extended to newspapers. That did not seem to me the heart of the matter. More important than such legal niceties was the attitude of the main political parties. The experience of four post-war General Elections seemed to have confirmed in the minds of politicians the view that broadcasting was too powerful, and too potentially dangerous a force to be set loose at election times, except within the confines of party political broadcasts. So long as this attitude prevailed at Westminster, no progress could be made with the reporting of elections on television because for that to be done we needed the co-operation of candidates and of party leaders to bring across the sight and sound of the election debate – and an election is nothing if not a debate. Yet the politicians if they chose could effectively veto such coverage simply by refusing to take part in it. Refusal by any one candidate could throw our coverage out of balance, and so bring us up against another Act of Parliament whose requirements were clear beyond doubt, the Television Act, with its insistence on impartiality in politics. We had to

---

1   H.G. Nicholas, *The General Election of 1950*, MacMillan, p. 126, 1951.

achieve, therefore, not so much a change in the Representation of the People Act, as a change in the attitude of the politicians. We had first to demonstrate to them that television could cover elections fairly, if we were to win them over to accepting broadcast news as part of the democratic electoral process.

Robin Day suggested a way of doing this by stages. We could cover the Melton campaign as if it were just another news story, but hold back the presentation of our report until the late bulletin on polling day. This would give our report immediacy, but would mean that it would not have gone out before the polls closed at 9.00pm, and therefore could not be held to have influenced the result. We would mount as it were a dry run of an election report, but broadcast it at a time outside the constraints of the Act.

So Day went off with a camera team into the mists of Leicestershire, to work out a pattern for constituency coverage of elections. A month later George Ffitch repeated the same process in the drab, bomb damaged streets of South Lewisham, followed by another report set against the hillsides of Carmarthenshire; all constituencies in which by-elections were held. In these reports we evolved a pattern in which we showed scenes of the constituency to establish its nature; we interviewed voters about the issues; and in particular we interviewed the candidates, securing from them a statement of their policies, so bringing the election argument for the first time clearly to the screen.

The next step was to apply these techniques to reporting an election whilst it was still in progress, by putting out the report some days before the polls closed. Early in 1958 an opportunity offered itself in a by-election at Rochdale. It had caught public attention because Ludovic Kennedy had announced that he was resigning from ITN to fight as the Liberal candidate – the first time that a television personality had turned politician. We were preparing our coverage when a new factor intervened. Granada, within whose transmission area Rochdale lay, invited the three candidates to appear in a series of programmes which they intended to mount. The Labour and Liberal candidates accepted, but the Tories held back whilst they took advice as to whether such appearances would breach the Representation of the People Act. I decided to meet this problem by not carrying the actual voices of the candidates, but by setting out the main points of their election addresses over film of them canvassing. This we blended with film of the constituency, and with interviews with electors about the issues. We got on with this report whilst the lawyers argued. So in our main bulletin on 31 January 1958 the first election report containing the arguments of the contenders in a Parliamentary election whilst the election was still in progress appeared on the British screen. *The Times* noted the fact the next day in a paragraph austerely headed 'Interview by ITN'. The *Manchester Guardian*, under a headline, 'Fair Shares at Rochdale' underlined the fact that this was the first ever broadcast of an election campaign. 'Whatever the complications to be sorted out by parties, Government and lawyers, the Rochdale by-election went on the screen last night, and ITN gave a substantial slice of politics and opinions in that most independent and 'awkward' of Northern towns.

'The Gothic gloom, the murky sky, the solemn, unshaken face of Rochdale were fairly shared among all three claimants. This was the opening, while George Ffitch, the reporter, stood there amid the mist summarizing the parties' claims, fairly, always fairly .... Then to the man and woman in the street. Here Rochdale showed a confident and canny face: nothing was given away easily. There was the bus conductor who, when asked about international affairs, said 'Well, the atom bomb seems to have something in it. '... To sum up, ITN's sally into by-election reporting – the first time it has ever been done – could do no harm, and might do much good, if only in making politics a little more real and down-to-earth for people far outside the range of Rochdale'.

Over the weekend the Conservatives decided that it would be proper for their candidate to be heard as well as seen on television, and five days later the first of two Granada election programmes were broadcast. In one the candidates were questioned, each in turn, by a panel of three newspaper editors. In the other each candidate made a statement about his policy, after lots had been drawn to determine the order of speaking. This was accompanied by film of the constituency and interviews with electors along the lines we had already made familiar. These two programmes carried the broadcasting of elections an important stage further. In them for the first time the voices of the candidates were heard arguing their own policies. After Rochdale the right of television and radio to report elections was never in any doubt.

The accuracy of our diagnosis that the key to establishing the right of the broadcasters to cover Parliamentary elections lay less in arguments about the law, and more in convincing the political parties that we could so fairly (which the early dry-run reports had demonstrated) was emphasized some five and a half years later, when we went ahead with the coverage of a by-election in defiance of one of the candidates. This occurred in the by-election in Perthshire in which Sir Alec Douglas Home sought a Commons seat after resigning his peerage on being made Prime Minister. There were seven candidates in the field.

One of them, the Liberal candidate, refused to allow his meetings to be filmed, and refused to co-operate in any way with the television coverage. He was a local man, Alister Duncan Miller, who had nursed the constituency assiduously over the years. He held that television, with its power to present candidates and issues swiftly to the public, conferred an unfair advantage on newcomers who were contesting the seat without having put in any such ground work. Nothing we said could persuade him to take part in the programme which we had planned.

This was the obstacle we had feared back in 1957 and 1958, but by 1963 the climate of opinion had changed. The televising of politics was by then a commonplace, accepted as a normal part of the political process. We decided therefore to challenge Mr. Miller's stance, and prepared a report which included film and interviews with each of the other six candidates including the Prime Minister. We filled the gap left by Mr. Miller's refusal by showing a still picture of him, and reading a summary of his policy over it. The Liberal Party protested, but not too much, and accepted the clear victory which Sir Alec Douglas Home subsequently won. The ITA had supported us in our action, though they banned a later Granada programme which, because the Liberals had refused to co-operate, was about to be presented with the Liberal case going unstated. It was a further small victory for the televising of politics, but it was to prove short lived. The Representation of the People Act was in due course amended so as to authorize the broadcasting of elections, but also to make illegal any reports which did not have the consent, and the co-operation of all the candidates, a position which prevails today.

A fortnight after the Rochdale by-election, political broadcasting took another big step forward when for the first time a Prime Minister agreed to be interviewed at length on the air. Mr Harold Macmillan, perhaps to offset the defeat his Party had suffered at Rochdale, agreed to be interviewed on the BBC's *Press Conference* and, three day's later, by Robin Day on a new programme we put out early on Sunday evenings, called *Tell the People*.

No previous Prime Minister had been prepared to submit to interrogation outside the House of Commons. Neither Sir Winston Churchill nor Mr Attlee would have contemplated giving an interview on radio, let alone on television, that medium which Churchill regarded as an unworthy upstart. Had he been younger, no doubt he would have mastered it, as he mastered radio. But the added visual dimension was not something which he welcomed. When in 1948 it was suggested that he and Mr Attlee should each make a television broadcast, Churchill spurned the proposal in these words. 'When I was very young, if one said something in one's constituency which might have led to trouble if it was spread abroad, nothing happened. Now one has to weigh every word, knowing all the time that people will be listening all over the country. It would be intolerable if one had to consider also how one would appear, what one would look like all over the land'. He never gave a Party Political Broadcast on television, nor appeared in any television programme – other than when filmed for the news as he went about his business – except to make a brief, moving and unscripted statement to the cameras after watching a BBC programme in which many of his friends paid tribute to him on his eightieth birthday in November 1954.

It was left to Sir Anthony Eden to be the first Prime Minister to grapple with television. By the time he entered Downing Street in 1955 this new medium had begun to establish the interview as a more natural form of communication with the viewers than the direct talk favoured by radio. Though Eden had used the technique of the direct talk on television as a means of addressing the country on three occasions – once during the visit of Bulganin and Khruschev, and twice during Suez – he had confined any interviews to brief occasions at London Airport. Harold Macmillan had followed the same pattern. It was in one of these short airport interviews that he had dismissed the resignation of his three Treasury Ministers as 'a little local difficulty'. His readiness to be interviewed at length in February 1958 represented therefore a distinct change of policy towards this new medium.

The Prime Minister's appearance before a team of three journalists on *Press Conference* on 20 February had made little impact. The basic defect of a panel interview had again been apparent, as the questioners cut across each other's lines of inquiry. *The Times* described the BBC inquisitors as 'a restrained group' and the Prime Minister seemed equally restrained in his replies. That was certainly not the case in *Tell the People*. Mr Macmillan was in good form from the moment when, in black coat and striped trousers, and wearing a red and blue Guards Brigade tie, he walked into ITN. He noted appreciatively that the producer of the day, Robert Verrall was (by virtue of his wartime service as Sergeant R. Verrall, Welsh Guards) wearing the same tie, and settled himself into a chair beside Robin Day. To facilitate the changeover with the newscaster, whose bulletin would finish in the same studio only a couple of minutes before the interview was due to begin, Day was due to occupy the newscaster's chair, which had a higher back and was altogether grander than that provided for the visitor. Mr Macmillan commented drily on these seating arrangements. Robin Day at once offered to change chairs. 'Not at all, not at all' insisted the Prime Minister, 'I know my place'.

The interview filled the front pages of the morning papers the next day, chiefly because Robin Day had raised the most sensitive political issue of the moment, the question of whether the Prime Minister had any intention of moving the Foreign Secretary, Mr Selwyn Lloyd, from his post. Though this was being widely canvassed in the papers, the *Press Conference* panel had not raised it. The Prime Minister took it in his stride, dismissing the idea as being 'not in accordance with my idea of loyalty'. The papers found Mr Macmillan as showing himself 'firm and confident in the face of vigorous cross-questioning, certainly the most vigorous cross examination a Prime Minister has been subjected to in public'. Mr Macmillan was later to say that it was in this interview that he first felt he had mastered television. Certainly from then on he was readily willing to appear before the cameras, to face up to, in both senses of the word, television as part of the democratic process.

In that Spring of 1958 we were still in the first flush of confidence in television as the new journalism. We luxuriated in its strength, in its capacity to offer the sight and sound of events as they happened, in the way we could bring familiar spectacles, like an opening of Parliament or a Cup Final, quickly or immediately to the screen, in our chance to range widely and with a fresh eye over our own land and the world outside. The cliche 'a window on the world' which *Panorama* proclaimed itself to be each Monday night seemed true enough. We spoke condescendingly of 'steam radio', and I argued with sincerity that had television been in existence in the thirties, it could have stopped the rise of Hitler. Under the candid lens of the camera, and under sharp questioning, he would have been seen for the monster he was. That he might instead have conned and charmed the mass of the public as skilfully as he did most of those Britons who were admitted to his presence was a possibility I rejected. We were sure we had in our hands a new instrument for securing the truth, and we brandished it with delight. That the camera's view could often be so narrow as to distort, that the pressures of time and the evasiveness of those in power might blunt much television questioning, above all that television might itself modify the world which it recorded, so that its appetite for action might itself breed violent action, were phenomena which were not then even to be glimpsed.

Our certainty that we were on the side of the angels owed much to the fact that the world which television news reflected was still the pre-television world, as yet unaware of the cameras and not yet playing up – or playing down – to them. Television was not a manifest presence, affecting the events it portrayed, but just one more recording instrument amongst the familiar ranks of the press photographers. The days of massed control vans and links vehicles and scanners and cars, descending on a location like an armoured division, and by their very presence subtly altering what they had come to portray, were yet to come. Crowds did not erupt across football or cricket grounds at the close of play, waving their scarves frantically at Mum at home, hoping to secure a bit part in the picture they would see on the screen that evening. Strike meetings at factory gates were intended to rally workers to the strike, not to provide material for that evening's bulletins. We could still portray a world largely unconscious of the cameras, and so rely on the genuineness of what we showed.

The spectacular headlines which were won by *Tell the People* can be seen in retrospect as marking the end of one phase in the development of television news in Britain. It was a phase dominated by the personality and skills of those who appeared before the cameras, whether as newscasters or interviewers, and by the quality of the writing of the scripts and of the news stories, only intermittently, as at Suez and in Hungary, had hard news on film been the dominant element in news bulletins. But as pictures became more abundant, pouring into London in small square bakelite boxes marked 'Film: Urgent', from all over the world, elbowing their way to the forefront of our bulletins, we entered upon a new phase, indeed upon a new era. Five centuries of a culture resting on the printed word were coming under pressure from this cruder culture based on the visual image.

29

News in depth

The next phase in the development of television news was to be dominated by current affairs programmes, and in particular by the weekly news in depth programmes, *Panorama* on the BBC, and *This Week* on Independent Television. From early 1957 onwards these were to be joined by *Tonight*, the news magazine which the BBC put out in the early evening on weekdays.

Though these were essentially news-based programmes, their development took place under quite different leadership from that which controlled the daily news bulletins put out by BBC Television News and by ITN. Within the BBC they were put out by the Current Affairs Department; in ITV, by a programme company. In adopting this pattern, British television departed from the practice not only of newspapers, but also of the American television networks. Newspapers had always accepted that the reporting of the daily news, and the analysing and commenting on it, should come under the control of one person, the Editor of the paper. The US networks had carried this system into broadcasting, placing not only the reporting of news, but its subsequent analysis and examination, under the control of a News Division – and indeed that, for good measure, giving that division the responsibility for documentaries as well. But in British television a split had been driven on the one hand between those who got and presented the news – BBC Television News and ITN – and those who examined, explored or indeed enlarged upon it. These further tasks within the BBC fell to the Current Affairs and Documentary Departments at Lime Grove, and within Independent Television to similar departments in the programme companies.

This was an artificial division, for indeed there are no clear boundary lines between hard news, and news in depth. It had arisen within the BBC because of the reluctance of BBC News, under Tahu Hole, to move into this new medium. That had left the way open for Grace Wyndham Goldie and her Young Turks at Lime Grove to seize not only the television equivalent of areas which, in radio, had come under Talks, but also the area of immediate analysis and development of the day's news, which in radio had been, in Radio Newsreel, the province of BBC News.

When Aidan Crawley had set up ITN, he was strongly of the view that television news, to be properly done, needed a weekly interpretative news in depth programme, of at least half an hour's duration, to supplement the daily news bulletins. His experience with *Viewfinder* had convinced him that many issues, particularly if they were abstract ones like the risk of inflation, could only be effectively dealt with in much longer time than was available in a daily news bulletin. But his plans were shot down both by the programme companies, who wanted to keep for themselves every minute they could of programme time, and by the ITA. Sir Robert Fraser saw documentaries and news feature programmes as 'the conscience of the programme companies'. 'If these were taken away from the companies and given to ITN' he told me later, 'the companies would be only entertainment makers, entirely given over to the showbiz mind'.[1]

The BBC's Television Talks Department, who had acquired as its head Leonard Miall, an experienced former BBC foreign correspondent, moved swiftly to take advantage of the ground they had won. Their first action was to turn their fortnightly news magazine, *Panorama*, into a major journalistic vehicle. *Panorama* had been launched in 1953 as a programme of short, gossipy items dealing with the theatre, cinema and books, more in the tradition of the old *Picture Page* than of journalism with a cutting edge. It had vitality and pace, and numbered Malcolm Muggeridge, then a newcomer to television, among its contributors. It was reorganized in September 1955, under the direct control of Grace Wyndham Goldie herself. She made a gifted young producer, Michael Peacock, its Editor, brought in Richard Dimbleby as compere, and set it the task of grappling with major issues of the day. It was given the somewhat portentous sub-title of *A Window on the World*, and then proceeded with remarkable elan to turn itself into just that. It sent out reporters and directors with film crews, to newsworthy areas to report in depth. Woodrow Wyatt, who had recently lost his seat as a Labour MP, soon proved himself an effective reporter in this new medium. Grace Wyndham Goldie invited me to flank him in this role, and I would have done so had not the chance to become Editor of ITN suddenly occurred at that time. The upheaval at ITN which had opened the way to the Editorship for me made, however, both Crawley and Christopher Chataway available as reinforcements to *Panorama*. The new format rapidly established itself as a major television journalistic enterprise, and was soon accepted as the most prestigious current affairs platform on television. Within two years it was estimated that one adult in every four in Britain watched *Panorama* on Monday nights at 8pm, and Ministers and other people in the public eye were always ready to appear on it. Technically, *Panorama* made a significant contribution to British television journalism by its use of sound cameras to record the reports of their reporters, with the reporter talking into camera on the spot.

In January 1956 Independent Television launched, in *This Week*, its own news magazine. Its first edition, presented by Leslie Mitchell, more an announcer than a journalist, contained nearly a dozen items, setting a style more akin to the early *Panorama* than to its later version. It had pace, covered more human interest and sensational items than did *Panorama*, and had film coverage of very high technical quality, since in its early stages its film work was done on 35mm cinema-style cameras. In the words of the official historian of ITV, 'this lively, sometimes frivolous news magazine did not however

---

1   Fraser to author, 1959.

Fig. 12. Robin Day interviewing President Nasser of Egypt, 1967.

shy away from serious subjects'.[1] Gradually it moved closer to the new format of *Panorama*, particularly after the bearded and urbane Brian Connell took over as anchor man, and when its reporting staff included Paul Johnson, Bryan McGee and Godfrey Hodgson. In this new style its work was often first class, even if it never overtook the lead which *Panorama* had established at the outset. It was a lead which the BBC held until in the mid-1960s new and younger producers changed the format of *Panorama* to that of a one-subject inquiry, often on film. That had the effect of making the programme, however well done, just one more in the varied series of BBC's documentaries, instead of the authoritative enquirer into the news of the week.

In February 1957 the BBC carried its pioneering of current affairs still further in *Tonight*, a 40 minute news magazine which went out on week nights in the early evening, and which swiftly became a spectacular success. It was designed at short notice to fill the gap in the schedules caused by the ending of the Toddlers' Truce. This was the name given to the blank hour, deliberately left on weekdays between 6 and 7pm, to give parents time to get small children off to bed, and to give older children time to get on with their homework. Donald Baverstock, a gifted young Welshman who, after a short but successful career in radio current affairs had moved to television, was given the task of producing a topical magazine to fill this space. With as his chief lieutenant a young trainee, recently down from Oxford, Alasdair Milne, Baverstock evolved a pattern of hard hitting studio interviews, skilled human interest and travelogue reporting on film, with satirical songs on contemporary issues sung to the guitar by Rory McEwan.

---

1 Bernard Sendall, *Independent Television in Britain*, Vol. 1. London: Macmillan, p. 355.

Two key elements in this formula were ones we had pioneered in ITN – the probing interview and the human interest story. After an uneasy beginning, *Tonight* settled into a pattern in which a studio interview, often ten minutes or more in length, with someone in the news, was a regular feature. These interviews, with the questions carefully planned by Baverstock and his team in advance, took a deliberately critical, often irreverent approach to those in power, an attitude deliberately designed to establish an editorial tone for the programme as well as to get at the facts. Grace Wyndham Goldie attributed much of the popularity of the programme to this editorial stance. There was, she argues 'a kind of national explosion of relief' at discovering that 'it was not always necessary to be respectful; experts were not invariably right; the opinions of those in high places did not have to be accepted'.[1] This studio component was flanked by filmed reports of originality and high quality, which probed with geniality and insight the foibles and quirks of contemporary life. Bank tellers competed to see who could most rapidly count piles of bank notes; boys in Hyde Park emptied their pockets to show the contents – mostly conkers, marbles and grubby handkerchiefs. (What would a similar probe today reveal – credit cards and flick knives?) Alan Whicker went to Whitehall not to interview Ministers, but to dance with the Mrs Mopps at an annual dance held in one of the offices which they cleaned each night.

Alan Whicker was one of several Fleet Street figures who found a new career with *Tonight*. When *Picture Post* became one of the first casualties to the competition of television, Baverstock gathered in from its staff Fyfe Robertson, Macdonald Hastings and Trevor Phillpot, and turned them into highly individual television reporters, who roamed Britain, mining the same seam of human interest material which Arthur Clifford had hit upon for ITN. In the words of Trevor Phillpot, the British public had not yet been ravished by television. Eagerly and often naïvely, they opened up to the cameras the rich variety of their lives, lives not yet standardized into one dominant culture by this new medium.

The ending of the Toddlers' Truce proved important for ITN, as it opened the way for us to have some of the extra time on the screen which Crawley had sought. Coming as I did from the world of newspapers, I had shared to the full the view that there should be no boundaries – other than those imposed by the nature of the medium – between television news and current affairs. But in the first 18 months of its life ITN had been too busy learning how to turn news into television – and above all how to do this on a shoestring – to have any territorial ambitions in current affairs. So when Associated Rediffusion asked us if we could mount a 20 minute programme on foreign affairs, once a week, to help fill the gap which opened up between 6pm and 7pm, it was an unexpected bonus.

Associated Rediffusion had anticipated at most a studio discussion, enlivened by occasional brief film reports, and gave it very small budget. But I was anxious to find further scope for our reporters, and decided to use it to film a mixture of overseas news stories, some hard news, some more of a travelogue type. I was in a position to do so because we had two new newscasters. Huw Thomas, a young Welsh barrister, had an almost

1   Grace Wyndham Goldie, *Facing the Nation*. Bodley Head, 1977. p. 216.

three dimensional quality for projecting himself on the screen. Antony Brown was quieter and less assertive, but was an admirably clear presenter of the news.

Two of my former colleagues from the *News Chronicle* had joined us, Brian Connell as a Foreign Correspondent, and Ian Trethowan as Political Correspondent and newscaster. Both were destined to have distinguished careers in television. Connell became the anchorman of *This Week*, and Trethowan soared to the highest rank in the BBC, that of Director-General, a post in which he was to gain a highly deserved knighthood.

By exploiting my own contacts, and the excellent contacts of ITN's film manager, John Cotter, we wangled free trips for this new programme from airlines and ferry companies to get by until success – which came swiftly – enabled us to squeeze a more realistic budget out of the companies. We called the programme *Roving Report*, a title which still exists, 38 years on, the series having been taken over in the 1960s by the international newsfilm agency, Worldwide Television News.

Robin Day rose magnificently to the challenge of *Roving Report*, setting for it a tone of searching, humorous, zestful inquiry. George Ffitch and Reginald Bosanquet in turn carried on his high standards. Though *Roving Report*, going out as it did in the early evening, never had the chance or the money to attain the stature of *Panorama* or *This Week*, it enabled ITN to demonstrate that a news in depth programme was a natural partner for a hard news operation. It showed its worth in striking fashion in the summer of 1957, when Robin Day carried out an interview which had considerable diplomatic as well as journalistic impact – the first television interview with President Abdul Gamal Nasser after the Suez crisis, at a time when diplomatic relations between Britain and Egypt had not yet been restored. It was a testing interview for Robin Day, still only in his second year as a television journalist, but he handled it superbly, questioning President Nasser firmly yet courteously, never letting the occasion degenerate into a propaganda exercise by Nasser on the one side, or into an occasion to stir up renewed trouble between Britain and Egypt on the other. *Time* magazine devoted a full column to a report of the interview, describing Nasser as having sent 'an amiable grimace into several million British living rooms'. In the *News Chronicle* James Cameron had no doubt about the significance of the interview. It was something which had never been done before in the history of international diplomacy. 'For the first time on record, a national leader, submitting a major point of national policy, by-passed all protocol and sent his message into the homes of another state at a time when the two were not in diplomatic relations'. With the Nasser interview we were entitled to claim that ITN had arrived on the world stage.

30

Demos on the box

███

A t home 1958 saw the emergence of the first demonstration specially tailored for television, the Aldermaston march. Demonstrations as a political technique were not, of course, new. The Chartists had filled Hyde Park with hundreds of thousands of people a century earlier. Trafalgar Square rallies had helped to win the dock strikes under Ben Tillet. The suffragettes who chained themselves to the railings of Buckingham Palace did not do so in the hope that a film camera would be in the offing. In 1913 Britain was a cauldron of protest without benefit of electronics. These demonstrations had, however, as their prime aim the showing, by sheer force of numbers, the strength of their arguments. The demonstrators were voting with their feet to show authority, and the public, how widespread was their support. The suffragettes may have had their eyes also on the newspapers and the hunger marchers of the 1930s on the cinema newsreels, but like the Labour rally against Suez, their chief aim was to impress by their presence. Yet the fact that the Suez rally had commanded substantial screen time may not have been lost on those who, in 1958, decided to launch a picture-worthy march to rally opinion against the development by Britain of the H-bomb.

Headed by Canon Collins of St. Paul's, and with Bertrand Russell amongst its chief supporters with the simple and forceful slogan of Ban the Bomb, the campaign for Nuclear Disarmament organized a march at Easter from Trafalgar Square to the nuclear weapons establishment at Aldermaston, in Berkshire. It attracted a level of support which surprised its organizers as well as the press. The generation born in the war years were now well into their teens, and were catching the restiveness and the resentment which had found expression in John Osborne's *Look Back in Anger*. The end of compulsory military service was in sight, freeing the 18- year-olds from the disciplines – and the activity – which had filled the first two years of adult life for their older brothers. We found a substantial number of marchers assembled with rucksacks and banners in Trafalgar Square on the morning of Good Friday – enough to make it sensible to probe the motives behind the march as well as record the sight of it. Reginald Bosanquet and a camera crew went off to talk to the marchers when they halted to eat their lunchtime sandwiches in Kensington Gardens. I had assumed, from experience of the 1930s, that the prime movers in the march could well be the Communist Party, camouflaged by a screen of pacifists, defenders of the countryside ('environmentalist' was a word yet to come) and undisclosed sympathizers with the Soviet Union. (The term 'fellow traveller', so apt for the 1930s and 40s, was already beginning to disappear from use.) Bosanquet pressed this point hard in his interviews. The results surprised me. The Communists appeared to be playing only a minor role. They gave no sign of being the main organizers, but seemed rather to be giving a shove to a wagon which had already had its own momentum. The same impression came through in interviews George Ffitch conducted on Easter Monday as the marchers reached the perimeter fence of the Aldermaston Atomic Weapons establishment. If the Communists were running this march, they had covered their tracks very well. What came across, particularly from the many young people, rucksacks on their backs, guitars slung across their shoulders, was a genuine desire to do something to lessen the risk of war. The ever-renewing tide of human idealism which twenty years earlier had welled up to support the Spanish Republic and to stand against Fascism, was finding an expression now in CND. Though at a later date there was evidence that the Communists had by then penetrated CND, there is no sign that they originated the movement.

This annual Easter march was, for nearly a decade, to provide for these emotions an outlet which fitted the mood of the times. It fitted equally well the needs of television. Not only was it pictorial, but it provided a continuing story over the Easter weekend, when other news tended to be scarce. The marching column, headed by Canon Collins and Michael Foot, flanked by Dr Soper and Ritchie Calder (both in due course to be made Life Peers by Harold Wilson), and by Jaquetta Hawkes, then one of the few writers concerned about the environment, provided the action which the cameras hungered for. Interviews with marchers dossing down in schoolrooms or halls at the overnight stops, nursing their blistered feet and singing to the guitars (which first emerged in this context as the musical instrument of protest) provided highly viewable human interest material. If it was unmistakably propaganda, it was also unmistakably news, commanding its place in the bulletins. We made an effort to set the Aldermaston march in perspective by interviewing onlookers, not all of whom agreed with its purpose, and by reporting the few Eastertime speakers who opposed its aims. But it was an event which merited recording, and year by year we recorded it. It was the start of a decade in which marching crowds and sloganed banners were to oust the street corner speech and the set piece mass rally as a form of public persuasion.

In 1959 the organizers of the march shrewdly reversed the route, starting at Aldermaston on Good Friday and ending at Trafalgar Square on Easter Monday. This ensured them an audience of Easter strollers in the London streets and around the Square. As the column got closer to London, its ranks were swelled by reinforcements ready to join in these more glamorous concluding stretches. By the time the late bulletin had been transmitted on Easter Monday evening that year, with shots of the massed banners of the marchers passing the National Gallery, the march appeared firmly established as part of the ritual of Easter, sure of its place alongside shots of traffic jams, the van horse parade in Regent's Park, and the canoe race down the canals and the Thames from Devizes to London.

By 1960 it was clear that a minority of marchers were not content with the ritual of the four day procession. They sought more dramatic action. They had learnt that near

Reading an area had been prepared as underground headquarters for local government in the event of war. When the column reached this point a score of so of marchers broke away and tried to scale the high wire fences surrounding the headquarters. This led to scuffles with the police, which, being vivid action, won a place in the bulletins – to the annoyance of the march organizers. A year later another contingent, described by the organizers as anarchists, introduced the further technique of the sitdown, with which they tried to block Whitehall. This added still further scenes of violence, as the police struggled to remove the squatters from the roadway. A pattern in which action escalated to catch the eye of the cameras was becoming clearly discernible. The sit-down protest was a technique first employed in India in pre-war civil disturbances against the Raj. It lent itself well to television. When the police moved in to move or lift individual demonstrators, they provided a picture readily recorded by the camera, made all the more vivid because there was time for the cameraman to zoom in and capture the faces of the demonstrators and of the police in close-up. Pictorially this provided a variant to the wide-angled shots of which most crowd material is by its nature composed. For the organizers, too, the sit-down brought a propaganda bonus. The police, grappling with struggling or merely limp and manifestly passive squatters, were cast in the apparent role of aggressors.

The sit-down became a favourite technique of a new group, the Committee of 100, which was now out-flanking the work of the CND. A month after Easter 1961, during which the Aldermaston march had been reported as a matter of routine, the Committee of 100 found they could win useful screen time by staging a major sit-down demonstration in Whitehall. Soon every Saturday bulletin – the day was shrewdly chosen because news on it was scarce – seemed to have shots of policemen linking arms to lift from a West End pavement, or from alongside the diamond meshed wire of a military airfield the frail, white haired figure of Earl Russell, or the compact, short haired and shouting figure of Miss Pat Arrowsmith. On 12 September 1961, Bertrand Russell was sentenced to seven days imprisonment for his part in one such demonstration. Five days later, a mass Sunday afternoon demonstration in Trafalgar Square brought a further and dramatic raising of the ante, both in the scale of the demonstration – 1,314 people were arrested – and in the manner of its coverage. ATV decided that it merited live coverage, and stationed their outside broadcast cameras around the Square, having convinced the ITA that the demonstrations had sufficient religious significance for such coverage to intrude into the zealously guarded preserves of time set aside on Sunday evenings for religious broadcasting. Scenes of squatters blocking the roadways as well as the Square, and being lugged away by the police, alternated with discussions by a panel of pundits. There was an abundance of martyrs, with Vanessa Redgrave, Sheila Delaney, John Osborne and Alan Silletoe appearing in court the next day to be fined for obstruction, and with a torrent of complaints against the police for the rough handling of demonstrators. The police retorted with accusations of violence by sections of the demonstrators, whom the organizers were quick to disown. It was an evening of significance, for this marked Britain's entry into the decade of street politics which was to characterize the 1960s, and which was to culminate in Europe and in the United States in the widespread street violence of 1968.

But by 1964 this interest was beginning to wear thin. The march rated no coverage at all that year on the first three days of Easter, gaining only brief coverage as it reached

Trafalgar Square on Easter Monday. This was partly due to the Campaign for Nuclear Disarmament having spread themselves too thin. On Good Friday they had held a vigil at St. Paul's, and a march to a US base at Ruislip, both of which we had filmed. On Saturday the Committee of 100 had won a mention with a demonstration at Rosyth. More significant, however, was the placing of the CND story on Easter Monday. It was ousted from the lead in the bulletin by a report of a sudden, unexpected outbreak of rioting by teenage mobs at Clacton – the forerunner of the fighting between Mods and Rockers which was to become for some years a feature of holiday weekends at seaside resorts. By Whit weekend the film list was showing 'Mods and Rockers clash, Margate. Mods and Rockers go mad, Brighton. Rampage on Margate beach'. In August they were at it again at Hastings. We had come a long way since that Bank Holiday in May 1956 when George Ffitch had reported on the quiet routine of Whit Monday at Southend, and indeed since that Good Friday morning in 1958 when Reginald Bosanquet had queried the scattered Aldermaston-bound groups as they ate their lunch beside the Albert Memorial.

31

Foreign coverage

B y the early months of 1958 both BBC News and ITN were using the new type of 16mm film, on which the sound was recorded on a thin band of magnetic tape running along the edge of the film. Together with the more sensitive directional microphones, this provided a much better quality of sound than had been possible with the old system of optical recording. These developments not only made it easier for the cameras to record the natural sound of events, but enabled them to be used more fully as a reporter's notebook. Reporters could be filmed on the spot, adding their own commentary to the pictures, much more easily than before.

A striking demonstration of this new style of reporting was given in May 1958 by Brian Connell, in his coverage of General de Gaulle's bid to return to power. At the press conference in Paris at which de Gaulle announced his intention to be a candidate for the Presidency, Connell stationed himself at one side of the ornate chamber, in a position where the camera could depict the General, huge and erect behind the conference table, or pull back to show Connell at one side of the room. Crouching low and speaking low, Connell translated into the microphone, sentence by sentence, the General's speech as he delivered it, giving the story virtually the force of a live outside broadcast. It underlined too our role as a newsgathering organization. Here was a big occasion – and here was ITN in the thick of it.

Ten days later Connell repeated the process. In the Place de la République a huge demonstration of left wing parties and trade unionists formed up to oppose de Gaulle and the Army in Algeria. The marchers, twenty abreast, filled the wide boulevard as far as the eye could see. The camera recorded this in long shot, and then moved in towards the politicians and trade union leaders who formed the front row of the marchers. It picked out in their midst the bearded figure of Connell. Microphone in hand, he walked with the leaders, interviewing them as they moved forward, and adding his own commentary as the march advanced. Once again we were giving the news, and giving it from the centre.

Foreign news became dramatic film news again when two months later US Marines moved into the Lebanon to counter a revolutionary crisis in Iraq. The Marines landed

Fig. 13. Brian Connell.

from their landing craft in classic D-Day style, on beaches to the south of Beirut. The Beirut dentist who was also our enterprising local cameraman drove fast to the scene, and arrived in time to film the landings head on. He caught the moment as the landing craft edged in, dropped their ramps and allowed the Marines, rifles and light machine guns in hand, to pour out through the shallow water and storm ashore, moving towards the camera with their faces set and ready for battle. But there was no battle. The landings not only took place unopposed, but on a holiday beach at the height of the tourist season. Bathers grabbed their towels and watched with astonishment as the Marines moved up the beach, fanned out into the sandhills, and began to dig slit trenches. It was an extraordinary comic opera mixture of the banal and the dramatic. Children, lollipops in hand, stood in wide-eyed groups around troops preparing positions and setting up their machine guns. The inevitable Middle Eastern touts, including even a carpet seller, were soon on the scene, offering their wares to exasperated and embarrassed Marine officers. The story was rounded off by shots of a powerful column of tanks and armoured troop carriers rolling on towards Beirut, headed by the American Ambassador in a long black Packard with a fluttering stars and stripes flag, whilst in the background the mountains of the Lebanon rose against a clear Mediterranean sky.

The Middle East crisis of the summer of 1958 marked a watershed in television journalism. During it, according to a Gallup survey, the public for the first time turned to television as their main source of news. Until then radio and the newspapers had vied for first place. Now research showed that during those tense days it was to television news that the people had turned night after night to learn what was happening. This development may have been accelerated by a recent decision of the BBC radio to move their main evening news from nine o'clock, the time hallowed by wartime practice. But it owed most to the growth in the ownership of television sets. Combined television and sound licences now outstripped those for radio alone. Increasingly when people said 'I heard on the news last night ...' they were referring to television news. Indeed they now frequently used the words 'I saw it on the news'.

We now had to be comprehensive as well as vivid, to face every evening the test of having covered all the main news – and covered it in picture. Fortunately the means for doing this had improved steadily throughout the past two years. All over the world cameramen had equipped themselves with the light 16mm cameras suited to television work. The product of their labours could also reach us more quickly. In July 1958 the first Comet airline service had started across the Atlantic, ushering in the age of jet air travel. This speeded up the transit of film, and enabled camera crews to be more rapidly deployed to the scene of the news. To this we added, in the autumn of 1958, the use of the Eurovision network not only to transmit news, but to allow it to be viewed live.

Plans for a week's trial exchange of daily news between five European countries, including Britain, had been laid for October 1958. Each day at midday the newsrooms of the five were inter-locked through the Eurovision control centre at Brussels and each made available its best stories free to the others. Just as this was getting under way, news came from Rome on 6 October that Pope Pius XII had died at his summer home at Castel Gondolfo, in the Alban Hills south of Rome. When his body was carried by road to Rome, RAI, the Italian broadcasting service, stationed their OB cameras at points along the route, providing coverage which was a blend of Italian showmanship and Roman Catholic ceremony that was spectacular and yet intensely and sincerely moving.

For more than two hours that afternoon the pictures poured out over the Eurovision link, as the cortege made its way through the drab working class areas of south western Rome. In front of the high, crumbling apartment blocks crowds, many of them kneeling, lined the pavements. This was the first time since the Coronation in 1953 that Eurovision had been used to cover hard news.

I had travelled this route on the morning Rome fell on 4 June 1944, making my way alongside the unshaven, dust-grimed American infantry moving forward in single file, as the Sherman tanks nosed forward to reconnoitre each street crossing. Now the cameras were bringing the sight of the Papal cortege, with its long line of dark shining vehicles, moving through lines of darkly clad onlookers, as sharply as if we were there again. As never before, the force of this new medium was carried in on me. Today we take such live coverage as commonplace, and would be indignant if we could not see every moment of a World Cup football match, or every second of an Olympic final, as it takes place. But that afternoon it was a new experience, demonstrating forcibly the power of electronics to widen our view of the world.

Yet, of the RAI coverage that October, ITV viewers saw only excerpts in the news bulletins, taken either from those OBs or from the Eurovision news exchange. The network was not yet interested in news at length. Of the many hours of pageantry which was also news, as one Pope was honoured in death, and another selected, only some 15 minutes in all reached our screens, in two or three minute excerpts in the bulletins. The BBC, in contrast, gave extensive coverage.

The European news rooms continued to exchange their daily news film intermittently throughout 1959. In May 1961 the exchange was put on a regular basis, with a daily closed circuit transmission at 17.00 hrs central European time, on which each European station offered its best news stories. In 1968 this was supplemented by a further exchange two hours later in the evening, and in March 1974 by a third exchange at noon. These developments owed much to the enterprise of the RAI cameramen in the sunlight of that Roman autumn.

When Fidel Castro finally won power in Cuba in January 1959, we were presented with a new editorial problem. For the first time we had on film the scene of an execution, of the deliberate taking of human life. A former police chief of the Battista regime had been sentenced to death. The CBS cameraman had shown him, in trousers and white shirt, hands bound, being taken in an open truck to a field. There he was tied to a post and blindfolded. Half a dozen troops lined up a few yards away, an officer's voice rang out and they fired. The policeman's body gave one sudden lunge, and then slumped in its bonds. The officer walked across, held a revolver to the lolling head and fired one final shot.

The moment of death, the sudden transformation of this living, if pinioned and helpless human being, into a sacklike object, was all the more hideous because one knew, up to the second, that it was coming. It conveyed a sense of drama, but also of shame, of the stirring of the basest of human instincts, the making of a spectacle of a fellow human being deprived of life. I decided that we would show all the sequences except the actual moment of death, when the bullets thudded into the tethered body. We had done away with public executions in Britain nearly two centuries previously. I saw no reason to restore them to the public gaze – and to the gaze in the sitting room, not even at Tyburn or New Palace Yard.

It is ruling which was to prevail in ITN when other such film reached us from other revolutions and other wars. I saw no reason to change it, even when other producers across the years have thought differently. Indeed one ITV current affairs programme a few weeks later showed the full Cuban execution sequence; another a year or so later equally gave every moment of the shooting, in a public execution in a street in Saigon, of a group of blackmarketeers. In the wider context of a current affairs programme these sequences had somewhat less shock effect than when packed into the confines of a news bulletin, where they were viewed alongside other very different news items. Even so, I held to my view that they had no place on the television screen. The reasons for banning executions from our streets are equally valid for banning them from our homes.

32

Covering a General Election

In the autumn of 1959 broadcasters for the first time embarked on untrammelled coverage of a British General Election. The precedent set at Rochdale had thrust aside the inhibitions which had limited radio and television election coverage in the past.

The BBC's self-imposed ban during previous elections had left us with no guide lines by which we could steer. We would have to devise our own methods and our own principles. We had learnt much from covering by-elections. But reporting a contest within a single constituency was much more manageable than one spread over 630 constituencies. Power was at stake in a General Election in a way which was not the case in a by-election, however significant its result might be. Our coverage would be watched with very sharp eyes by the politicians whose fates we could influence, and by the press which until now had held a monopoly of the reporting of election campaigns. If we got it wrong, we would not halt the televising of politics. That had now a momentum of its own. But we could damage the reputation of ITN, and of Independent Television as a whole. Though the system was too firmly established now for the Labour Party, if they won the Election, to carry out their threat to abolish ITV, it could be burdened with new controls if it was decided that we had been unfair. Amongst the Tories there were still the old opponents of commercial broadcasting to be reckoned with, together with some new ones suspicious of this new power in the land. And there was always the risk that, however fairly we might cover the Election, the loser might seek to blame television, would emerge crying 'Foul' against the cameras.

Yet we moved towards the Election with reasonable confidence. Ffitch, Bosanquet and Connell had all had experience of covering by-elections on television, and Trethowan and I had our newspaper experience of the past three General Elections to draw on. This confidence held even though in May 1959 Robin Day announced that he would not be with us during it. He had accepted an invitation to contest Hereford as a Liberal candidate. Under rules which the Board had adopted when Ludovic Kennedy had announced his sudden entry into politics, this meant that Day would have to give up newscasting immediately, in order to ensure not only that we were impartial, but were seen to be impartial. We paid him a retainer, and I helped him get a contract to write a weekly column for the *News Chronicle*, which he did with pungency and humour.

Election Day was set for 8 October 1959. The newspapers were quickly on to us to ask about the principles which would govern our coverage. I replied that we would cover the election as we covered any story – on the basis of its news value. This is a good broad journalistic term which covers a multitude of interpretations. I had no doubt in my own mind what those news values were, in the context of a General Election. They meant ensuring that the share of time devoted to the sayings and doings of each political party should be roughly in proportion to the number of candidates it had in the field, and that within individual constituencies the amount of time devoted to each candidate should be equal. A General Election is a contest confined within certain rules, which in turn impose their own rules upon any broadcaster working under an obligation of impartiality. The only test we could apply to ensure – and to be seen to be ensuring – impartiality was that of time, of minutes and seconds allocated to parties and to candidates. Our by-election coverage had made plain that an election is above all an argument, a clash of conflicting claims and conflicting statements by different politicians and different parties. What criterion, other than the stop watch, could be used to decide the news values of these arguments, the relative space which should be accorded to them? What might seem to a person of Conservative inclination to be a statement of great interest and importance, might seem an irrelevance, or a downright falsehood, to a Labour opponent – and so on, to and fro across the whole political spectrum. No news editor aiming to present a fair picture could do other than fall back on the clock to guide him. The sharing of time would not have to be exact within any bulletin or any one electoral report. Different issues would arise on different days, different leaders would be playing varying roles from day to day, and these differences would have to be reflected in each day's coverage. But over the period of the campaign as a whole, the amount of time devoted to the various parties must be broadly in line with the part they were playing in the election – which in turn meant the number of candidates they put into the field.

We had learnt from our by-election coverage one further important lesson. The principle of fair shares must apply to the facilities used to cover a story, as well as to minutes on the screen. The technical equipment employed to turn political argument into television could affect the impact of those arguments. This was most noticeable in coverage of a speech. If we used the sound camera, so enabling the candidate to state his argument of his policy in his own voice, the outcome was more authentic, and the impact undoubtedly greater, than if his words were relayed by the neutral voice of a commentator. This impact was liable to be all the greater if the politician was speaking in the emotionally charged atmosphere of a party meeting, with the applause of the faithful to reinforce his message. Similarly election news reinforced even by silent film would have greater force than news relayed only by the newscaster. We would therefore have to allocate our cameras, and in particular our sound cameras, with care. We were, in fact, applying in television terms the principle which the farsighted John Reith had laid down in 1923, that 'if on any controversial matter the opposing views are stated with equal emphasis and lucidity, there can at least be no charge of bias'.[1] To secure that equal emphasis and lucidity, I defined, therefore, the basis of our coverage of the Election as one of 'news values plus parity of technical resources'.

We secured from the network a slot of 10 minutes every weekday evening of the campaign for a special programme, *Election Report*. Trethowan and Connell presented it, and I edited it myself. It was a task which brought back the intensive daily rhythm I had known during Suez, with days that stretched from a morning planning conference until the night's *Election Report* had finished its run at 11pm. Once again exhilaration was to outweigh exhaustion. For we were not just making television. We were forging a new way in which Parliamentary democracy could operate, finding methods by which this formidable new technology could fit into the complex organic structure of the British political system. Though this further, deeper goal was very much in my mind, I took care not to proclaim it. Good journalists armour their sensitivities with scepticism, and I knew that even those who thought as I did – and there were plenty in ITN who did – would not thank me if I put such thoughts into words. Better to base our approach on the hardened newsman's attitude that we were out to dominate the story and outpace the opposition.

On the opening night of the campaign both the Conservative and Labour leaders planned important platform speeches, Macmillan in Manchester, Gaitskell in Bristol. The Prime Minister's speech presented no difficulty. The Free Trade Hall where his meeting was being held was close to the Granada studios. We could cover the speech with a sound camera, have the film processed and cut in Manchester in time for it to be piped down to London. But with Gaitskell the task was more thorny. Sound coverage was possible only if we could rush the film to Cardiff, to the TWW studios. As for the Liberals, their leader, Jo Grimond was well out of range in the Orkneys, and so would have to wait a day or two before we could give his meetings sound coverage.

Harold Macmillan's speech went according to plan, and well before the time of our Election Report we had a neat segment of it cut and waiting in Granada's telecine. But Gaitskell's speech ran late. Though the cameraman drove madly with film of it from Bristol to Cardiff, we were too late. It was still in the processing plant by the time we went on the air.

The contrast was marked. Harold Macmillan was seen and heard, vigorous, confident and witty, against a background of cheering supporters. A silent, overcoated Hugh Gaitskell hurried along a station platform, to be greeted by a handful of supporters. From the studio in London George Ffitch gave a summary of Gaitskell's speech. This was clear, but manifestly at one remove from the real thing. Logistics were obviously going to be as important as editorial assessments in securing 'equal emphasis and lucidity'. As soon as I got to my desk the next morning Transport House were on the phone seeking explanations, and demanding that we redress the balance.

We were able to reassure them that justice would be done that evening. Gaitskell was due to speak at Battersea, on our very doorstep. To make sure that no hitch would occur, we had put two sound cameras in the hall, which was something we had long

1   Charles Curran, *A Seamless Robe.* London: Collins, 1979, p. 71.

wanted to do, in order to pick up the audience reactions as well as the speech. Macmillan was off to the remote mountains of Wales, and could not be covered on sound anyway. Still suspicious that we might have been playing in with the Tories (whom the Labour Party saw as the friends of commercial television), Morgan Phillips, the Party Secretary, agreed to wait this extra day before making any formal complaint. 'But you had better get it right this time' he told me, 'or I will throw the book at you'.

I was not worried. Special lights had been installed to supplement the hall lighting. Every possible precaution had been taken. If ever we had mounted a belt and braces operation, this was one. To make doubly sure, George Ffitch went off with the camera crews to Battersea Town Hall. Gaitskell was due to speak at the reasonably early hour of 8pm, ample time for us to get the film back, and have it ready for *Election Report* I was in the preview theatre, watching film of Harold Macmillan starting off on his Prime Ministerial progress when the phone rang. It was George Ffitch. 'I don't know whether to laugh or cry when I tell you this' he said. 'But when Gaitskell came onto the platform, and we switched the lights on, the load proved too much for the electricity system. We blew all the lights in the hall. Not only is there no film, there's no meeting either'.

Hugh Gaitskell was a big-minded man. Instead of bursting out in wrath, he continued the meeting by candlelight. Meanwhile the ever resourceful John Cotter had got one of the camera crews to gather up its gear, and hurry across the river to Hammersmith, where Gaitskell was due to address a further meeting. We could give him coverage only from a handheld camera, with the cameraman being jostled by interjectors and cheering supporters. Not much of Gaitskell's policy came across, but the outcome – for we had silent film of the candlelit meeting as well – was at least viewable. Gaitskell laughed the whole matter off. 'So it was you, was it'? was his only comment to George Ffitch at the end of the evening. 'I thought it was either the Empire Loyalists or the Communists'.

Even Morgan Phillips, though the humour of it escaped him, had to admit that we could plead *force majeure*. He accepted my assurance that a further close range speech by Gaitskell the next evening, at Harlow New Town, would give us a further chance to get matters back into balance.

We very nearly failed to do so. The despatch rider, bringing back the film from Harlow, skidded on an icy road, and was hurled into a ditch. The film broke from its container, and was ruined. This time I knew no amount of explanations or apologies could meet the situation. Whatever the reasons behind the screen, we were not giving the public a fair picture of the election. I rang Kenneth Dick, Editor of the BBC's international news agency, Visnews. In my days as a radio news analyst we had often found ourselves at adjoining desks in the Egton House newsroom, as he finished his long night shift as Duty Editor and I came in in the grey light of dawn to dissect the day's news for Australia and New Zealand. Could I borrow a cut of their coverage of Gaitskell?

I could, and did, and the crisis was over. We were able to make a speedy repayment. A day later it was Waldo Maguire, Head of BBC News on the line to me. Their film of Jo Grimond, flown down by air from the Orkneys, had been late. In an effort to speed up the processing the temperature in the developer had been raised – but raised too high. The emulsion had been boiled off. The afficianados of political coverage might have detected a marked similarity on those two evenings between the BBC's film reports and those of ITN. But no-one in our respective hierarchies seemed to notice, and Waldo and I saw no need to draw their attention to the fact.

The relatively primitive technical conditions of the time helped to set in train another characteristic of televised elections – the dominance of the election campaign by the Party leaders. Because the sound film camera quickly established itself as the main instrument of news coverage, and because such cameras were relatively scarce, television news editors were bound to give priority to coverage of the main speech of the day by the leaders of Conservative and Labour Parties, and reasonable prominence to a speech by the Liberal Leader. The outcome was that the Leaders were, night after night, heard as well as seen on the screen, whereas less but still prominent figures might appear only in silent film sequences. Harold Macmillan's genial confidence, Hugh Gaitskell's searing earnestness soon established themselves on the screen. Coverage of the Liberals was somewhat more widespread. With their leader far away most of the time in the mists of the Orkneys and Shetland, they had to be represented by Liberal speakers closer at hand. As a result the Liberal Chief Whip, Frank Byers, shared star billing with Jo Grimond. One back bencher whose speeches we covered on three occasions was Sir Winston Churchill. I was determined that in this, the last General Election in which he was likely to take part, his words should be recorded by this new medium. A Labour name which did not figure on our coverage list was that of Harold Wilson. He was not then ranked high in the Party hierarchy to merit special attention – nor indeed had he yet demonstrated his skill as a speaker before the cameras. Similarly disregarded was another star of later Elections, George Brown.

By the time we had reached the last few days of the campaign I knew that, providing nothing went wrong in the final straight – and nothing did – we had met successfully the challenge of covering for the first time a General Elections on television – and indeed of covering it for the first time in any form of broadcasting in Britain. The coverage logs which I had carefully compiled morning after morning showed that the two main parties were within a minute or two of each other in their total screen time. The Liberals' proportion had been equally fair, though we had had to scour the country in the second week to find suitable Liberal meetings to keep the records in trim. The minor parties had had a reasonable share of our scanty time. We had brought through the main arguments, shown the main personalities, reflected something of the cut and thrust of electioneering. None of fears of unfairness or of partiality which had inhibited coverage during the four other post-war Elections had proved valid. From now on General Elections would be reported by television and by radio as a matter of course.

Our results programme on Election Night was out-pointed by that of the BBC. They had Richard Dimbleby, then at the peak of his fame, as their main presenter, and Grace Wyndham Goldie as producer, with not only her natural flair, but the experience of three previous Election Nights to draw on – for there had been no inhibition on reporting the results, as distinct from the campaigning, in earlier Elections. Nevertheless we were in the battle right through the night. Our dual presentation team of Trethowan and Connell – foreshadowing the *News at Ten* pattern – were clear and authoritative. We could claim, too, to have been first with the moment of highest drama of the night. For it was on ITN that Hugh Gaitskell conceded defeat only four hours after the polls had closed. This was the first occasion on which a British Party Leader had conceded defeat on Election Night, and certainly the first on which he had done so on television. Gaitskell had spent the evening at Leeds Town Hall, where the votes in his constituency, South Leeds, and those in neighbouring constituencies were being counted. Towards 1.00am, in a small, temporary studio inside the hall, he was interviewed for us by Neville Clarke. Opening his hands, then pressing his finger tips together, he said 'it is obvious there will be a Conservative Government'. Television, by capturing and presenting this moment, had shown its power not only as a new form of journalism, but as an essential part of the democratic process.

BBC Television had confined their reporting of the Election to their news bulletins, which had been extended for the purpose. They had proclaimed strongly that they too would cover it on the basis of news values, but at the end they, like ITN, emerged with coverage which was roughly equal between the two main parties, and with the Liberals having less screen time, but still a substantial amount. The BBC had cancelled *Tonight* for the duration of the campaign, and had kept all politicians off *Panorama* and *Press Conference*. They tried one series of special programmes, which they entitled *Hustings*. Candidates appeared in regional television studios, or in local halls in front of OB cameras, and were questioned by invited audiences. In order to avoid any suggestion of political bias, the audiences were selected on the advice of the three main parties. This proved a recipe for noise and disruption, as it meant that two-thirds of the audience would be against the speaker. It was not a method which commended itself either to the politicians or to the BBC, and fifteen years were to elapse before party spokesmen could again be lured before a studio audience at election time.

One significant fact about the 1959 television election coverage was that neither Macmillan nor Gaitskell was interviewed on television. We had seen our task primarily to use this new medium to portray the type of campaigning which had existed in the days before television, rather than to shape or influence the campaign to the needs and strengths of television. That was a process which was to follow soon enough.

33

New faces and new techniques

The BBC's coverage of the 1959 General Election had taken place under new leadership. In 1958 a change had been brought about in the BBC hierarchy which was of great importance for the development of BBC News and current affairs. Tahu Hole, that most reluctant convert to television news, gave up the post of Editor, BBC News. In his place came Hugh Carleton Greene, who was given the new rank of Director of News and Current Affairs, a role which put him direct charge of all BBC News, on both radio and television, and which gave him supervisory powers over the current affairs programmes at Lime Grove.

Greene, who had been a *Daily Telegraph* foreign correspondent in Germany before the war, and had covered the outbreak of war from Warsaw, had headed the vitally important BBC's German Service during the war. His post war career was mainly with the External Services at Bush House. On his appointment to the post of Head of News and Current Affairs he moved swiftly to, as he put it, 'restore freedom to the News Division, which had become the Kremlin of the BBC'[1] – a metaphor applying to what Greene saw as its secretive and highly centralized administration, rather than to any political stance. Greene brought in new men from Bush House, and appointed a committee of lively young producers, mostly from Current Affairs, to advise on new methods for television news. Out of these changes emerged, in the early 1960s, as Editor of BBC Television News, an Ulsterman with a real flair for television news, Waldo Maguire. He was to bring a sharply competitive edge to the BBC Television News bulletins, delighting in the battle to be first with pictures of the news.

These developments at the BBC came at a time when ITN was also facing change. After the Rochdale by-election in 1958, Ludovic Kennedy did not return to ITN, but moved over to *Panorama*, which offered him wider scope for interpreting the news. Robin Day who had failed in his bid to win Hereford for the Liberals, also sought the

---

1   Sir Hugh Greene, *The Third Floor Front*. The Bodley Head, 1969, p. 122.

chance to develop further his talents. *Roving Report* had provided such a vehicle, but, going out early in the evening at a time when the critics and opinion formers were not watching, lacked the prestige of *Panorama* or *This Week*. So when *Panorama* invited him to join their already very talented team, which included Robert Kee, James Mossman, Christopher Chataway, as well as Kennedy and Richard Dimbleby, Day parted company with ITN. His going was a loss not only to ITN, but to the televising of daily news. *The Spectator* noted that no one had done more to 'create the persona of Independent Television News, to show that it is possible to be forthright without being prejudiced, fair without being mealy-mouthed. When ITN began, Chataway made the more immediate impact, but it was Day who developed and perfected the technique of newscasting in a way which made the BBC television newsreaders by contrast dull and not infrequently embarrassing to watch.'[1]

The haemorrhage of talent from ITN revealed one major problem posed by the newscaster system. It called for people of personality and talent, yet by definition such people were likely to find the role of presenting the news, night after night, restrictive. They needed wider outlets than television news bulletin could provide. Yet the nature of the ITV system denied to ITN the type of news in depth programme, properly funded and broadcast at an hour which could command the right type of audience, which could hold the best people. Though at least one remarkable screen figure, Reginald Bosanquet, was to emerge from within the ranks of ITN's younger recruits, finding newscasters who could match up to the standards set by the early pioneers like Robin Day and Ludovic Kennedy became a constant problem for ITN, until the establishment of the half hour news in 1967 provided a durable answer.

These difficulties were intensified by the policy of the ITV programme companies of keeping ITN on short rations of both time and money. In 1959 they cut back the length of the ITN main evening news from just under a quarter of an hour to ten minutes, as the price of promoting it to the peak hour of 9.25pm. The move had not been made to accord news pride of place. It was because, to the programme schedulers, the main evening news was a nuisance, a chunk of programming which broke the evening into two halves.

News was also proving to be an expensive type of programming. On the face of it, this should not have posed a problem. Independent Television had moved swiftly into very lush times, with advertising revenue pouring in in tidal waves, giving force to Roy Thomson's claim that Scottish Television's franchise was a 'licence to print money'. But the companies were reluctant to spend this money on the programmes of a subsidiary company which, however much prestige it might win for ITV as a whole, brought them, as individual companies, little in the way of praise or reputation. The programme companies were aware that their initial licences had been granted for a period of only nine years. When that time was over, and the time came to seek a renewal, it was on the quality of their own individual programmes that they would be judged. They did not believe that a history of strong support for the news service of ITN would count for much in allocating the next round of licences. And they judged rightly. For when, in 1967, the ITA had to decide whether Rediffusion should continue as the London week-

---

1   *The Spectator*, 17 April 1959.

Fig. 14. Andrew Gardner.

day contractor, Rediffusion lost out even though it had for the previous decade been ITN's best supporter among the companies.

The reduction of ITN's time on the air in 1959 to 10 minutes mid-evening came, moreover, at a period when news on film was becoming more plentiful. Not only were cameramen in many parts of the world equipping themselves with 16mm cameras, but the arrival of the jet age meant that film could reach London and New York more quickly – and British and American camera teams could fly out more readily to cover big stories. More film too was coming in over Eurovision, and, very importantly, from regional newsrooms throughout the United Kingdom.

Regional news had become a growth area. In the early phase of television news, both the BBC and ITN had placed cameramen in key regional centres such as Manchester and Glasgow. These were staff men from the central news rooms, supplemented by freelance cameramen in other parts of the country. From early 1957, however, the coverage of local news was steadily taken over by regional news services, developed to supplement the national news bulletins by regional news programmes. The first of these within the Independent Television system was set up by ATV, the Midlands weekday contractor, in Birmingham in 1957. It not only provided a programme of local news, which went out immediately after the early ITN bulletin, but provided coverage of Midland stories for ITN itself. This pattern was to be repeated in each ITV region, as the network was extended to one area after another. A similar system was developed by the BBC. This was to bring into being a very important aspect of news coverage, supplementing the national and international news by grass roots stories of great interest and importance to local people. The provision of news from the regions to the national BBC and ITN bulletins was facilitated by the spread of the two-way co-axial cable network, which enabled television signals to be sent not only from London out to the transmitters in the provinces, but from the provinces to London.

This cable network was made all the more valuable by another technical advance of great importance to television news. This was video recording. It was a system developed in the United States in the mid 1950s, in the form of an American recording apparatus, the Ampex VRX 1000. The Ampex recorders could produce a recording which was almost as good as the original, and was incomparably better and faster than the telerecordings which had, until then, been the only way of providing a copy of pictures which had been broadcast.

The early Ampex machines were cumbersome and costly and the editing process, which depended upon the actual cutting of tape by razor blade, difficult. But their existence transformed television news. It was now possible to use recorded excerpts from live broadcasts, particularly from sporting events, where in the past the alternative had been to rely on grainy telerecording or on costly film coverage. Ampex also provided the essential link in the transmission of film by cable, because it allowed such film to be transmitted in advance of the programmes in which it was to be used. This facility was to become doubly important when the further great development of transmission by satellite followed in the early 1960s.

The pattern of short, film-packed mid-evening bulletins was to last in British television for the next seven years. The bulletins were gradually lengthened, until on the BBC they totalled 15 minutes and on ITN 13 minutes. In the summer of 1962 our main ITN news was put out at 9pm, that hour sanctified for news in the great days of radio. The move owed less to a feeling in the programme companies that this was the right time for news than to a hard scheduling battle in which they were engaged with the revivified BBC, who had brought their own main news forward to 9.15pm. But whatever the reasons, the change brought us to the peak of the evening in a most gratifying manner.

Yet this placing was to cramp ITN's development for the immediate future, because no one wanted to take risks with audience at peak time by experimenting with any considerable lengthening of the bulletins. At the same time, despite the ingenuity of producers, these shortened bulletins could not cope effectively with big news occasions. This led to the development in the early 1960s of the technique of the ad hoc special news programme. In this a big story was treated not just as news but as programme material. If it was urgent or dramatic enough time would be cleared, even in peak hours. When Dr Voevord, the South African Prime Minister, was stabbed to death in the Parliament building in Cape Town, ITN was given the half hour from 9.30–10pm for a news special. On the opening day of the Cuban missile crisis in 1962 both ITN and BBC filled the hour between 9pm and 10pm with film reports and studio discussions, in the course of which the American reconnaissance photographs, with their vivid evidence of missile sites being cleared in the Cuban countryside, were shown to the British public for the first time.

European broadcasters, stimulated by the RAI coverage of the funeral of the Pope in

1958, vied with one another to offer live coverage of events. Highly televisual figures bestrode the world's stage – the new young President John F. Kennedy of the United States, and his beautiful, enigmatic wife; the ebullient, unpredictable Nikita Kruschev; President de Gaulle, towering behind his ornate desk in the Elysée Palace as he made brilliant use of television to sustain his public support; Pope John XXIII, who was to make equally skilful use of television to make the Papacy more human and yet more powerful. These were personalities who could readily command huge audiences, and whose meetings and journeyings were widely covered on Eurovision. New links with the broadcasting services behind the Iron Curtain through Intervision enabled us to meet the avid, if brief curiosity in the West for the great Soviet annual occasions such as the May Day and 7 November parades in Red Square. An adroit use of that link by the BBC in April 1961 enabled them to secure a spectacular scoop – live pictures of the first astronaut in space, Yuri Gagarin, being greeted in Red Square by the Soviet leadership and by a parade of Soviet troops and civilians.

Within Independent Television special news programmes had begun in the autumn of 1960, when Kruschev visited the United States Assembly in New York, where he was expected to announce a new blockade of Berlin. He did no such thing, but his unique mixture of clowning and menace provided some memorable pictures. The UN cameras did not, alas, catch the moment when he took off his shoe and hammered it in protest on his desk in the Assembly. But it did record the scene when he stood up, shouting an angry objection to a statement by Mr Harold Macmillan, only to be met by a roar of laughter from the other delegates when the Prime Minister, with exaggerated courtesy, asked 'Could we have that translated please'? But the event which established firmly the news special in our techniques was Hugh Gaitskell's speech at the Labour Party Conference at Scarborough in 1960, when he defied the ban-the-bomb majority with his declaration that he and his supporters would 'fight, fight and fight again to save the Party we love'. Granada put OB cameras into the hall, and recorded the whole morning session, from which an hour and a half special, with commentary by Ian Trethowan, was prepared. It caught the atmosphere in a way the film cameras, with their more limited duration, could not have done. Gaitskell's speech was not great oratory. He was too tense for that, his voice and manner too strained. But it was great television, winning for Hugh Gaitskell overnight respect and support far beyond the confines of the Labour movement.

In February 1962 the scope for special programmes was dramatically extended when Colonel John Glenn made the first American space flight around the world. Though Major Gagarin had done the same for the Russians ten months earlier, the Soviet authorities released no film of either the blast-off of their rocket or of the recovery of the astronaut. No such inhibitions affected the authorities at what was then Cape Canaveral. On to our screens poured, as the United States space programme got under way, coverage of the astronauts reaching the launching site and mounting to the capsule in their gleaming space suits; of the tense moments to the countdown; of the flaring and billowing as the great engines ignited; and of the rocket making its steady way into the sky. Even in the monochrome coverage of 1962 this was compulsive viewing.

In March 1962 both the BBC and ITN covered a by-election result live for the first time at Orpington, where a Rediffusion OB camera caught the moment as the returning officer announced that the Liberals had won this apparently safe Tory seat. A month later the companies made available two and a half hours of time in the afternoon for ITN to present for the first time a special programme on the Budget. David Windlesham, then a current affairs producer for Rediffusion, mounted it for us, and used OB cameras to bring in the scene outside the Houses of Parliament, even if we were debarred from the Chamber itself. It was a day of clear April sunshine, outlining the stonework on the Palace of Westminster and the hands of the clock on the Big Ben tower. From the Commons we provided a running commentary of the Chancellor's speech and the tax changes – running in more senses than one, for it involved a series of reporters sprinting from the Press Gallery to give their news into camera, or to phone it over to the special news room we had constructed in Studio 9 in the basement of Television House.

The most durable form of special programme came, however, in the autumn, when for the first time continuous live direct coverage of the three Party Conferences was mounted. Granada again took the initiative. Two of the three conferences that year, those of the Liberals and the Conservatives, were at Llandudno, within the Granada transmission area. The Labour Party was at Brighton and Southern Television followed Granada's lead and offered comparable live coverage from there. Ian Trethowan and George Ffitch provided commentary for the pictures, identifying the speakers and explaining the procedures. The BBC, who also had their OB cameras in the halls, confined their direct coverage to highlights, such as Party leaders' speeches, so enabling ITV in this instance to claim another important political first. Only a year later did the Corporation too begin continuous live coverage of the conferences.

It was the year in which the Macmillan Government was seeking entry to the Common Market and debates on the Market provided highly televisual material from all three conferences. This was particularly true of the Labour Party at Brighton, with Gaitskell strongly opposed to entry, and George Brown, usually his close ally, equally strongly in favour. On the night after that debate the two men continued the argument late into the night in the ITN office at the Conference with Trethowan, Ffitch and myself. Gaitskell that evening was at his best, combining intellect not only with passion – as he did in public – but also with a humour which rarely came through on the platform or in the Commons. George Brown was too in good form, aggressive without being truculent, demonstrating what Richard Crossman was later to say of him, that 'when George is good, he is very very good. When he is bad ...' This talk, coming at the end of a long day, with an equally long day ahead, and continuing into the small hours, was a reminder of the bull-like strength which a politician must possess. It was well after one in the morning when I walked back with Hugh and Dora Gaitskell to the Metropole Hotel along the deserted Brighton seafront, the last time I was to see him before his death four months later.

34

A two-tiered news?

S pecial news programmes, valuable though they were when big news broke, did not meet the need for more time to cope with the flow of less spectacular but nevertheless important news. Not only was more news in pictures available from around the world, but more news was being deliberately cast in visual form. The success of the Aldermaston Marchers in securing access to the screen was noted by others wishing to carry their case to the public.

In industrial disputes the unions had at first seen television mainly as a way of arguing their case, through their union officials, in interviews. But in 1961 one of the least militant of unions, the nurses, secured wide screen coverage by marching to Parliament. From then on the mass demonstration became a major form of union pressure. Smaller groups followed suit – mothers seeking a pedestrian crossing at an accident black spot, conservationists wanting to block or divert one of the motorways which were beginning to spread across the countryside. The habit spread, as other less reputable elements found they could, by violence or even by unruliness, win a place on the screen which they would otherwise not have merited. Seaside fighting between mods and rockers became part of the Bank Holiday scene. By the midsixties the normal, staid ending to football matches had been replaced by the spectacle of crowds erupting across the pitch, waving their scarves and banners in frenzied gesticulations, determined to be in the picture even if it meant spoiling the picture, a warning of television's tendency to modify, by its presence, the events it had come to report. And in 1958 we hcd within our camera sights the first flaring of the new phenomenon of racial violence, as street fighting broke out in Nottingham and Notting Hill.

All these events called not only for film coverage, but, equally importantly, for probing and explanation, for not all demonstrations were what they seemed. This underlined the need for longer news bulletins. Though in December 1960 the main 9.25 p.m. bulletin had been extended to eleven minutes, it was still too short. This led me to formulate the idea of the two-tiered bulletin, with one segment in mid-evening time in which the most urgent news could be presented, and a second segment set around 11.00 p.m. in which that news could be amplified and explained. I put this idea to the ITN Board in April 1960, who told me to put it up again later when broadcasting hours

Fig. 15. David Nicholas, appointed Editor of ITN, 1977.

had been extended, and to the Committee under Sir Harry Pilkington, who were then in the midst of investigating British broadcasting. For good measure I argued to the Pilkington Committee that ITN should produce a weekly news in depth programme, like *This Week* or *Panorama*, and a morning news at breakfast time.

My belief in the value of a two-tiered bulletin was reinforced when, in the autumn of

1961, Rediffusion gave us the chance to produce a late evening ten minute news analysis programme. They had at first asked ITN to provide ten minutes of local London
news at that time. But local news did not sit easily at such a late hour, though one item,
a study of the newly elected MP for Finchley, Margaret Thatcher, was to prove very-
durable, finding its way over the years into innumerable film portraits of Britain's first
woman Prime Minister. After three months John McMillan of Rediffusion suggested we
turn the programme into a nightly scrutiny of the main story of the day. This we did,
under the title of *Dateline*, establishing a pattern for late night news in depth which is
today institutionalized in the BBC's *Newsnight*.

We found a good producer for *Dateline* in Brian Wenham, who had joined us as a
young scriptwriter from ATV, and who was to develop on *Dateline* the skills which
were to carry him in time to the leadership of BBC2, and then on to the satellite world
of the ill-fated BSB, and into the new ITV era as a director of Carlton Television. There
must have been something in the late night air of Kingsway in those days which stimulated ambition, for another producer of *Dateline* was an ebullient young man called
Gordon Reece. After leaving ITN he was to become a national figure in the 1980s as
the producer who modified Margaret Thatcher's hair style, and the pitch of her voice,
and who guided her through three victorious General Election campaigns, becoming Sir
Gordon in the process.

As well as pioneering techniques in scrutinising the day's news in depth – some years
before the need for this was suddenly discovered, and sanctified by John Birt and Peter
Jay in their celebrated enunciation of television's 'bias against understanding', *Date-line*
played, along with *Roving Report*, a key part in enabling ITN to discover and develop
new talent.

Four newcomers to our ranks in the 1960s were to play major roles not only within
ITN, but in shaping the future of television news.

David Nicholas joined ITN from *The Daily Telegraph*, where he had been a sub-editor.
He had a Welshman's delight in the skilled use of words, and soon showed a comparable skill in handling film. He had, too, a gift for the leadership of journalists. In 1963
he was appointed Deputy Editor, going on to be Editor, to be made CBE, and knighted
for his services to journalism.

Donald Horobin also came from the newspaper world, having been News Editor of the
Birmingham Gazette. In 1961 Arthur Clifford moved on to become head of News and
Current Affairs at Anglia Television. I had heard reports of Horobin's drive and flair,
and though he had had no experience of broadcasting, I offered him the post of News
Editor. I never made a better choice. Horobin's fierce, keenminded, unremitting pursuit
of the news was to make him an ITN legend.

The third recruit, Nigel Ryan, was to succeed me as Editor of ITN. I had been struck
by the quality of his work as Reuter's correspondent in the Congo and offered him a
post as a reporter on *Roving Report*. On his first assignment he secured a scoop,
gaining the first interview with Jomo Kenyatta, soon to be Premier of Kenya, but then
just released from jail in Nairobi. Ryan, tall, independent-minded, with a cavalier dash
in his bearing, graduated rapidly from reporter to producer to Assistant Editor.

The fourth man was William Hodgson, who joined ITN in 1960 as General Manager. This was a key post, for he was the Deputy for the other half of my task, that of managing, as distinct from editing. A very tall, lean, quiet man, Hodgson had been a Fleet Air Arm pilot in the war. A Londoner with a grammar school education, he had become a feature film editor, working with Jean Renoir, before he moved into management. He was to prove an ideal colleague, clear headed, methodical, forthright, never flinching from difficult decisions. He was to play a major part in building up UPITN, the worldwide television news agency we were to found in 1967.

Two women who had been amongst the first recuits at ITN also came to the fore in the 1960s. Diana Edwards-Jones, who had started as a studio floor manager, became a studio director, a post she was to hold for 25 years, and in which she was to win an OBE. Jo Hodgson, who had joined ITN as a sub-editor, rose to be Chief Sub-Editor, the first woman in television news to hold that rank.

In 1960 the programme companies, awash now with money, allowed us to expand our premises and enlarge our studio. We moved the editorial and administrative areas of ITN from the first to the seventh floor of Television House, bringing them at last alongside the technical areas. We were able, too, to enlarge and re-equip the studio, though we could do nothing about raising the ceiling, which continued to limit the lighting of our programmes, and which made the studio dangerously hot if we used it for long periods.

35

News by satellite

The techniques of this new journalism were revolutionized by one huge technological development in the summer of 1962, the satellite transmission of television pictures. The development of rockets to carry man into space (and to allow nuclear warheads to be delivered over long distances) brought as a by-product the capacity to put a communications satellite into orbit. The first satellite, code-named Telstar, was launched from Cape Canaveral on 10 July 1962. The Post Office engineers agreed, with some reluctance, to let us broadcast live the first pictures the satellite was due to send back. We placed an OB camera in position at the GPO tracking station at Goonhilly in Cornwall, and Ian Trethowan stood by ready to comment.

Telstar passed across the surface of the globe at an angle which permitted messages to be sent up to it, and relayed down from it, for only twenty minutes at a time, and then only at certain periods of the day. The first such pass – we were soon learning a new jargon – would come at 3am on 11 July. All we could show the viewers in our main bulletin and in *Dateline* on 10 July were the preparations at Goonhilly, at the French tracking station in Normandy, and at the American transmitting and tracking station at Andover in Maine.

At midnight the network went off the air. But at ITN we were as busy as if this was a peak hour, as we stood by ready to record on videotape the first transmission. As the clock moved towards 3am the control room was crowded. Diana Edwards-Jones, now an experienced director, was in charge. On our monitors we could see Ian Trethowan at Goonhilly, backed by the ranks of Post Office monitors in the tracking station's control room. The monitor linking the satellite with Goonhilly showed only a blank, flickering screen. Diana had an open line to the CBS control room in New York, whose engineers were talking to the engineers at the station in Andover, Maine, from which signals would go to the satellite. More new jargon reached our ears. 'Are you talking to the bird yet'? queried the CBS engineer. 'Any moment now' came back the laconic reply from Andover.

Suddenly the blank monitor screen at Goonhilly began to quiver, and break up. Through the crackle of static, the shaking, wavering lines of the screen gradually formed into the face of man. 'We have a picture – a man in picture', came Trethowan's voice, triumphantly. And there, clumsy, incomplete, but recognisable, was indeed the face of a NASA official in New York, seen in the first picture transmitted by satellite. A new era in communication was, for better or for worse, upon us. Next morning the film list for our planning conference began proudly 'First pictures from space'.

We were able to tell the story in the bulletins that evening and to show the recording of these first shaky pictures. The next evening and at 11.40pm, when Telstar came within range once again, we were able to transmit direct to the viewers a series of items from America. President Kennedy presided at a news conference; a game of baseball at the Yankee Stadium unfolded its complex ritual; the contestants for Miss Florida paraded in the sunshine.

The quality of the transmissions rapidly proved to be good, showing that the fears of the Post Office had been misplaced. A formal two-way programme, with Richard Dimbleby as anchor man on the European side, was broadcast at ten days later, and carried on both ITV and BBC, as well as by all other Eurovision stations. Bison charged over hillsides in Montana; the huge sculptured faces of Lincoln and Washington showed from their North Dakota mountainside; Europeans sat in cafes and sailed on lakes. When it was all over, the wonder of Telstar had become commonplace. The critics were soon busy expressing doubts as to whether the programme makers would live up to these new gifts the technicians had brought them, and posing the question 'What are satellites' to be used for, anyway'?

On the answer to that question I had no doubt. Their main use must be for news. Immediacy was the quality which above all satellites added to inter-continental broadcasting, and immediacy was an integral part of news. I was therefore delighted when the programme companies decided that when both broadcasting channels were to be given access to Telstar, for ten minutes apiece, ITN should use the time allocated independent television. I did not regularly keep a diary, but on this occasion I jotted down some notes of the next three days' events, heading them as 'From the Diary of a Space Age Editor'.

10 am. Friday, 27 July. Meeting at the GPO of the ITV-BBC Consortium for Telstar programming with the officials of the Post Office who control the Goonhilly Downs transmitter. Formal high ceiling conference room is hung with portraits of earlier Postmasters-General. Reversal of roles since our previous planning meetings here. Then it was the engineers who, under their studied calm, showed some hints of the strain of this immense experiment. But since last week's successful first tests, and Monday night's spectacularly successful programme exchanges, they are easy and relaxed. The tension is on our faces now – the programme planners. My sense of time is completely blurred by incessant conferences, incessant telephoning across the Atlantic and up and down the ITV network. Can it be really only four days ago that the first formal two-way programme exchange took place? Now we are meeting to agree on another unexpected offer of satellite time next Monday evening.

The quiet voiced official confirms that the American Telephone and Telegraph Company are offering the United Kingdom 20 min of time on Pass No. 187 on Monday evening, between 8.20 and 8.40. This suits BBC well for *Panorama*, and they accept

Fig. 16. ITN News from New York, 1962.

with alacrity. ITV has no magazine programme that night, so I make a quick bid for it for the ITN news. Argue that news is what Telstar is best suited for, anyway. Bid accepted. My mind is only half on the rest of the conference, as I suddenly tot up the problems involved. We have no regular New York correspondent, no staff on the ground, and only a weekend – and no city is so dead as New York at the weekend – in which to organize a programme. But we can rely on our good colleagues of CBS for help with studios, film, links. 11am. At last conference ends. Sprint down four floors of handsome GPO staircase, grab taxi back to Kingsway. Brian Connell is in the corridor as I come in. He had already booked a seat on the 4pm plane to New York, just in case we got the job. 'All systems go'. But we must send a producer as well. Robert Tyrell handled the Scott Carpenter fight from New York, knows the city and CBS. He comes out of the viewing theatre where he has been working on our film for the Radio Show.

'Like a weekend in New York, Bob'? 'Why not'? 'All right, you're on the 4pm flight with Brian'. Norman Clark ITN's foreign editor, has called CBS, secured a promise of studio and other assistance. What are the news prospects for Monday? Lousy – Not a decent story stirring anywhere. Not even a flood? There's always a flood or a fire somewhere in the States. Not even a flood. There was one in Texas, but it has gone down. Hold on, there is one story – a good one. An Arizona court is due to rule on the thalidomide baby case. But it probably won't rule until after our transmission.

6pm. With planning for the day's normal ITN bulletins finished, Telstar looms up suddenly again like a nagging tooth. We must get some Americans talking into camera. We must let Telstar do its other big job – of letting people of one nation see and meet ordinary people of another. But this is a news programme. How are we to do this? Move around the office questioning harassed executives for ideas as they get on with the nightly rush to get the 9pm bulletin on to the air. Out of all of it comes one plan. We must book an OB unit for Monday and use it to go out into the streets. We can surely find some news story we can follow up wi th live interviews. Norman Clark is on the 'phone to John Cooper and Bob Little, CBS's admirable overseas planners. Yes, we can have an OB unit. They suggest Grand Central Station as a setting. No, we must have the New York skyline in the shot. I know we are certain of plenty of people in Grand Central, but it is indoors, it might be anywhere. Anyway, book the unit and we'll place it later.

8pm. John Macmillan is on the 'phone from New York. A-R have a *This Week* unit with Desmond Wilcox as reporter in New York, in the hope Telstar might have been available in their programme time. Now that we have had the luck of the draw, John generously offers us their help. Grasp it thankfully. Desmond Wilcox is just the reinforcement we need. And he has producers, secretaries with him. Discuss with John placing of OB. What about Coney Island? What about the amusement park, 'Freedom Land'? Not too keen on the latter. Too much like the Seattle World Fair, the only dud item in the American space programme earlier in the week.

9pm. John Macmillan on the 'phone again. Jones Beach. The main middle-class summer playground near New York. Atlantic rollers, Americans holiday-making. Sounds ideal. Ask CBS to fix. Desmond Wilcox and unit hurrying back from Washington.

Saturday, 10am. Check with news room. Any news stirring in America for Monday? Not a thing. Dead as can be. Summer slack period has set in. Decide best thing is to play a round of golf and forget it all. Play round, but don't forget it all. A ten minute programme filled with a dreary lack of news looms up between me and every shot.

1pm. Saturday. Call Connell and Tyrell. Catch them at breakfast time. Shouts of 'Put the orange juice on the table', in the background as we talk. Situation pretty grisly. Jones Beach no good. Will be deserted Monday afternoon. So will Coney Island. Opt for Central Park. Skyscrapers in the background will give us an opening title. Tyrell breaks in with suggestion that we track down an agency which specializes in American holidays for Britons, and get them to divert a bus load of British tourists towards our cameras at transmission time, which would guarantee us people for Wilcox to talk to.

Fig. 17. Geoffrey Cox with BAFTA award, 1962.

Are there ordinary British tourists in New York? I thought only the rich can afford it. It seems there are cut price tours. Ask them if they really can do it on 15 dollars a day. That should be of interest to ordinary viewers. We settle on Central Park, plus American passers-by (we hope) plus British tourists. Connell breaks in with good news that Charles Collingwood has agreed to flank him in the CBS studio on Monday, giving us a two-man newscast, which will look different to ordinary bulletins. We have the bones of a programme. All we need now is some news to put the flesh on it.

My diary notes ended there, as I became absorbed in the task of ensuring that we had enough news to justify all this high cost technology. We were scheduled to come on air in Britain at 8.26pm – which was 3.26pm in New York, very early in the day for there to be any flow of hard news, particularly on film. At the UN the Security Council was discussing the Congo. That would provide at least one hard news item. In Albany, Georgia, the Reverend Martin Luther King was leading a protest about segregation in schooling. CBS would get him interviewed on the spot for us. But the only story which would grip the minds of most viewers was in a courtroom in Arizona. The thalidomide story was then new, and tragically fresh. A young American mother, Mrs. Sheree Finkine, already the mother of four healthy children, had been treated with the drug whilst awaiting the birth of her fifth baby. She had applied to a court for the right to have an abortion. The hearing was set for this Monday, the day of our transmission. This should provide us with enough news to give force to the programme.

But we had reckoned without the weather. At six o'clock our time – lunch-time in New

York – an anxious Robert Tyrrell was on the phone from his hotel room overlooking Central Park. A sea mist had rolled in, covering the whole city. Visibility was down to a few hundred yards. He had rushed out to the OB site in Central Park. Not a single sky-scraper, not a trace of the New York skyline could be seen – only forlorn dripping trees.

Sea mists are a rarity in the New York summer. For one to plague us now was cruel. Yet it was out of the question to change to an inside site. Could CBS perhaps rig up another camera at their Studios, to give us the alternative skyline shot we needed for the opening title, to establish we were in New York? No, that was out of the question. I assumed a confidence I did not feel. 'I know these New York mists well' I assured Tyrrell. 'They roll away by mid-afternoon without fail'. I checked hastily with the CBS correspondent in London. He whistled his sympathy. 'That's bad. Once those summer mists settle, they just don't move'.

But the reverse was to be the case. As the clock ticked down towards the time of transmission, a light wind sprang up in Manhatten and a triumphant Tyrrell assured us he had a usable picture. We were due to follow 'Panorama', and as their picture came through I saw, to my relief, that they had opted for a magazine format, instead of going for hard news. Richard Dimbleby came on screen interviewing a policeman in Rockefeller Plaza; James Mossman talked to customers at a drug store food and drink counter, explaining that a hamburger cost three shillings. We had the news field to ourselves.

Diana Edwards-Jones and the CBS director in New York were talking to each other as calmly as if they were in adjoining studios in Kingsway. The figures on the time-elapsed clock on the control room wall flipped down towards 20.26. Then suddenly there were the towers of Manhattan on the skyline, a bit hazy, but unmistakable, and Central New York was in our midst – and in the midst of a multitude of British sitting rooms. A moment later and the familiar ITN News caption was superimposed, with an added line to it 'From New York' and the sound of *Non-Stop* was played on the disc which Tyrrell had taken with him to New York. Even better luck was in store. Mrs. Finkine came out of the courtroom a few minutes before our transmission, and, on the verge of tears, told the waiting CBS reporter that the Court had refused to allow her to have an abortion. (She got one a month later in Sweden.) It was a strong human story, which would have crossed any national boundary. Told on the steps of this sunlit Georgia court house, and almost instantaneously heard and seen on the other side of the Atlantic, it was doubly poignant. The United Nations debate flared into argument in front of the cameras, Martin Luther King denounced the school authorities with vigour; Desmond Wilcox drew out his British visitors wittily as well as determinedly. Connell and Collingwood were authoritative, confident and highly professional. The picture quality throughout was excellent. Our ten minutes of satellite time flashed by. We switched back to London to bring in three more stories, to round off the bulletin.

It was good programme by any standards, matching the occasion. Our colleagues recognized this, for six months later it was to win us a special award from the Guild of Television Producers. The critics liked it too, preferring it to *Panorama*'s 'flabby travelogue' – which had been 'better seen on film anyway'. ITN's report was 'something with a real sense of actuality about it, one of the few occasions on which the BBC has been beaten at the sort of game it generally commands'.

Telstar fairly quickly wore itself out, to be replaced by Telstar II. But before it finally disintegrated Telstar was to help transmit from America film of the biggest news story since Suez and Hungary – the Cuban rocket crisis of the autumn of 1962, when we moved to the very threshold of nuclear war. Though it was available for only brief periods of the day and night, it brought to us the scenes of confrontation between Adlai Stevenson and the Soviet leaders in the Security Council, and the ominous shots, filmed from American reconnaissance planes, of the long, canvas enshrouded shapes of the rockets on the decks of the Soviet cargo vessels heading for Cuba. It also enabled for the first time filmed reports from our own correspondents in New York and Florida to be brought immediately to the screen, so hastening the day when British television news would have to have a full corps of its own reporters to cover all the main stories, instead of relying to the degree we did then on agency reporters; a development which was to make inevitable the introduction of the half hour news.

36

Newsyear '63

T he flood of news in 1963, that *annus mirabilis* or, if you choose, *annus ter-
ribilis* for news, swamped the bulletins and made special programmes almost a
regular part of the schedules. The year opened with Britain snowed up in the
worst winter for years, and saw soon the death of Hugh Gaitskell and Britain's exclusion
from the Common Market. Racial strife mounted in America, and guerrilla strife in
Vietnam. Pope John XXIII died, and his successor was crowned. President Kennedy
visited Berlin to proclaim 'Ich bin ein Berliner', and County Wexford to visit the village
from which his forefathers had emigrated to the USA. Harold Macmillan resigned and
the 14th Earl of Home became Prime Minister. And winding through all these major
events was, like a stained thread in a carpet, the squalid tale of the Profumo affair.

The Profumo affair posed for television a peculiarly difficult problem. It was a scandal
reflected not just in gossip or allegations, but in the sworn evidence of the two trials of
Dr Stephen Ward, in the privileged statements of a full scale debate in the Commons,
and in the findings of the judicial inquiry conducted by Lord Denning into the security
aspects which arose because Christine Keeler had numbered among her friends the
Soviet Naval Attaché as well as the British Minister for War. Material from these sources
was unmistakably news, and as a result the Profumo scandal involved television, essentially a family medium, in handling material which told of sex orgies and two-way mirrors, of perversions and practices which until then were to be found only in the pages
of Kraft-Ebbing or Havelock Ellis, or in pornography smuggled in from the Continent.
We were not yet into the era of pornography on open sale in Soho, let alone soft porn
on the shelves of the corner newsagents. I considered whether we should suppress or
at least bowdlerize the evidence which emerged. But to do so would have been to distort
and indeed falsify the news. Squalid conduct was the basis of the story, and it could not
be reported with any meaning or any truth if that squalor was hidden. We deliberately
bowdlerized our reports for the early evening bulletins, when children were likely to be
viewing. But for the main bulletin our reports were frank, though shorter than the copious details offered by the press.

Court cases about scandal in high places were not new. In 1918 the Billing libel action,
in which allegations were made (which proved bogus) that German spies had compiled

a black book of the sexual weaknesses and perversions of British political leaders, had filled many newspaper columns. But its details were not spoken aloud in sitting rooms where families were gathered, and given added importance by the very fact that they had been broadcast. Long established taboos, both of language and of subject, were swept aside during the Stephen Ward trials. The Profumo scandal was the booster rocket of the permissive age. When in August that year it was joined by the robbery of the century, the sense of a society in disarray was further intensified. For it was on 8 August 1963 that the Glasgow to London mail train was ambushed in Buckinghamshire, and Great Train Robbery passed into the mythology of British crime.

The final manifestation of the Profumo affair came in September when, at the extraordinary hour of midnight, we mounted a special programme to summarize and discuss the Denning Report – a programme which even at that hour commanded a substantial audience. From the window of my office I could see the queue outside the Stationery Office in Kingsway, stretching out of sight round the corner, as people waited for the Report to come on sale at midnight. Denning put paid to any question of security risks, and to virtually all the other rumours as well. Mandy Rice-Davies, the other girl in the case, provided her own pictorial postscript to the affair by being filmed, a copy of the Report in hand, as she wiggled her way in tight fitting jeans across the muddy farmyard of a farmhouse in Warwickshire in which she had sought refuge.

October 1963 saw the arrival on the screen of that other phenomenon of the 1960s, the Beatles. That month they made their first appearance on the stage in London, in *Sunday Night at the London Palladium.* After the show our cameras recorded a group of frenzied, shrieking girls chasing the four as they ran through the darkened street to their car. How far we had filmed a genuine manifestation of teenage feeling, or how far a carefully contrived publicity stunt was never clearly established, but certainly from then on Beatlemania was a part of British life and of British news bulletins.

We were to see a lot of the Beatles in the months ahead, for from time to time they appeared in Rediffusion's pop programme *Ready, Steady, Go.* This was mounted in the same basement studio in Kingsway from which we had presented the Elections, and the Beatles' presence there put Television House into a stage of siege. Police cordons guarded all doors of the building, and traffic in Kingsway was brought to a standstill. Our camera cars could not come and go, and even motor cycle despatch riders had difficulty in battling their way into the building any evening that RSG was on the air. The floor of the basement studio was crammed with rapt faced boys and girls in their early teens, jiving intently but silently (the least noise during the broadcast meant that most terrible of fates, instant expulsion from the studio) the girls wearing exaggerated make-up that looked as if it had been hastily applied as they rushed here from school. A smell of sweat, chewing gum and popcorn hung in the hot, brightly lit air, as the music, muted though it was by later disco levels, reverberated in the packed studio. The Swinging 1960s were under way on our doorstep, encouraged, enlarged, and no doubt to a degree created by this new medium which reflected these trends immediately into a multitude of homes.

37

Death in Dallas

Massive though the news stories of the first three quarters of 1963 had been, they were all to be over-shadowed by the story which broke in Dallas on Friday, 22 November. At the time that the John F. Kennedy motocade was approaching the Dallas Book Depository, many of the chief figures in British television were gathering at the Dorchester Hotel for the annual awards ceremony of the Guild of Television Producers and Directors. I was having a pre-drink there when word reached me that Kennedy had been shot at, and wounded. In my dinner jacket I ran along Park Lane to my parked car and drove back to Kingsway as fast as the Friday evening traffic would permit. I knew that ahead lay not only a long night, but a long week.

One concern was uppermost in my mind – that the federal structure of ITV, with its thirteen companies all broadcasting from different points, could lead to delay in putting out a news flash, particularly if the President had died of his wounds. The BBC was a unitary system, with most of its programmes going out from London, able to break into transmissions immediately. But Independent Television had to wheel all its stations into line before they could take a news flash from ITN. Though there was an interlocking telephone system, with red telephones which rang simultaneously in all control rooms, the process of arranging a news flash could be as cumbersome as changing the course of a convoy at sea by use of a semaphore.

I reached my office and turned on the set in the corner in time to see *Emergency Ward 10*, the medical soap opera of the day, faded out by Rediffusion, and replaced by Sir John Barbirolli conducting the Hallé orchestra. We had given the official announcement of the President's death a few minutes earlier, within two minutes of its appearance on the Reuter tape. The BBC had been ahead of us with the first news flash of his death, which they had got from a source not available to ITN, their monitoring service at Caversham, which listened to all the main foreign broadcasts around the clock. Caversham had picked up an unofficial report of the President's death, put out by the Voice of America the official United States overseas radio service. This report was based on statements made by a priest who had just left the hospital in Dallas, and anticipated by several minutes the official statement from the White House. The BBC were at the time transmitting the *Tonight* programme live, which enabled them to put out the Voice of

America report without delay – though they took the considerable risk of hardening it up from being an unofficial report into a categorical statement that the President was dead. Granada, who had managed to get a line through from Manchester to New York – all lines through London were jammed – phoned through the same unofficial report to us after it had been broadcast on NBC radio. But there was no way in which we could get it on to the air through the cumbersome ITV system in time to match the BBC's centralized operation, which had the additional good fortune of having an easily interrupted magazine programme on the air in which to flash the news.

The Hallé orchestra continued with its programme of classical music until nine o'clock, when we put out an extended news bulletin, followed by a filmed profile of President Kennedy which we held ready against such an eventuality. This was to be the start of three days and nights of extraordinary news pressure, during which ITN was to fill six hours of airtime, and the current affairs programmes many other hours as well. From breakfast time onwards the next morning we were on the air with special bulletins, in which we were able to show the first film, transmitted by Telstar, from Dallas. Throughout the week end people turned to television as never before, seeking not only information but also to share the widespread and deep emotions this event had stirred. This was particularly so in the United States.

> The full acceptance of television as the nation's supreme forum was earned only by its performance over the assassination week end ... Sitting with friends in Harriman's parlor and watching the tube was to be in touch with reality, to be part of the national grief.[1]

Film of the moment of the shooting did not reach the screen for a day or two, when United Press circulated the only film record of it, made on 8mm colour film by an amateur cameraman. But the other scenes had been widely caught by the cameras – the ambulance racing to the hospital; the anxious, tearful faces in the sunlit hospital corridors; the square and the Book Depository; the arrest of Oswald; the swearing in of the new President by a Texas woman judge in the cabin of the Presidential Aircraft, U.S. One; Jackie Kennedy emerging from the plane at Washington airport with her suit still marked with dark bloodstains. Then on the Sunday evening came the extraordinary moment when the American television cameras caught, live, the actual shooting of Harvey Oswald as he was being escorted down the stairway in the police headquarters.

Though we did not yet have colour on British television, the poignancy of the later ceremonies was almost unbearably sharp. In the Rotunda of the Capitol the cameras caught the moment as Jacqueline Kennedy, erect and set faced in her widow's black, led forward her ten year old daughter, Caroline, to touch the Stars and Stripes which draped the President's coffin. Other cameras followed the funeral procession on its slow measured way past the Lincoln Memorial across the Potomac, and up through the trees of Arlington Military Cemetry. The burial was at an hour when Telstar was in a position to carry these scenes to Europe, so that many millions on this side of the Atlantic watched and shared those moments with the American public. It was fitting the television should have marked in this way the passing of John F. Kennedy, for he was the first new leader of the television age. He was little known outside the United States until he reached the White House; yet within three years he aroused deep personal affection

---

1   Theodore H. White: *In Search of History.* Cape, 1979, p. 517.

amongst millions. His hatless, striding figure and ready – but not too ready – smile, depicted alongside veteran leaders like de Gaulle and Macmillan, or warily studying an ebullient Kruschev alongside him on a Vienna sofa, or talking to Irish families amid the mud of Wexford, or with his voice ringing out in confidence and hope against a background of the Berlin Wall, had been portrayed by the cameras to a multitude of people and had given the sense that they knew him personally. He had come to embody for them hope, and it was the death of that hope which made these days and these scenes of his funeral so deeply moving.

38

The first truly
TV election

T he General Election of October 1964 was the first truly television election, the first in which television coverage was of supreme importance to the candidates and the parties. In 1959 our role had been new. We were still regarded as an interesting extra to the established means of election communication, rather than as the central forum. During that election the way the parties used television for their party political broadcasts attracted as much attention as the way the broadcasters reported and analysed the contest. But by 1964 television had assumed a much greater significance. The ITV system had spread over most of the country. Some 90 per cent of homes now had TV, as against 70 per cent in 1959.

ITN'S coverage of the campaign followed the same pattern as five years earlier, though we had double the amount of time – 20 minutes a night – for our special Election Reports. We relied mainly on our film cameras for coverage of meetings, but on eight occasions also made use of outside broadcast units. These added so much authenticity and vividness that it seemed obvious that at least one major meeting of each of the main parties should have been broadcast in full, instead of the brief excerpts which were all that found their way into our reports. These excerpts no doubt gave the heart of the matter, but in cutting out the heart, we killed the sense of occasion. Recordings of full meetings could have been shown late in the evening, but to do so would require the broadcasters to surrender large amounts of time, and for the parties to surrender some of the time they use for their own party political broadcasts. This has never come about. Television has been broadcasting the annual party conferences live since 1962,and now broadcasts Parliament, but television has never yet broadcast in full an election meeting during a General Election campaign.

ITN covered the 1964 General Election with a new chief Political Correspondent. In 1962 Ian Trethowan had, too, felt the gravitational pull of the BBC, and had moved over to Lime Grove, setting himself on the path which was to carry him to the post of

Director General of the BBC. His replacement, Alastair Burnet, came to ITN from the prestigious role of Assistant Editor of *The Economist*. He was to develop into one of the greatest of British television journalists, winning in due course, as an ITN newscaster, not only a knighthood, but a standing with the British public comparable to that gained by Walter Cronkite in the United States. Two other new recruits to ITN, Andrew Gardner and Peter Snow were also at this time starting on long and highly successful television careers. With another newcomer, John Whale flanking Burnet in the coverage of politics, ITN was able to approach the 1964 Election with a confident professionalism.

The BBC concentrated its day by day coverage of the campaign in its news bulletins, which were extended for the purpose. To this they added one important development in the television treatment of elections. Grace Wyndham Goldie devised a means of getting the leaders of the main political parties to be interviewed during the campaign. Entitled *Election Forum*, it took the form of three interviewers putting to each main party leader in turn on consecutive nights a number of questions selected from questions sent sent in by the public. Of three interviewers Ian Trethowan and Robin Day (the third was Kenneth Harris) had been ITN newscasters. The programmes were seen as a considerable success, and paved the way for the more direct interviewing of political leaders by broadcast journalists in the future.

The prominence of television in the 1964 campaign led to much discussion about the telegenic strengths and weaknesses of the Party leaders. 'Image' had become a cult word among Party managers. Harold Wilson, the first British politician to come through to Party leadership in the television age, set about mastering the techniques of the medium, and gave every sign of enjoying their use. He swiftly learnt to tailor the key point of a speech to a passage of some two or three minutes in length, providing an ideal cut for a busy film editor. The hideous American term 'sound bite' had not yet gained usage in Britain. In handling hecklers, Wilson soon realized that the microphone seldom picked up their words. He would therefore repeat what they said, so winning marks for fairness – and at the same time giving himself time in which to think out a riposte.

Television has undoubtedly magnified the histrionic element in politics, but it did not invent it. Churchill's cigars and hats were used as deliberate props in the role which he set himself to play. That the role and the man were one and the same did not disguise the fact that he, consciously or subconsciously, projected a picture of himself. This was clearly to be seen at Westminster in the years of his final Premiership, in the early 1950s. As the time for questions to the Prime Minister approached, Winston Churchill could be seen waiting in the shadows of the lobby behind the Speaker's Chair – a stumpy, pale, loose-jowelled figure, shoulders bent under the burdens of age and responsibility. Then, as the House neared on the Order Paper the questions to the Prime Minister, he would suddenly draw himself upright, square his shoulders and stride into the Chamber, his chin thrust out his step purposeful, very much the old lion ready for the fray. It was as if he had suddenly drawn on, like a garment, his public person.

In Sir Alec Douglas Home this histrionic element was slight. The inner circle of the Conservative Party which had ensured for him the Premiership in 1963 had paid scant regard to his potential as a television performer. He made no pretence to be one. He went his way, waging exactly the same type of campaign his predecessors had done, leaving his aides to anguish over the inescapable fact that he was certainly not a natural television figure, and that no amount of presentation tricks or camera angles would make him one.

Yet Sir Alec was by no means an ineffectual television figure. In the studio he may have been stiff and abrupt and have given the impression that he regarded the questions as slightly offensive, if not himself, certainly to the office he held. But in the field he came over differently, particularly when facing the hecklers who during this Election pursued him everywhere. The lean, upright figure who stalked from his car through noisy crowds to speak in a market square or on a building site had the assurance of a colonel checking his troops under fire, a man of courage and cool headedness, if not always a master of the deft answer. This was certainly true of the uproar, verging on a riot, which marked Home's meeting in the Rag Market in Birmingham, a week before Polling Day. It was covered by outside broadcast cameras, and the presence of their scanners and vans and lighting trucks may have drawn in crowds of would-be trouble makers. Only the fact that he had the microphone, whilst the crowd had only their voices, enabled him to get his message across to the viewing public, if not to the audience in the hall.

The most difficult question which arose during the campaign turned on the great unspoken question of race: Enoch Powell had not yet thrust the issue of immigration to the fore, and all the leaders avoided it carefully. But in the Midland constituencies it was not to be avoided. In particular in Smethwick the Tory candidate was giving voice to the resentment felt by many whites at the influx of coloured immigrants into their area. Every canon of news demanded that we should cover this development, so I agreed that we should include Smethwick in the list of constituencies on which we would present special reports. Once this news reached Transport House the Labour leadership reacted with vigour. A senior official told me that they saw our action as highly irresponsible. It could stir up racial feeling in a most dangerous way. The BBC, I was told, had had similar plans for *Panorama* but, on Sir Hugh Greene's direct instructions, had cancelled them. I thought this was no way in which to confront a key issue in a democracy. If immigration was a matter of deep concern in a constituency, and yet was to be classed as one which could not be openly argued at the time of an election, we were inviting people to seek non-democratic ways of sorting out their problems. I became more convinced than ever that we must cover Smethwick. We could not,I knew, go ahead with a balanced constituency report unless the Labour candidate took part. I told the labour party that if Gordon Walker refused to do so, ITN would have to announce that that was his decision. We had already made approaches to the other parties. The fact of Labour's ban could not be kept secret.

Such a ban would have done great harm to Gordon Walker's already threatened hold on the seat. Transport House saw this, and yielded to our pressure. Alastair Burnet went to Smethwick and on Saturday 10 October, five days before Polling Day, we presented a report on the constituency which neither avoided nor stressed the racial issue.

Throughout the campaign we once again worked closely by the clock, totting up our coverage figures every morning, and keeping the screen time of the parties within justifiable distance of one another. Once again when the parties and the press, and the

Fig. 18. Election Night, 1964.

now greatly widened ranks of the academic researchers probed our work, they decided that by and large it had been fair.

For the *Results* programme on Election Night we had in the studio a small but knowledgeable team of commentators. Alastair Burnet was flanked by William Rees-Mogg of the *Sunday Times*, and John Freeman, Editor of the *News Statesman*. Since Burnet was about to return to *The Economist* we had assembled the next Editor of that paper, the next Editor of *The Times* and the next Ambassador in Washington. Robert Kee chaired their group, and Hugh Berrington of Newcastle University added expert psephological expertise. Kenneth Harris stood by in another studio to interview victorious or defeated candidates, peers, experts and others with something apt to say. Amongst those he interviewed were the Beatles. They chorused 'Don't take our money away, Mr Wilson'. They had no need to worry. In Harold Wilson's first Honours List they each had the MBE.

Once again we built a newsroom in the basement studio of Television House. When I visited it just before we came on the air on Election Night the scene on the crowded floor was as bright, under the lights, as on a sunny Mediterranean beach. Our secretaries and typists were as radiant as actresses; the teleprinters chattered in their corner; cameramen and other technicians waited by their equipment; the short sleeved journalists were already busy at their desks. At the long curved central desk Burnet and his colleagues radiated a quiet confidence, looking more like a group of dons at a Senior Common Room table, or experts in a Whitehall conference room-settings into which they could readily have fitted – rather men about to come under the scrutiny of millions.

I was sure that we would deliver a good programme – and we did. What unfolded on our screen until the small hours of that night, and throughout the long drama of the next day, until Labour scraped into power by a margin of half a dozen seats, was television news at its best, swiftly presented and clearly explained. It was certainly the best live broadcast Independent Television had mounted to that date, and even in these technologically more advanced days the recording of it merits study. It sustained its quality up to the final moments when, on the Friday afternoon, our camera outside Buckingham Palace picked up in a dramatic long shot Sir Douglas Home's car in the traffic in the Mall, as he made his way to offer his resignation to the Queen. An alert cameraman filmed him later leaving, as defeated Premiers are wont to do, by the garden gate at the ear of No 10, just before Harold Wilson swept up to the front entrance. In the new Premier's entourage that bustled into the corridor of power behind him was to be glimpsed the tall figure of Marcia Williams.

The viewing figures showed that even if we had not yet completely turned the tide which flowed the BBC's way on great public occasions, we had done much to stem it. The audience on Election Night was split only marginally in favour of the BBC. J.D.S. Haworth, writing in *Contrast*, an admirable early venture into the professional discussion of television, observed that it is 'curious how, at times like the Election, viewers switch over in droves to the BBC for the 'traditional' portentousness of Dimbley and Co. For the first time, however, there was not much to chose between the two channels. If anything ITN had the more consistent sense of urgency'.[1]

---

1   *Contrast*, Vol. 4, No. 1, p. 16.

39

Live election coverage

When the General Election came in April 1966, it followed so closely on the heels of the 1964 contest as literally to seem to be *déjà vu*. One of main contestants, Edward Heath, was a newcomer to star status. But otherwise there was a sense that this was a re-run, rather than a fresh take.

The most remarkable television coverage of the campaign came during Harold Wilson's meeting in the Rag Market at Birmingham, where Sir Alec Douglas Home had been howled at, if not howled down, in 1964. The Prime Minister's speech there on 16 March was planned to run from 8.30pm to 9.30pm, a span which straddled, by accident or design (one never did know with Harold Wilson and his entourage) the time in which our main bulletin went on air. I decided to carry a segment of the speech live in the bulletin, and stationed myself in our VTR editing room to select it. When the Prime Minister took up his place on the platform in Birmingham, it was clear that the meeting was already in a turbulent mood. He began slowly, lingering over the sentences of his written speech, certainly not reading swiftly through the earlier passages – as he could often do – before coming to the key points. This leisurely approach stimulated the hecklers, and for the next twenty minutes we were treated to a virtuoso performance by a remarkable television political performer, as Harold Wilson varied his replies from scorn to wisecracks, from derision to apparent indignation, seeming deliberately to tease the audience. He was certainly in no hurry to get on to the main parts of his speech. The reason was not hard to guess. He was playing the audience along, playing for the time until 9 o'clock, warming them up as the compere of an entertainment show warms up his audience, until he was ready to come in. And come in he did, right on the stroke of the clock which marked the start of our bulletin. As the second hand on the big clock on the recording room wall moved towards the opening minute of our bulletin, and our titles came up on the screen, Harold Wilson's whole manner changed. He dropped the attitude of the jesting debater, and, almost as if he had changed his very garb, became in a flash the serious statesman. By the time we had switched over to the live feed from Birmingham, and millions of homes in Britain had joined me in this ringside view from the Rag Market, the entertainer had been replaced by the political leader. Gravity now marked his features, as he set out the core of his argument swiftly and vigorously.

The audience, which had by then passed from heckling to uproar, with Conservatives shouting at Labour supporters, and students shouting at them all, were taken by surprise, and for a moment silenced. But within a minute or so they were back on the attack. At home the audience saw the Prime Minister seeking to expound his policy to the country, being shouted and yelled at, but battling on in the face of uproar, steadily putting his message across, pausing only to deliver an occasional riposte. It provided some of the most remarkable television ever seen in a news programme. Now you could indeed 'see it happen on ITN'. I let it run for four and a half minutes and then cut away for the rest of the bulletin.

The BBC did not show the meeting live. Their hierarchy, I was told, had ruled against it on the grounds that, by allowing live material into a bulletin, one had lost editorial control of its content. That seemed to me an excessively purist approach and certainly did not deter the BBC, 14 years later, from putting out live coverage of the siege of the Iranian Embassy in London and of the Defence spokesman's announcement of the sinking of HMS Sheffield during the Falklands campaign. The test must surely be whether we could reasonably assess in advance what the material was likely to be and judge its newsworthiness. The two earlier occasions on which we had used live material in a bulletin – the first arrival of President Kennedy in London, and the breakthrough of the final section of the new St Bernard tunnel under the Alps – had passed that test. It was a reasonable assumption – and one which proved true – that a major setpiece speech by a Prime Minister would be equally newsworthy.

For Election Night we adopted the same basic pattern as in 1964, though this time we had two computers on the job, both installed in the scene Dock of Studio 9, alongside the area where the area where the news room had been set up, and where the commentators faced the camera. Alastair Burnet, who had continued to appear before the cameras for *This Week* after leaving ITN for the Economist, was again in charge of the programme on the air. This time we did all the planning and organization within ITN. David Windlesham was now a senior executive of Rediffusion; so David Nicholas, having got ITN Reports well under way, took over the producing of this Election programme, as he was to do triumphantly during the next four elections.

This was the first General Election since 1950 in which Richard Dimbleby did not head the BBC team. He had died of cancer three months earlier, Churchill's funeral having been the last great occasion on which he had presided at the microphone. But Cliff Michelmore, well known for his work as the compere of *Tonight*, filled the central role admirable for the BBC, where he was flanked by those two ITN graduates, Day and Trethowan.

In the outcome the battle on the night between us and the BBC was very even. Once again Alastair Burnet was at his skilful best, switching from area to area and person to person with deft, brief remarks that gave the whole programme form and point. He sustained this task without any apparent fatigue or flagging right through the next day, when his work was the more difficult because, with the result long decided, there was none of the cliff-hanging suspense of 1964. When at five o'clock in the afternoon of the second day, Burnet finally signed the programme off the air, the team in the studio – the cameramen, recordists, journalists, telephonists and studio hands – spontaneously burst out clapping, emerging from the shadows around their cameras and desks in this tribute to a true professional.

The incident of the 1966 Election which caught the headlines, and bulks large in the academic studies of the campaign, occurred not in the studios of Kingsway or of Television Centre, but on the train from Liverpool to London on the morning following Election Night. The BBC had put electronic equipment on to the train which would enable them to transmit live an interview with the Prime Minister. But he refused to give them an interview, though he readily gave one to John Whale and the ITN crew who were also on the train. The reasons for the Prime Minister's attitude to the BBC throughout his period of office and afterwards during the row about *Yesterday's Men* have been frequently analysed, but still remain obscure. I was sorry at the time, and remain sorry, that they took the shape of this refusal to share out his interviewing time between both organizations. We wanted any scoops we could get against the BBC, but we wanted them to be on a free-for-all-basis. John Whale's interview, too, would have stood up to any competition, shot at the breakfast table with a bottle of HP Sauce well in view, and full of sharp, clear questions.

In this campaign the BBC supplemented its news coverage with a special late night programme, along the lines which ITN had adopted from 1959 onwards. A perceptive analyst noted significant differences between these special programmes. While ITN's *Election '66* adopted a hard news approach, presenting 25 minutes of extracts from speeches supplemented by interviews, the BBC's *Campaign Report* was more of a magazine, with feature items, discussions, interviews and analyses of the polls overshadowing straight reporting.

> ... Between the two approaches of straight reporting and of commentary with analysis, television had still to find an ideal balance in communicating the substance of campaign arguments while scrutinizing and advancing them.[1]

ITN's emphasis on the reporting rather than the analysing of the Election was an act of deliberate policy. I held the view that the role of television, once a General Election got under way, was primarily to enable the contestants to use this new medium to put their policies and their arguments before the public. The time available, within the bulletins and the special reports, for reporting the election was limited; so too was the attention the public was prepared to give to the Election news. It seemed to me right, in the interests of the functioning of democracy, that time should, during an Election period, be left to the politicians to use, rather than being taken up by journalists. There was a role for the questioning of politicians during the campaign, but the proper place for that was in feature programmes like *This Week* and *Panorama*. Within the news reports, we should get out of the frame, and leave the screen clear for those who sought to govern us to put their own case in their own way. We should concentrate on the journalistic task of ensuring that the politicians' words and activities were presented as fairly and accurately as possible. There was, too, in my stance something of the newsman's dislike of the attitude of those current affairs producers who seemed to think that events only had validity if they took place within a television studio.

---

1   Professor Martin Harrison of Keele University, in D.E. Butler and Anthony King (eds.) *The British General Election of 1966*, Macmillan, 1966.

40

News needs time

In May 1965 a further technological development made plain that the time allocated to daily news on television in Britain was far too short. That month a greatly improved satellite, entitled Early Bird – *La Matinuelle* the French technicians called it – was put into orbit. Unlike Telstar, with its chancy 20 minute periods of transmission, Early Bird was available for 18 hours a day. At £3,000 an hour, it was too costly for ITN – and even for the BBC – to use regularly. But we now had the reassurance that satellite transmissions would be available when big news broke anywhere in the world.

This meant more pictures to crowd into the twelve minutes which were allocated to ITN for its main evening bulletin, and to the 14 – soon to be 15 – minutes of the main BBC News. Both services had, too, the facilities with which to garner the day's news in visual form. ITN's financial position had been significantly improved by the findings of the report in 1962 of the Pilkington Committee. ITN had been the only part of the independent television system for which the Committee had praise. It had damned the programme companies and the Authority, but of news it wrote:

> Our general conclusion is that the country is well served by the national news bulletins of the BBC and ITN. The selection and presentation of both services is fair and objective. For the television news services, a particular but important part of television broadcasting, competition has worked well. Each of the two services is good in itself; each is different from the other in style and approach. Hence they offer the viewer a worthwhile choice, and stimulate one another.

The report went on to endorse my claims for a second nightly news bulletin, and for a fully financed and properly scheduled weekly ITN news programme.

This praise, and these proposals were endorsed by the Government in a White Paper, and by many speakers in both the Commons and the Lords. The Television Act 1963, which greatly increased the powers of the Authority over the companies, laid down that there should be adequate time for daily news, and that that news should be adequately financed.

But the decision as to what constituted adequate time for news was still one which the broadcasters had to take. Expert opinion, in the BBC as well as in ITV, was that a bulletin of quarter of an hour in length was all that the public wanted, or would watch, during peak viewing hours. One outcome of this stance was that news tended to spill over, not just into news specials when big stories broke, but into regular programmes dealing with particular aspects of news. Sport and the arts had long since developed their own outlets, with the BBC leading the way with *Sportsview* and *Monitor*. Politics found its own outlet in the BBC's weekly programme, *Gallery*, and in ITV's *Division*. Regional companies, and particularly Granada, with its programme *Scene*, went into the business of news analysis and news in-depth in a way which carried them close to what had always been regarded as ITN's territory. News feature programmes, too, were tempted to use their abundant time to stray across the boundary from news analysis into news coverage. *Panorama*, particularly when it was under the leadership of the daring and thrusting Paul Fox, secured a news scoop by doorstepping President Kennedy, and interviewing him in a London street when he was on his way to dine with the Queen at Buckingham Palace. On another occasion Robert Kee made brilliant use for *Panorama* of the sound camera to give a running account, recorded on the spot, of French paratroopers moving into action against Algerian guerrillas on the outskirts of Algiers. His report had virtually the force of an outside broadcast, and was striking proof of the powers of a good reporter working with a sound camera. But to have that effect, the report needed time. Kee's Algerian story had lasted 12 minutes – the length of an entire ITN bulletin.

The arrival on the scene in 1963 of Granada's weekly current affairs programme *World In Action* provided another outlet not only for investigative journalism, but for programmes which came close to hard news. Its Editor, Tim Hewart, was an Australian who had learnt his journalism on the *Daily Express* in Fleet Street. Hewart had a streak of real genius in his use of television, even if this went hand in hand with a readiness to disregard the requirements of the Television Act regarding impartiality. His techniques were in one sense old fashioned. He never showed his reporters in vision, but reverted to the style of cinema documentaries like *This Modern Age*. An off-screen, unidentified voice – indeed in those pioneering days, two voices, of alternating commentators – delivered the commentary. Though this denied *World in Action* the impact which the personality of Richard Dimbleby gave to *Panorama*, it established the programme itself as a personality. But there was nothing old fashioned in Hewart's determination to get to the heart of an issue, and to present the truth as he saw it. The official historian of independent television has declared that 'No single ITV series was the occasion of more discussion between Authority and company than Granada's *World in Action*. In connection with no other programme was the Authority's censorship more patently displayed nor more regularly challenged'.[1] But it was not these controversial investigative programmes which caught our attention in ITN. What we noticed was the impact made by the programme when it used its ample time and ample resources to cover hard news in feature form.

It did this, for instance, when its cameras followed British troops going about their duties during one day of the struggle against Greeks irregulars on Cyprus, or when a *World in Action* camera team joined in a sit-down strike in Whitehall, covering the demon-

---

1   Bernard Sendall, *Independent Television in Britain* Vol 2, London: Macmillan, p. 301.

stration from within its ranks. These were further proof of the power of the reporter with a sound camera. But it was a power that, within the narrow limits of the daily bulletins, we had little scope to use.

By the early 1960s both the BBC and ITN had enough camera crews to ensure that most action stories were covered with the accompanying sound. There were also enough to allow reporters increasingly to provide at least an into-camera on the spot introduction to a story, even if the bulk of the commentary was still written by a script writer in the news room. But a story with a reporter in vision took up more time than a purely picture story and so added to the pressures which were making the main evening bulletins burst at the seams.

The American networks had met these pressures by, in the autumn of 1963, going over to the half hour news. This was an easier step for them to take than it was for us. In the United States the early evening, between 6 and 7pm, had become established as the hour for the main news bulletins. It was possible to put a longer news at that time without risking a loss of audience. But in Britain 9 o'clock was deemed – rightly – to be the earliest hour at which the news of the day could be fully presented.

Yet in Britain in 1963 half an hour of news at 9 o'clock, or even at 10 o'clock, was out of the question. The programme companies would have rejected out of hand any gamble with the audience. Nor were the technological conditions for such a leap yet in existence. Telstar could bring us in some film quickly, but only for short periods, and at times of the day often unsuitable for our bulletins. A much wider satellite service would have to be developed before we could be sure of having enough of the day's news on film to be able to hold the audience for half an hour in prime time.

I therefore decided to propose the pattern I had put to the Pilkington Committee, that of a two-tiered system of evening bulletins. One segment would go out in prime time, and a second would follow at about 11 pm. A blueprint for this existed in the London area, where *Dateline* provided hard news in depth. An obvious step forward would be to turn *Dateline* into a hard news programme, and network it to all companies. In 1964 I pressed strongly for this to be done. But the plan foundered on the rock of regional programming. Many of the ITV companies used the late evening as a time in which to transmit programmes specially tailored to their own local audiences. Since most companies were far from enamoured of any extension of time for ITN, as this would mean an extension of the funds they had to pay to us, the companies outside London argued strongly against the networking of *Dateline*.

The issue was referred to the ITA. They faced a dilemma. The Authority favoured more time for news: they also favoured more time for regional programmes. So they compromised. They ruled that there should be a late night in-depth news programme in all areas on week nights. Companies could either make their own, or take *Dateline*.

It sounded reasonable, but in fact it defeated our object to get more time on the air for news, and not just for news in depth, though I had always planned that the second segment of a two-tiered news would contain a good deal of analysis. A second ruling by the ITA diminished the value of their compromise even further. They decided that the late night news need not be put out simultaneously, across the network, but that each company could put it out at a time which suited it best. This meant that those companies which took the ITN late programme did so at different times, involving night-marish transmission problems for us.

Yet we had made some gains, for at the same time the Authority ruled that *Roving Report* should be given more time and more money. This meant that *Dateline* and *Roving Report* – which we renamed *ITN Reports* – became valuable vehicles for re-cruiting and training new talent. The men and women who worked on these pro-grammes were to be an invaluable reinforcement when the time was ripe for a half-hour news.

Many of those whom I selected at that time were to become household names. Sandy Gall came to us from Reuter's, and Andrew Gardner from pioneering work on Rhode-sian televison. Alan Hart, who was to win fame in the early days of *News at Ten* had, as Editor in his twenties of a newspaper in Nyasaland, slept at night with a revolver under his pillow. John Edwards had been a teacher in a tough secondary modern school. Julian Haviland was an Old Etonian who was to become, in time, Political Editor of *The Times*. John Whale was to become our Political Correspondent, and to write two perceptive books about television and politics, before going on to edit the *Church Times*. Michael Nicholson and Richard Lindley were other recruits, and Gerald Seym-our, who was to draw on his experiences as an ITN reporter to write *Harry's Game*, the first of the bestsellers which have since made him a rich man. A trainee system I instituted for university graduats brought in Peter Sissons, Peter Snow, Gordon Honey-field and Richard Whiteley, who has combined success in journalism with compering Channel 4's *Countdown*. Susan Tinson, who rose to be an Assistant Editor, and to be made a Dame in 1990, was a graduate trainee from the University of Hull. Sheridan Morley did a stint in our newsroom before he decided that his proper career lay in writing about the theatre. All were new to television, and all gained their basic training on the seventh and eighth floors of Television House, established now as the barrack square for a new generation of television journalists.

With our plans for a two-tiered news frustrated, a half hour news became, from then on, ITN's main goal. It was to take two years of lobbying and arguing, of dry runs and experimenting, to bring it about. But when the time came, in July 1967, it was to revolutinize television news not only in Britain, but in Western Europe, giving television the opportunity, which it has grasped firmly, to become the dominant news medium.

41

A half hour news?

It was clear, from early 1965 onwards, that the best chance for ITN to win approval for a half hour news would come in 1967, when the programme companies would have to apply for a renewal of their contracts. They certainly could not take such a renewal for granted. The ITA had now an energetic new Chairman, Lord Hill, who had the toughness and guile of a seasoned former politician. There were signs that other significant groups would come forward in 1967 to challenge the existing companies. That would put the companies on their best behaviour, and in a mood to listen to ideas like that for a half hour news. Within ITN, therefore, we based our strategy on forcing the pace for a half hour news during 1966, the year before the new contracts were due to be decided.

At first the omens for a half hour news were not good. When the idea was discussed at an ITN Consultation on News and Current Affairs in January 1966, the producers of current affairs programmes in the companies showed themselves unanimously hostile to it. ITA officials produced the results of a survey they had had made of viewers' opinions. This showed that 83 per cent liked the main ITN evening news at its present length of just under 15 minutes. Only a third wanted it lengthened to half an hour. This did not worry me. All newspaper experience shows that the public does not know, and cannot know, what it wants until someone offers it to them.

Sir Robert Fraser, the Director General of the ITA, in summing up the outcome of the Consultation, said nothing in support of a half hour news. Instead he laid stress on the view of one regional News Editor of 'the danger of a surfeit of news and current affairs in the late evening if a half hour news were introduced at 10 o'clock'.

The success of regional news programmes, both in the early and the late evening, had certainly intensified the struggle for time on the air. The popularity of these local programmes had been one factor in dislodging the BBC's *Tonight* from the early evening slot it had occupied so splendidly ever since 1957. It was moved to the late evening, and then replaced by a new programme, *Twenty Four Hours*. This was a news analysis programme, along the lines we had pioneered in *Dateline*. With ample resources, and a nationwide outlet, it paved the way for today's *Newsnight*. The quirky human interest

Fig. 19. Geoffrey Cox, 1964.

items which had leavened the mix of *Tonight* proved to be an ideal element in local news programmes, and in time became the staple fare of a new BBC early evening programme, *Nationwide*. This element reached its peak – or its nadir, according to your choice – in a story about a duck which enjoyed riding on a skate board, an item which became *Nationwide*'s trademark.

Even more worrying for ITN were experiments which BBC News were conducting on BBC 2 with an extended news programme late in the evening. Had they continued with these, and brought the programme on to BBC 1 at a better hour, they could have been first on the air with a half hour news in prime time. But they held back, leaving a chance for ITN to grasp.

During the spring and summer of 1966 ITN produced two pilot programmes for a half hour news. This proved to be a formidable task, as we had no spare staff, and few spare resources. The first pilot proved scrappy, but the second, using the material available on Derby Day, was strong enough to win the approval not only of officials at the ITA, but of Sir Robert Fraser. He viewed a videotape of the programme in August and decided – with the eye of an old Fleet Street hand – that it was a workable format, and agreed that half an hour of news around 10pm was the goal at which ITN should aim.

I had a scare in November, when Sir Robert came back from a visit to the United States with a belief that a better time for the half-hour news would be the early evening. The main evening bulletins in America went out between 6.30 and 7 pm. If an ITN half-hour programme was placed at such a time the Authority would be able to avoid a battle with the programme companies, since the news would have been placed outside prime time.

Eager though I was eager to secure a half-hour slot for ITN, I realized that an early evening timing was no answer. By 7 pm in Washington most of the main news of the day is in. Congress does not sit in the evenings. In Europe, five or six hours ahead of America, the working day is over, and the news it has yielded has reached American newsrooms. But the reverse is true in Britain. News from the States, copious in those days of space development and the Vietnam war, was barely on its way by 6–7 pm – early afternoon in America. At Westminster Parliament still had four hours of news-making ahead of it. So I lobbied and argued strenuously against the idea of an early evening half-hour news, and the idea got stalled.

Meanwhile, unbeknown to us in ITN, events within the ITV system were moving in our favour. The BBC was steadily gaining a bigger share of the audience, particularly with situation comedy shows like *Dad's Army* and *Steptoe and Son*. The ITA decided that the time had come to use the new powers conferred on it under the 1963 Act. In the summer of 1966 they called on all companies to take a fresh, hard look at their schedules between 7.30pm and 10.30pm. When this produced no real improvement in the companies' output, and when viewing figures continued to drift downwards, the ITA decided upon a bold move. Early in 1967 they drew up proposals for a major shake up in the weekday schedules. The corner stone of their plan was a half hour news at 10 o' clock.

The big networking companies were horrified. They were convinced that half an hour of news at 10 o'clock would kill the late night audience. But the companies were realists. They knew their ground was weak, not only because their contracts were at stake, but because the schedules they had devised themselves were not holding the audience. They did not disguise the fact that they found the plan unpalatable, but they yielded to *force majeure*, and accepted it in principle. On one point, however, they sought a modification up to the last minute. They argued that the 10 o'clock news should be only twenty minutes, not half an hour. A longer time would take the flexibility out of the late evening programming and put the audience at risk. The advertising agencies disliked the idea of a half hour news. Revenue could be lost. If the longer news failed to hold the audience, even more revenue would be lost. 'I resisted *News at Ten* – and I was wrong' Lew Grade, with his customary forthrightness, told a Commons Committee four years later.[1]

On 8 March the final decision was taken, and the schedule was adopted. It included the half hour news at 10 o'clock. There was to be one commercial break, half way through the news. I had readily agreed to this. I knew that mounting a half hour news would be full of snags, editorial and technical. A commercial break would give us a chance to sort out any problems. What none of us envisaged that was, by this decision, the most valuable commercial spot in Independent Television's schedules was being created – a spot from which, a decade later, the revenue would be huge. The half hour news at ten was in the first instance to be only for a trial period of three months. If, as the companies

---

1   Second Report from Select Committees, Session I, 1971, P. 159.

confidently expected, it had not proved effective within that trial period, the ITA would look again at its plans. We had won the time: we had now to prove that we could use it effectively. The long battle for the half hour news which I had waged within the ITN Board, the long hours of lobbying and arguing and persuading were over. What loomed now was the battle for the audience at 10 pm.

42

Creating News at Ten

W e had only three and a half months in which to prepare the new programme, months in which we had to keep our existing service running at full blast. We could not halt operations for a week, or even a day, in order to organize the changeover. We could – and did – halt *Dateline* for a week before the new programme was due, and cut out two of the final issues of *Reporting 66*. But the daily bulletins would have to continue unbroken. It was rather like changing over a production line from making Minis to making a new saloon car without interrupting the flow.

This did not worry us greatly. There is no way in television in which you can tip-toe into experiments. There is only one end in television, the deep end. The longer you stand shivering on the bank, the worse you are likely to fare. You can only dive in and swim your hardest. I knew that the Napoleonic maxim which had guided me in the past – 'On s'engage et puis on voit' – would apply with even greater force in this development.

We were certainly not lacking in advice, both private and public. Two points were repeatedly emphasized from within the companies and in particular from Sir Robert Fraser. The new programme must be markedly different from the existing mid-evening bulletin and it must be built around a strong central personality. In a feature article in *The Times*, Clive Irving stressed the need for a major anchor man to execute the role which Walter Cronkite for CBS, and Chet Huntley and David Brinkley for NBC carried out in the United States. Irving listed only three figures in British television as being capable of undertaking the task – Day, Burnet and Kee. It was an influential article – so much so, that one leading commentator, whose name was not included by *The Times* on its list, considered suing for libel simply because he had been left out. It would have provided an interesting case had it come to court.

Since the central part of my case for a half hour news had been the need to keep with ITN broadcasters of stature, and since two of the three men listed by Irving had been brought into television and had come through to stardom with ITN, we hardly needed to be taught this basic fact of our trade. Nor did I retort that anchor men do not exist ready made, standing like tree trunks around which the ivy and clematis of a daily news show can grow and proliferate. Major newscasters are created and developed to full stature by the news programmes in which they appear. They need daily exposure to the public, and to the flow of news, as surely as crops need the sun. Walter Cronkite was as much a product of the CBS early evening news as he was in due course to make it his own show. When I first had contact with him late in the 1950s he was the newscaster of a much lesser news programme, the CBS news at 1.00pm. Only his skill at handling the special programmes at the conventions and on election nights had indicated the potential he so rapidly developed once he had star billing in the early evening. Huntley and Brinkley, then at the peak of their fame for NBC (Cronkite had been promoted to counter their grip on the audience) had not come together as a team because someone had spotted them as two established performers. They emerged because NBC decided to run a programme with one newscaster in New York and in Washington. On air the two men had proved naturally complementary in style and in approach to the news, the stalwart Huntley, the essence of reliability; the swift, wry, Brinkley, the embodiment of the informed commentator. I was confident, therefore, that even if we did not immediately find the right man for the job, we could find one who would grow into it.

Two men were ideally fitted for the job – Alastair Burnet and Robin Day. But Burnet had left ITN in 1965 to become the Editor of *The Economist*, and Day was too firmly established in the BBC to be drawn back into a venture which, if the companies got their way, would have only three months' life. Clive Irving's third man, Robert Kee, who was to do a distinguished job launching ITN's *News at One* in the early 1970s, was fully committed on other programmes and in any event might have seemed too much up market, to have a shade too much of the senior common room about him for our mass audience at that stage of television's development. Ludovic Kennedy was not going to be tied down in a studio year in and out. Robert Robinson, still at that time a relatively new face on the screen, seemed to me a likely contender, but he decided the role was not for him. Ian Trethowan was firmly settled into the BBC, where attractive executive prospects were opening before him. We clearly had to look in-house, within ITN itself, for our talent.

The lack of any one outstanding figure strengthened a view I had already formed, that the programme should be presented by two newscasters. Since all other news programmes at the time had a single anchor man, a two man team would, at a glance, establish *News at Ten* as something different. The format would also have practical advantages. It would give a longer programme a variety of image and pace; it would enable one newscaster to keeping up an unbroken front to the viewers whilst the other sorted out snags, or dovetailed new information into the copy. These provided powerful arguments for the two-newscaster format, which was to become one of the hallmarks of *News at Ten*. Commentators have in later years suggested that we took the idea from the Huntley Brinkley show. That programme was an encouragement to us, but was not the origin of our plan. It grew – as so much good broadcasting grows – from solving an immediate problem.

I was sure that a combination of either Gardner and Snow, or Gardner and Bosanquet, would quickly come through as a highly effective team. Peter Snow, however, made clear that he did not want to continue as a newscaster. He wanted to report in the field, and above all to develop techniques for clarifying and explaining complicated news stories and news situations – something he was to carry to a fine art. That left us with Andrew Gardner and Reginald Bosanquet. I had no doubt at all that they would measure up to the task, but I had equally no doubt that to the companies and to Sir Robert, who was taking an almost hourly interest in our proceedings, they would have the fatal defect which attaches to prophets in their own countries.

I decided that we must flank this home-grown team with a major figure until the programme was safely launched. So I asked Alastair Burnet if he would present the new programme for the crucial three months trial period. It seemed a preposterous idea to put to the editor of the major intellectual weekly of the day. But I knew that Burnet had a Scottish lust for work, and that his talents gleamed the brighter under pressure. To my delight he agreed to broadcast the programme on Mondays, Tuesdays and Fridays. On those days he would be flanked by Andrew Gardner. On the other two nights Gardner and Bosanquet would form the team.

This formula met the doubts of the industry and provided us with the necessary big name for our advance publicity. To support this team, and to strengthen our hand on the early evening bulletins we were lucky to find Leonard Parkin, an excellent correspondent, at that moment footloose and resistive in the BBC. He was just back from a stint in Washington, and was too forthright and too straight a reporter to find favour with the trendy producers of 24 Hours and of the other cult BBC programmes of the time. He gave a quick 'Yes' to our invitation, so bringing into ITN a man whose steady and stylish contribution was of great value over the next two decades.

The title for the new programme suggested itself. *News at Ten* admirably told the viewers exactly what the programme offered and had the further great advantage, by stressing the hour of transmission, of publicizing the fact that we were not only offering a new style of programme, but also offering it at another time than the sacred hour of nine o'clock.

The other main point which we were objured to observe by those who wished us well – and those who wished us ill – was that the new programme must not be merely the existing mid-evening bulletin extended to double its length. The half hour news must be something new, different, clearly distinct from the prevailing pattern of news bulletins.

This was an easy aim to define. How it was to be achieved was more difficult to say, and I resisted many pressures to forecast our methods. These could be devised only by experimentation on the air. I decided we would start with a formula along the lines of the Derby Day dummy run, with an opening segment of hard news, followed by at least one item of news in depth – a *Dateline* in miniature – with other, more extended news reports to complete the programme. This amounted to amalgamating the existing bulletin with a mini *Dateline* and a mini *Reporting 67*, and would serve to get us under way, provided we were ready to modify it swiftly as changes suggested themselves.

When on 9 May 1967, just six weeks before we were due on the air, the ITN Half Hour News planning committee held its first meeting in my white-walled office on the seventh floor of Television House, the first task we faced was to find a title sequence which would underline from the outset that this was a new type of news programme. We tried a number of designs based on still pictures, including some of the first views of the earth form outer space which the American space explorers had taken. We tried some specially shot film sequences. None seemed effective. Then I remembered a highly effective shot of the Houses of Parliament from the South Bank, which in December 1966 we had used as an opening for the first programme sent by satellite to Australia. We had this filmed, and discovered that by opening with a longshot from downstream of Westminster Bridge, and zooming towards the Clock Tower, we had an excellent sequence. At the risk of appearing traditional, even old fashioned, we had a title which demonstrated that the news was coming from the heart of the nation's capital, and underlining that it came at the new hour of 10 o'clock.

This also enabled us to use the chimes of Big Ben as part of our opening sound sequence. We experimented with these one afternoon in the studio, bringing a recording of them up under the final frames of the film of the clock face. It became at once clear was that we could not utilize all ten strokes of the bell to establish the hour. A pause of at least a second intervened between each stroke, leaving a gap which, on the air, seemed much longer At the most, we agreed, we could accept; two or three of these 'bongs', as Diana Edwards-Jones quickly termed them. She was experimenting with a first cut of the filmed title sequence, and a recording of the bongs, whilst Andrew Gardner in the studio was intoning at intervals the opening sequence which was due to follow the titles. 'Good Evening. Here is the news' followed by half a dozen potential headlines: 'The Torrey Canyon is bombed; more border raids around Gaza: trade figures worsen: the West Indies win the toss and pile up a big opening score'. A misunderstanding by the sound mixer brought up Gardner's words in the midst of the bongs. Diana's swift ear noticed that the gap between one bong and the next fitted almost exactly the time needed for a news headline. She got Andrew Gardner to trim the words, and fit his speech to fill each gap with a headline. It worked admirably. I was listening on the monitor set in my office, and the outcome seemed so exactly right that I sprinted up the stairs to the control room and agreed the pattern then and there. It is a technique which has lasted to this day, providing, with the interweaving of bell and words, an admirable sense of emphasis that is free of portentousness, as well as being an economical use of time. One of the enduring hallmarks of *News at Ten* had come into being.

This called for a change in the title music. *Non-Stop*, with its jaunty cheerful vigour did not fit into this more formal scene. We tried many alternatives, including themes specially composed and specially recorded. None was right and almost in desperation, close to the day of our first transmission, we settled on *Arabesque*. It seemed to me overemphatic, bordering on the strident, and many viewers reacted against it when it was first used. I wanted indeed to change it after we had been on the air a month, but feared that if we did so, we could appear to be losing our confidence in our product. So it remained – and remains to this day, when perhaps because we live in harsher and more strident times, it now seems to match the hour.

To make the studio set look different we helped ourselves to a device the BBC had utilized during the General Election, the Eidophor projector. This enabled a television picture to be thrown, enlarged, upon a cinema screen at the back of a studio. It could show not only still pictures, but also film. We could use this to bring the opening sequence of film stories up on the screen behind the newscaster, before filling the screen

```
HALF HOUR NEWS


Which brings us to the end of this, the

first News at Ten.  Our aim is to bring you

every weekday evening a half-hour news in

depth, at a peak viewing hour, a new venture in

British television.  For television itself is

now better equipped to cover the world's news

than it was when the old, short news

bulletin was devised.  We know it means asking

you to develop a new viewing habit at 10

o'clock every evening; but we mean to make it

worth your while.  Goodnight.
```

Fig. 20. Footnote to script for first night of *News at Ten*.

with them. This would not only be a new method, but also would interlock closely the work of the newscasters with the film they were introducing.

When we had tracked down one of the rare Eidophor projectors in Britain, we came up against a problem which was to dog us throughout the early months of *News at Ten*. Our studio on the eighth floor at Kingsway was too small. It provided only some 1,100 square feet of floor space, and -because it was on the top floor right under the roof – was just over 10 feet in height. There was no way in which the Eidophor projector could be fitted into this space. We had to beam its pictures around a corner, using mirrors to carry its images from the scene dock which lay at the back of the studio. This involved the use of a huge magnifying lens, for which Europe had to be scoured. And no rehearsals of the Eidophor were possible until two days before the programme went on the air, because key elements of the apparatus had been booked for Billy Graham's crusade at Earl's Court. But it was there, and working on the night. Our Chief Engineer, Bill Sweeney and his staff knew their jobs.

The next problem was temperature. The low ceiling meant intense heat from the studio lights. Air conditioning could cope with the heat engendered by a quarter of an hour bulletin preceded by about 25 minutes of rehearsal. But a half hour programme, with all its complexities, needed an hour's rehearsal. This cooked the studio to such a heat that the temperature had reached the 90s before transmission time had been reached. The dry runs which we carried out in the closing week of June, mounted in the mornings or the late evenings (for the regular bulletins had to go out as usual in early and mid-evening) showed newscasters glistening with sweat, brought production assistants close to fainting and had cameramen's sweating fingers slipping on the controls. Nor did the weather hold out any hope of relief. Sustained hot weather was forecast for the first ten days of July – and the forecasters were to prove right.

There was no time to enlarge the air conditioning. The roof could not carry the additional weight of new plant. Bill Sweeney came up with the suggestion that we use a mobile refrigeration plant, of the type trundled out to cool down aircraft on the tarmac of airports of hot countries. The vehicle could have been parked in the yard, eight floors below. But this proved impractical, for it meant that a hole would have to be cut in the studio wall – and that was not on. The only realistic answer was to bring trays of ice into the studio and blow the cold air from them with electric fans. This we did. People coming into the studio to be interviewed on this new and revolutionary style programme would stare with disbelief when they were ushered to a chair backed by a series of ice trays which made the place look like a storage room in a fishmongers.

We had a strong team of executives to produce *News at Ten*. David Nicholas and Brian Wenham would alternate as Duty Editors, taking turns to put the programme on the screen. Nigel Ryan, flanked by Stephen Wright, an experienced newsman who had come to ITN from the *Manchester Guardian*, and David Phillips, who had been producing *Reporting 67*, were available to ensure a flow of truly televisual stories. Ryan and Phillips went to New York to study American methods, and came back convinced that the key to the success of *News at Ten* lay in the use of integrated film packages to cover the news. This style of coverage – with the film camera in due course being replaced by the handheld electronic camera – has, ever since those formative days in the 1960s, been the norm for television news. It opens with a shot of the reporter, set against a background which establishes that he is on the scene of the story, whilst he speaks to camera the introduction to his story. He continues his report in words which serve as commentary to the filmed scenes which follow, and which is interwoven with any interviews he has conducted. The story is rounded off with a closing passage from the reporter, once again filmed in the heart of the story's setting.

In 1967 this technique was widely used in news feature programmes, but only rarely in news. We relied mainly on the technique devised in the early days, under which the commentary which held the report together and conveyed the main facts was written, not by the reporter in the field, but by a script writer in the office, and read over the film by an unseen voice in a commentary studio. The reporter might provide a filmed into-camera opening and closing sequence, and would do any interviews necessary. But he would not be responsible for the final working or the final shape of the report. This pattern was technically simpler to prepare than a fully integrated, on the spot report. It took less time, and so enabled a reporter to cover more news in a day, as he could move on to other locations or to other interviews whilst the finished story was being completed back at the studio.

The integrated news package had however two major advantages. It was a smoother, more artistic, more finished job. Each story formed a compact little television programme in itself, readily watchable. It gained also both unity and authority from having only one voice on it, that of reporter, instead of two – reporter and the studio commentator. It was manifestly the work of the man on the spot, conveying the same authenticity as does an outside broadcast. It also represented a significant shift in the roles of the journalist and the film technician, tilting the balance in favour of the reporter as against the film editor. In an integrated news package the editor cut the film to fit the reporter's words rather than the script writer writing words to match the film. By allowing scope for such news packages the half hour news widened significantly the function of the reporter in television – and made it essential for television news organizations to gather much more of their own news, instead of relying extensively on the agencies. But we could not go over to this new technique at a stroke. It called from more camera teams, more editing units, more reporters – in short for much more money. The most we could do was to employ the method in a special unit I set up under Nigel Ryan to supplement our other coverage.

It was a crowded spring and early summer, for in parallel with these preparations we had been carrying through a merger between the ITN syndication service and the film news service of United Press International, the first of the international newsfilm agencies. This brought into being UPITN which quickly established itself as one of the two main world-wide agencies providing news on film, and soon, news on videotape, delivered by satellite-to television stations throughout the globe.

Throughout the time we were preparing for the half hour news we, too, had to keep moving the conveyor belt of our existing news programmes. The news which passed along it was big news. In March 1967, when the final negotiations for *News at Ten* were at their peak, Francis Chichester (he became Sir Francis some weeks later) sailed his yacht Gipsy Moth IV round Cape Horn and headed for home, on the final stage of his single-handed voyage around the world. His venture had gripped public interest, as if Swinging Britain was thankful to find that it had some other heartland than mini-skirted King's Road or denim-trousered Carnaby Street, some other gods than the Beatles or Mick Jagger.

The BBC got the first pictures from Cape Horn, and we got the first from the Western approaches to the Channel, in a contest in which both the BBC and ITN chartered sea-going ships on which to place OB cameras, aircraft to circle overhead and relay the pictures back to land. The reporter's expenses for the story included surely one of the strangest items ever to get on to a journalists expenses account – the cost for 300 tons of gravel, needed as ballast for the Dutch coaster we had hired. Meanwhile another sea spectacular had occurred. The giant Liberian tanker Torrey Canyon ran aground off the Scillies, and was bombed and set on fire by the RAF to check the pollution her oil was spreading to nearby coasts.

Soon afterwards planes were flying in deadly earnest in the Middle East. On 5 June war broke out between Israel and her Arab neighbours. It lasted just under a week, earning the title of the Six Day War, and provided Europe with its first experience of covering a war in the satellite age. It was a heavy extra burden for us to carry, but it provided our reporting teams with experience which was to prove of great value when we came to produce longer news programmes.

A week after the war had ended, and only thirteen days before we were due to mount the half hour news, we held our first dry run of *News at Ten*. We recorded it hard on the heels of the mid-evening news. It was a hot night, the studio was stifling, and the the outcome was not impressive. We had one more trial run that week, followed by three the next week – on the Wednesday, Thursday and Friday nights – before we were due to go on air. With each we got more grit out of the works, though the problems of preparing double the amount of material within the one extra hour before transmission proved formidable. But the Eidophor had at last been installed, the title sequence was distinctive, and the dual newscaster format worked well. By Friday evening I was confident that we had a programme which looked different, which looked good, and which provided a framework within which we could widen and deepen our treatment of the news. What we needed now was a good spate of news to carry us through our opening days.

One welcome visitor in that run-up week was Richard Salant, President of CBS News. With his own experience of launching a half hour news fresh in his mind, he was both cheerful and disconcerting. 'Don't worry too much if it doesn't work out smoothly at the start' he said. 'It took us two or three months to get the bugs out of the system. Some of our early half hour shows were amongst the worst CBS News ever produced'. But I knew we had no such margin of time. Neither the programme companies nor the ITA would give us a margin of weeks, let alone months, to get the product into shape. Unless it could hold the audience quickly, it would either be off the air, or pushed back to the early evening hour which Sir Robert had so strongly favoured.

I noted with relief that the BBC showed no desire to try to pre-empt us in a move to half hour news. Their only action was to put *Twenty-Four Hours* directly against us, apparently confident that in Cliff Michelmore they had a star who could outshine any we could offer. J.D.S. Haworth, of *Television Today*, who had close contacts with the BBC, interpreted this as meaning that 'both *BBC News* and *Twenty-Four Hours* have sufficient respect for ITN to await *News at Ten* with unease, but this unease is tempered by a delight that Geoffrey Cox had seemingly decided to take such risks, committing himself so fully to a gamble whose failure could have done the BBC much good'.

As we came closer to D Day, interest in the press grew steadily and my commitment became increasingly public. I found myself having to deploy to the press the arguments I had for so long used in private in favour of the half hour news. I summed up our aim as 'trying to prove that the news of the day can fill half an hour either by its sheer dramatic quality or because it can be more readily assimilated if it is presented with analysis at the time'.[1]

The journalistic trade press took us seriously. The *UK Press Gazette* saw *News at Ten* as 'a frontal assault on morning newspaper readers'. The *World's Press News* said 'this could be the biggest competition newsmen on the dailies have had to face since television started'. And *Television Today*, under the headline 'Sir Geoffrey's revolution'

---

1   *TV Times*, June 1967.

commented that this development 'represents the most daring upheaval in the organization of television reporting ever seen in this country'.[1] The *Yorkshire Post* chided me for 'grandiose generalizations' when I said we were out to change the viewing habits of a lifetime. I was well aware that I was giving hostages to fortune by the claims I had made, but we needed every bit of publicity we could get to attract the substantial audience which alone could mean success.

1   *Television Today*, 25 May 1967.

43

A close run thing

What we needed above all on Monday, 3 July, was a real flow of news. Yet when we gathered for the morning's conference, with *News at Ten* for the first time featuring on the film list, I knew that the luck which had helped us so often in the past had deserted us. After the big stories which had crowded the schedules for weeks, the list was drab and threadbare. The main story was a negative one. A strike of freight services on the railways, called as a protest against containerisation, had been called off. This was important news, but was neither exciting nor visual. The Middle East was quiet. Fighting which had flared up on the West Bank of the Jordan, and had given us some vivid film 24 hours earlier, had flared down. We were due to interview King Hussein of Jordan, but he had been frequently interviewed of late, and allowed himself to say little. An interview with an Egyptian commander on the Suez Canal produced little more. Wimbledon alone offered some excitement, with Roger Taylor from Sheffield bidding to be the first Englishman for many years to get through to the semi-finals. If we were not faced with making bricks without straw, we were likely to be making them with at best a few scattered whisps. I was thankful that the Ryan unit had two in-depth pieces under way – a report by John Whale on the Montreal Exhibition, Expo 67, which the Queen and the Duke of Edinburgh were due to visit that day, and a report by John Edwards on the way the Israeli seizure of Jerusalem had destroyed at a stroke the considerable and lucrative tourist trade which the Kingdom of Jordan had developed when its territory included the Old City.

This news list would have been meagre enough for a shorter bulletin. For *News at Ten* it was scanty rations indeed. But at least we had no major late-breaking stories to interrupt rehearsal. In sweltering conditions, for it was not only a hot but a humid evening, Alastair Burnet and Andrew Gardner steadily coped with delayed film and with studio cameras which played up in the heat. Julian Haviland recorded an into-camera report on the progress of the Bill to legalize homosexual practices between consenting adults – a significant measure, no doubt, but not one to sit easily in a peak time programme, even in our new-found progressive age.

The studio, despite its ice trays, was like the hot room of that disappearing institution, the Turkish bath, when I went in five minutes before transmission to wish them well.

In the control room Diana Edwards-Jones was volubly undismayed. I went back to my office, switched on the monitor in the corner, saw the commercials come and go, and heard for the first time on the public air our new theme music. Then the titles came up, and the camera zoomed in across the Thames to the clock face of Big Ben and I heard Andrew Gardner's steady, confident voice announce the headlines between the strokes of Big Ben. For better or for worse, the half hour news was launched.

But only just. As the programme unfolded, it seemed often off key. There were several technical hitches, with film slow in coming up, a wrong map displayed, a still picture which failed to materialize. But these were minor errors. Its central flaw was that it lacked shape and personality as a programme. The individual stories were efficiently done, as well as could be expected on a night of thin, dull news. Burnet and Gardner worked well together and the two-man technique was both new and strong. The commercial break fitted in naturally, providing a sorely needed pause for getting the second half into shape. Yet these adequate pieces did not add up to an adequate whole. The programme lacked pace, lacked flow, lacked an integrated style. Though I could not put my finger on these defects at the time, I knew that at the end of that long day when the final caption came up, and the cameras caught Alastair and Andrew instinctively turning towards each other in the studio – an action which was to become a hallmark of the programme – that we had not got it right. But we had got it on the air, and that in itself was a great achievement. I hid my anxieties and spread my congratulations and thanks around the weary technical crews, the weary newsroom and the remarkably unwearied newscasters. Yet I went home a worried man.

The papers the next morning gave me grounds for that worry. They were unanimously critical or disappointed. The *Yorkshire Evening Post* found us 'an unimpressive adversary for the BBC's *Twenty-Four Hours*'. *The Times* felt 'that the right balance between the programme's various ingredients had not been struck'. The *Daily Telegraph* pointed out that we had not used the later hour to bring in later news: 'Most of the items had been broadcast by the BBC in their 8.30 news'. Nancy Banks Smith in the *Sun* wrote, 'every journalist knows that the birth of a new news venture is attended by pangs not comprehended outside the trade. I won't assume to judge *News at Ten* on the basis of one edition. Suffice to say that sober competence rather than excitement prevailed. What I don't understand is how anyone could suppose that the new programme is revolutionary ... I doubt if its news interleaved with in-depth format will allow it to compete with *24 Hours*'. The *Daily Express* found the close up of Big Ben striking one stroke for each headline 'as irritating as it was old fashioned'. The *Morning Star* declared that there was nothing in this new project which had not been done as well as in the *BBC Late News* or *24 Hours*'. Others attacked us for the way we 'machine gunned the headlines over the chimes of Big Ben'; for a 'dramatic over-Americanized introduction'; and for presenting no more than 'a very simple news round-up relieved by a few minutes of commercials'.

It was Peter Black, shrewdly perceptive as ever in the *Daily Mail*, who offered me the first hint as to where the trouble lay – and how it could be cured. 'Nobody does anything for the first time without a nervous edge, and the first edition of ITN's *News at Ten*, all the news that is news, screwed up tension almost audibly ... The overall disappointment was in the lack of momentum and of narrative verve one got from the old bulletins ...'

The only parts which won praise, I noted, were John Whale's report on the Montreal Exhibition and John Edwardes' report on the collapse of the Jordan tourist trade. These were both news packages, integrated picture and commentary pieces from Nigel Ryan's department, and had the polish and pace which so much else of the bulletin had lacked.

As always, these morning papers lay in their serried ranks on the table in my room as we met for the morning conference on the second day of the programme, with ahead of us another twelves or thirteen hour day. From the programme companies, even from those producers who wished us well, there was only an ominous silence. When the day's news and film list was distributed, I knew we were in for another thin day. The only home story of any strength was a White Paper on Road Safety, the epitome of a worthy but dull subject, only very slightly relieved by a proposal that driving lessons should be introduced into schools. We would have to lead on a story which we had organised in advance, an interview which Reginald Bosanquet had recorded in Salisbury with Ian Smith on Rhodesia under sanctions. It was good stuff, but it was another static story, visual radio rather than active television. It posed, too, the same problem as the rail strike story had done the day before. To be fairly and fully presented, it needed to be set in its perspective. We arranged for a group of three MPs to come in and discuss the issue live on air. Michael Foot was amongst them, which promised that it would be a lively discussion, but once again it was static television, even if we separated it from the interview, and placed it in the second half of the programme – a structure which I suspected had contributed the night before to the lack of momentum which Peter Black had notice.

When we came to rehearsal time I realized that we had a programme which, with its jerky lack of rhythm, its lumpy disproportion between items, was very similar to that of the first night. Only one item, an on-the-spot report from Sandy Gall, on the Allenby Bridge between Jordan and the occupied West Bank, really held the attention. One home story which had developed during the day had a quirky interest, but had proved hard to cover. The chairman of the Housing Committee at Crawley New Town had been accused of demanding from housewives who sought new homes assurances that they were of good moral character. He suspected apparently that they might use Council property for illicit love affairs during the day. 'Chastity Test on Housewife', was the evening paper headline. But the councillor was on holiday in the Isle of Wight, seemingly out of range of the cameras, and without his version the story had in more senses than one little body to it.

Yet it was to play its part in regaining our momentum. Shortly before transmission Don Horobin arrive eagerly in my office. Southern Television had tracked down the Crawley councillor and could give us an interview. We looked at the schedule. The only way we could fit this interview in at that late stage was to scrap the discussion on Rhodesia. In the Green Room, opposite my office, at that moment, Michael Foot, Lord Byers and a Tory spokesman were with George Ffitch, ready to go up to the studio. Was it practicable, let alone courteous, to cancel their discussion at this stage? What kind of impression of this major new programme would they carry back to their colleagues at Westminster if a key issue like Rhodesia was kept off the air to make room for a story

Fig. 21. Alastair Burnet and Reginald Bosanquet in *News at Ten* studio.

of this kind? I hesitated. Don Horobin read my mind. 'I've no doubt which story the viewers would prefer', he said, fixing me with that intent gaze which had reporters grabbing their coats and rushing out to get the story whatever the cost. It was late in a long hard day. I drew a deep breath and said to Don 'Well, this is what editors are paid for'. I walked across the corridor and faced the assembled MPs. 'Gentlemen', I began, 'I hope you will all one day write your memoirs, because what I am about to say will I am sure merit at least a footnote in them. I am going to ask you to hold over this discussion to make way for an interview with a councillor who imposes a chastity test on would-be council tenants'. There was an utter, chilling silence before Michael Foot burst into laughter, and the moment was saved.

By the time I got back to my room, the second edition of *News at Ten* was under way. It was free of technical hitches of the first night, and the chastity test interview certainly lifted the second part. But it was once again jerky and ill-shaped, broken apart rather than linked by the commercial break, and exuding this time, for all Burnet's and Gardner's self-possession, traces of a lack of confidence. Wearily we crowded into the lifts, saying little in our dismay, hiding our disappointment as we went our different ways in the hot London summer night.

I was too tired to think further that night but when I woke in the morning I saw suddenly the reasons for our failure, and a possible cure. We were making a programme with no clear goal. Its task was not, as had been that of the old bulletins, to tell and portray the news of the day. It was not to analyse and probe the main stories of the day, as had been *Dateline's* remit. It was not required primarily to tell one or more big stories in depth, as did *Reporting 67*. It was a mixture of all three, and each was blunting and obscuring the role of the others. We were doing this primarily because of a desire to meet the demand, voiced insistently at the ITN Board and by the programme controllers of the companies, that *News at Ten* should be something different from news at 8.55 pm, must at all costs not be just the old mid-evening bulletin writ large. This had obscured our aim. We were guilty of that cardinal sin, which at his wartime planning conferences General Freyberg had always emphatically denounced, the failure to define an objective clearly.

I knew I had to act quickly. So on that third morning of the programme, when the planning conference assembled, I came to the point at once. 'We are getting things wrong because we do not know clearly where we are going. Amidst all the demands for new patterns, we have lost our way. Forget all about the need to make something different. We will go back to what we know how to do well – to tell and depict the day's news. Put out of your minds the question of doing something different. Just make a normal ITN bulletin, at twice its old length'.

I felt a sense of relief sweep the room. It persisted even though the film list was again thin. The new Anglo-French swing wing aircraft had been grounded; Roger Taylor was virtually certain to be knocked out in the Wimbledon semi-final (as he was); LBJ had been filmed with his grandchild on his launch. These were the best on offer.

But the gods were with us. An hour later an exultant Don Horobin was in my room. In Aden the Argyll and Sutherland Highlanders had made a dawn raid into the Crater district. Alan Hart and our camera team had gone in with them. Hart had what he claimed to be some spectacular film. Here at last was an action lead.

And it was a beauty. Hart had recorded his commentary live, as the action unfolded. He and the camera crew had ridden in one of the foremost armoured cars. They gave us a report which had almost the impact of live coverage, as they captured not only the scene of the action, but also the sound of the clipped orders, the sudden bursts of firing, the shouts in Arabic and Glaswegian as the patrols seized crouching gunmen. The boyish figure of the Argyll's commander, Colonel Mitchell – Mad Mitch – who directed the action, spoke to Hart in the midst of the shuttered streets as this No Go area was brought back under British rule. We let the story run for every second it was worth, cutting it to 6 minutes 24 seconds – an unprecedented length for a story in a regular news bulletin.

It transformed the night's programme. It was for this that we had sought the extra time, to enable us to use television to tell the news as only television can do, and we had done so with clarity and verve. The drama and pace of the story not only gave us a strong opening, but also carried the other heavier items along with it. It made even the problem of the swing wing aircraft seem relevant and gave point to an otherwise heavy Commons debate on defence. After the break the tennis provided further action, if disappointing action, as Taylor went down to defeat. Princess Grace, on a visit to London, added elegance. LBJ with grandson was corny, but even a President's grandson can be a scene stealer. A packaged film report about putting the Crown Jewels on permanent show in the Tower proved palatable as a final item.

When the titles came up at 10.30 against the longshot of Westminster I knew that we had shown what a half hour news could do. Even more importantly, I knew we had clarified our goal. We were back firmly at our old task of telling the day's news. There were many problems of technique yet to be ironed out. But no one could deny that this programme had been eminently watchable, and eminently informative. We had found our feet.

The next day Aden provided us with another strong story. Francis Chichester began his journey up the Thames in brilliant sunshine. We brought the women's semi-finals up into the first half of the programme, showing Britain's Ann Jones win her way through to the final by beating Rosie Casals. And another packaged film story, this time from the home front, dealing with hippies taking drugs at the National Gallery, held the attention without difficulty for nearly four minutes.

On Friday, to round off this first week, we had abundant action. Sir Francis Chichester arrived at Greenwich and knelt, with the Royal Naval College as a spectacular background, to be knighted by the Queen; the Israelis patrolled the banks of the Suez Canal, observed by Sandy Gall in a story which matched Alan Hart's for immediacy, if not for drama; Newcombe won the men's final at Wimbledon. And from Pamplona Richard Lindley caught with deft commentary the atmosphere of the stampede of the bulls through the streets, a scene then still as genuine as when Hemingway had first portrayed it, not yet reduced to a tourist cliché.

These action stories had done much to restore the momentum Peter Black had found lacking. But we had further lessons to learn in pacing a longer bulletin. Early in our second week, on the Tour de France cycle race, one of the few British international cyclists, Tommy Simpson, collapsed and died of exhaustion under the midday sun of mountain road in the Pyrenees. The race was covered by mobile OB cameras of French television, and the moment of his collapse was recorded on videotape. There was no doubt that it merited being the lead story. But the action pictures called for considerable interpretative material, both about Simpson and about the hazards of sport driven to its limits. This could be provided only by studio or film interviews which would inevitably slow down the pace of the bulletin. Could we risk placing this interpretative material in a chunk at the head of the bulletin, delaying the rest of the news, or should we hold it over till later, as we had done with the rail strike on the first evening, and had planned to do on Rhodesia? We decided that the action pictures of the rider's collapse were so dramatic that they could carry the viewer's interest through the interpretative material, and so we kept all elements of the story together. This proved to be the right decision. There was little or no sense of the lead story being top heavy; the impression was rather one of significance being added to intrinsically interesting news. From then on we very seldom separated interpretation from reporting. By doing so we restored – though this had not been our conscious aim – a further element of cohesion, for by taking two bites at the same story, we had inevitably put a strain on the concentration of viewers.

We knew, however, that the key to our immediate future lay in using to the full the wider scope for action news which the longer bulletin gave. Not only did this allow us to let people 'see it happen' more adequately, but also longer news stories helped to make *News at Ten* look and feel different from the older type of bulletin. Big action stories were not, however, easy to come by. Early in our second week we faced the problem that one such story had taken place at almost the extreme limit of our range, and very close to transmission time. During the evening of Tuesday, 11 July the agencies flashed the news that Margo Fonteyn and Rudolf Nureyev had been arrested and held by the police of San Francisco anti-drug squad at a party in Hyattsville, the hippie area of San Francisco. This was the heyday of the Flower Children, and Fonteyn and Nureyev, who were dancing in San Francisco, had been touring Hyattsville when the raid occurred. Strenuous telephoning disclosed that ABC Television in America had camera coverage of the two stars being questioned in the Hyattsville precinct police station. If we had been willing to wait until ABC brought it to New York for their own bulletin, it would have been available to us at a reasonable cost. But the difference in time zones made that too late for *News at Ten*. The only way we could get the story on time was to pay the high costs of transmitting it by land lines across America and by satellite to London. By all our previous standards, the costs – between £5,000 and £7,000 – were prohibitive. But with the fate of the new programme still in the balance, I agreed to the money being paid.

The result outdid our expectations. Here was the stuff of innumerable American crime serials in real life. In a crowded office, against a background of metal filing cabinets and of desk tops littered with documents and paper coffee cups, a short-sleeved detective asked 'Noo-ray-eff? Say, how do you spell a name like that? N like Nobody, U like United States ...'? whilst a cool but concerned Margot Fonteyn waited to be questioned in her turn. John Whale provided good clear commentary. We had it entirely to ourselves. All the BBC could muster was a series of still pictures. The sense of immediacy, of late news of keen human interest being brought to the screen from half way round the world came through strongly. It transformed what had threatened to be a routine programme of short, run-of-the-mill stories – an investiture at Buckingham Palace, a protest march about school meals, a visit by King Hussein to Nasser – into a news report truly of the satellite age.

We needed this reinforcement. Although we were sure, from the moment Alan Hart's Aden report had reached the screen, that the new pattern would work, and had dismissed the two opening days from our consciousness, others had not. To our rivals, our foes and some of our owners, the disappointing programmes and the bad press of our opening nights had been proof that the experiment of a longer news had gone wrong from the start. Warnings reached me from Jim Coltart[1], in his role of ITN Chairman, that his phone was busy with calls from doubters in the programme companies. One company had, after the first two poor programmes, called for an early special meeting of the ITN Board, to discuss scrapping the whole project at once and reverting

---

1   James Coltart, Chairman of Scottish Television and Chief Executive of Thomson Newspapers.

to the older style of bulletin. The forebodings of those advertising agencies who had predicted that a half hour news would kill the late night viewing figures seemed to be coming true.

The weekend critics had been uniformly hostile. Stuart Hood, writing in *The Spectator* with the authority of a former Editor of BBC News and a former Controller of BBC Television, expressed 'a keen sense of disappointment'. Milton Schulman in the *Evening Standard* said that *News at Ten* had had 'more teething troubles than a student dentist with the palsy. It merely lengthened the news ... giving an overwhelming impression of padding for padding's sake ... ITN had neither the personnel nor the resources to produce a news programme commensurate with their hopes and their ambitions'. The *World's Press News* thought the whole concept 'thoroughly misguided. The programmes were trite compared to 24 Hours, ragged compared with the following day's newspapers'. And when on Monday, 10 July, the *UK Press Gazette*, whose voice was keenly listened to in Fleet Street, devoted a full page to a scornful appraisal of *News at Ten*, I detected even in the stalwart Jim Coltart a trace of real concern. The *Gazette* said that when *News at Ten* had first been announced newspapermen saw in it in a danger. 'It could make hell of first editions and prove particularly embarrassing for London printing times. Then came the show and everyone relaxed again'.

To this chorus of informed disapproval, the viewers gave their answer. On Wednesday, 12 July John McMillan telephoned me. He had problems enough of his own at that moment for his company, Rediffusion, had been shot from under him in the reshuffle of contracts, having been reduced to the role of junior partner in London. Rediffusion's constantly staunch support of ITN had clearly counted for little with Lord Hill and his colleagues on the Authority when they came to award the new contracts. But McMillan found time to ask me if I had seen the ratings for *News at Ten's* first week. I had not. 'All five issues were in the Top Twenty', John said. 'Two of them in the first ten'. When the weekly blue-covered TAM ratings volume came in the next day, with its sharply outlined black contours on the squared pink or pale blue paper, the proof was there that the public had found the programme eminently viewable. Night after night *News at Ten* stood out clearly, a peak in the mountain range of the evening's viewing, with audiences ranging from 4.45 million million homes to 6.9 million homes. At no time did *24 Hours* reach more than half of these totals. There was one worrying sign; we did not hold the audience evenly throughout the half hour. There was a falling away after the commercial break. But we had held a far higher audience than that gained by the shows which had previously occupied the slot between 10pm and 10.30pm. Far from diminishing the audience later in the evening, we had strengthened it. In programme making terms, this was a striking success.

I knew that we had won only the opening round in a long contest. We had not yet secured a permanent grip on this segment of viewing time. But we had won the chance to continue the experiment. Audience figures like this would put paid to any early efforts to hustle us back to shorter bulletins, particularly if the trend continued. And it did. The next week four of the programmes were in the top twenty, with this time three in the top ten. I shared my delight with Coltart. Bernard Sendall, the Deputy Director General was soon on the telephone from the ITA to express their pleasure. From the programme companies, other than Rediffusion, I had not one call of congratulations or approval. But their silence was to me golden enough, for it meant that for the time being at least what we had, we held.

44

Bridgehead consolidated

Action news continued to provide the most significant element in *News at Ten* throughout this early period. It reached a peak in early August in an *eye witness* report by Alan Hart of the white mercenaries seizing the Congo town of Buka-ville, on the border of Ruanda, in what was to be the last spurt of the long Congo civil wars. Hart was working with one of our best cameramen, Len Dudley, and an equally skilled recordist, Barry Martin. They set up the camera on the Ruanda side of the short bridge which marked the frontier between the two countries, a point from which, with a long range lens, they could survey, as if from a grandstand, the Congolese hillside opposite. Hart recorded a running commentary as refugees, laden with huge bundles, came slowly across the bridge. Then, with shouts that the mercenaries were coming, the refugees began to run, to be elbowed aside by fleeing Congolese frontier guards, who handed over their rifles to the Ruanda soldiers at the eastern end of the bridge. In this panic a crippled girl on all fours was trying to drag herself across the bridge.

It was a false alarm, and in a few minutes the Congolese troops were furiously demand-ing back their rifles. But soon, on the white road winding down the hillside, the camera picked up the mercenaries, in single file on the jungle edge, their torsos looped with belts of ammunition, heavy automatic weapons in hand, as they skirmished their way towards the frontier. 'Here come the mercenaries, with Black Schramm's battalion lead-ing' commented Hart, in the exact style of an outside broadcast. It provided a report of such impact that we decided to run it for thirteen minutes – as long as the whole mid-evening bulletin had been a year earlier. 'These are the rare moments which electrify the electronic embalmer' wrote Maurice Wiggin. When the story evoked a telephone call of praise from Robin Gill, Lew Grade's chief lieutenant, I knew this aspect of our formula was working.

Action news was moreover abundant in that summer and autumn of 1967. With one African civil war ending in the Congo, another even bloodier one was getting under way

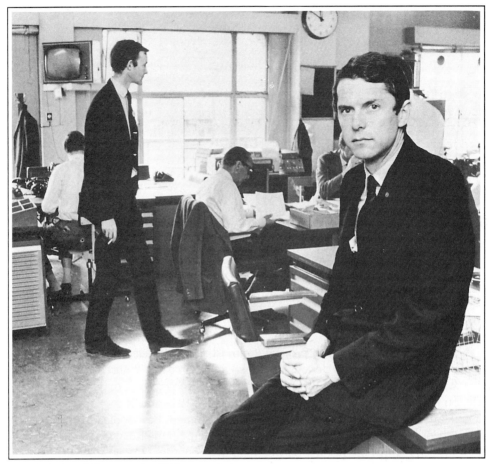

Fig. 22. Nigel Ryan in the ITN newsroom.

in Nigeria, where the Federal forces based on Lagos were determined not to let the oil-rich province of Biafra go its own way. Sandy Gall, working with the camera teams of our new ally, UPITN, was soon sending back pictures of this war, as huge black troops in jungle uniform, commanded by elegant officers speaking Sandhurst English, probed the in slow and cautious way along yet another series of white tree-lined roads. And from the United States the long hot summer of black rioting erupted before the television cameras. We began the fourth week of *News at Ten* with coverage from Detroit, as fires lit up the sultry night air, looters smashed shop windows, and National Guard troops in steel helmets, rifles at the high port, moved along the streets as if in an enemy country. The American networks provided copious film of this, even though, in an effort to help reduce the violence, they had adopted a self-imposed ban against showing live coverage of rioting on their own screens. Soon Newark, Syracuse and Milwaukee were adding their quota to this bitter story.

To get this material to Britain, we used the satellite lavishly. John Whale added his own commentary to the American network pictures, reinforcing the sense that our own reporters were on the spot. We had not yet hit upon the device of ending each story with the reporter signing off as 'This is Sandy Gall, for *News at Ten*, Nigeria', or 'John Whale, for *News at Ten*, Plainfield, New Jersey'. That simple yet highly effective method of simultaneously reporting the news and publicizing the programme was a touch added by Nigel Ryan when he took over the editorship.

This action coverage involved not only skill but risk. A week before they sent off their block buster from the Ruanda border, Hart, Dudley and Martin had spent ten hours in a Congolese gaol in Bukaville, accused of being spies for the mercenaries. They managed to throw a note out of the gaol window, which a passer-by took to the German Consul. He got them freed just when a firing squad was forming up to deal with them. In Hong Kong, Ernest Christie was roughed up during a street riot. His camera was smashed, and he was saved form serious injury only because he laid out an attacker with a karate chop. In Cairo Mario Rossetti and Alan Hart went in search of the exiled President of Ghana, Kwame Nkrumah. Rossetti was waiting in a car in a suburban street whilst Hart made inquiries when he suddenly felt small cold circles pressing against his temples from either side. A voice said, first in Arabic, then in English 'Don't move a millimetre'. Two Egyptian secret servicemen, guarding Nkrumah, had come up behind him. Rossetti's alarm was rapidly mixed with indignation when Alan Hart strolled nonchalantly by, never acknowledging by so much as a glance that he had anything to do with such a suspicious character, But once round the corner, Hart sprinted off to get the aid of the British consul, who in due course got Rossetti freed.

A month later what might have been a major tragedy occurred in the Yemen. A plane carrying an ITN crew had to make an emergency landing at a desert airstrip after smoke had been seen coming from the box containing their cameras. In the box were found eight sticks of explosive and eight detonators, which had apparently been placed there whilst the baggage was being loaded. Six of the detenators had gone off without detonating the main charge. This seemed proof that ITN teams bore charmed lives – and indeed, given the constant risks they faced, casualties were few. But a year later Peter Sissons, doing a reporting stint in Nigeria, was shot through both legs in a Biafran ambush. ITN flew a London surgeon out to him, and he came through safely to take a more static but extremely successful role as a newscaster.

Side by side with this action material we carried, particularly in the second half of the programme, a steady element of interpretation and background, often in the form of studio interviews. We persisted with this despite the continuing signs in the graphs that the audience tended to slip back after the commercial break. Material from these interviews steadily began to find its way into the morning papers. This was certainly the case when we interviewed Michael de Freitas, leader of the British section of the Black Muslims. De Freitas, who was later to be murdered in the Caribbean under his new name of Michael X, had hinted in a speech at Reading that Britain might see racial rioting like that in America. Strenuously cross-examined by George Ffitch, he alleged police brutality and injustice in the courts towards the blacks. We countered this with an interview with Mr. Duncan Sandys (later to be Lord Sandys) who not only called for a ban on all further coloured immigration, but said that 'steps should be taken to reduce the number of immigrants already here'. This remark, made a year before Enoch Powell's Wolverhampton speech, was widely reported – but roused little reaction. The West Indian

Standing Conference did call upon the police to prosecute Sandys, but dropped the demand when it was refused.

When the satirical series 'Mrs. Wilson's Diary' was translated from the pages of *Private Eye* to the stage at Stratford, in the East End, we filmed an excerpt from the dress rehearsal. This we presented on the play's first night, followed by a debate between the author, John Wells, and Quentin Hogg about the ethics of attacking public men through their wives and families.

The added impact which resulted from such longer and deeper surveys of the day's news became even more apparent when a group of people of varying degrees of importance and renown took a full page advertisement in *The Times* appealing for the smoking of marijuana on private premises to be made legal. Heading the signatories, listed in alphabetical order, were Jonathan Aitken and Tariq Ali. The name of Tom Driberg, MP followed that of David Dimbleby, whilst Paul McCartney had been careful to add MBE after his name. The appeal posed an issue which needed not only to be reported, but also to be probed. We gave full details of the appeal and showed on the screen the page of *The Times*. We interviewed an Anglican nun who ran a centre for curing drug addicts. She was a woman of such calm serenity, and the girl addicts who were under treatment were so horrifyingly young and horrifyingly ravaged, that their claims that soft drugs lead on to hard line drugs like heroin were convincing. Tom Driberg protested to me that we had been unfair in placing this counter argument in the same report as that which carried the pro-pot appeal. He agreed that it had its place, but argued that that was a day later, after people had had a chance to think for themselves about the appeal. I countered by pointing out that he was echoing Nixon's complaint that the US networks had immediately followed his latest appeal on Vietnam by presenting a panel of pundits who tore him to pieces, and that anyway I was only doing my duty to give both sides of the story. 'That is hair splitting', was his answer. 'You are editorializing, and you know it'.

The public continued to find this formula palatable. Week after week the ratings continued to be good. During the first five weeks of the programme *News at Ten* was in the Top Twenty on all but three week-day nights. We had double, sometimes three times the audience of *Twenty Four Hours*. 'It is a clear knock out victory, one which Auntie cannot disregard' said *The Guardian* on 4 August. Criticism too veered round sharply in our favour. *Variety*, the main organ of American show business, which was by now required reading for every British television executive, headlined its view that 'British Buffola News on TV'. It went on to report that 'as never before the citizenry has begun to devour news mileage in such volume as to make the IAM Top Twenty ratings look like a guide to video journalism'. This development, it declared, was 'entirely a triumph for the commercial network'. At home the *Northern Despatch* decided that 'ITN seems to have found a formula for making politics and current affairs in general into exciting and dramatic entertainment. This gutsy television may not always look at events in depth, but by golly it makes the viewer aware that these events are taking place'.

Such comments and above all such viewing figures clinched our fate. In mid-August, after only half of our three month trial period had elapsed, the companies decided that *News at Ten* would be continued throughout the rest of the year. The very important autumn schedule would be built around a half hour of news at 10 o'clock. Though I sensed that the battle was not finally won (for what television struggle for a place in a crowded schedule is ever final?) it would take now a massive counter-attack to dislodge us. We could turn to the next phase of development, that of ensuring that we had the reinforcement of talent, and of money, to keep up this pace over the months, and then the years ahead.

The viewing figures held up well in the autumn, which was a relief, as we had to carry a good deal of lumpy material from the Party Conferences and from the TUC, even though sharp interviewing from Ffitch and Burnet made these the more digestible. These were the last appearances which Alastair Burnet made as a newscaster for *News at Ten* in its formative phase, as he had to return to the very full time task of editing the Economist. *News at Ten* was the work of many talents, but Alastair Burnet's contribution was cardinal to its success. Had he not been with us to launch the programme, *News at Ten* might never have got under way. Not only did Burnet give it style with his authority, his incisiveness, and his subtle and supple use of language, but he made it look and sound new. Though Andrew Gardner and Reginald Bosanquet were the team who, over the next decade, were to embody the half hour news, the programme companies – and perhaps the public – would never have accepted them as an opening pair.

They proved well matched. I had always seen Gardner as a key man in a half hour news, with his natural presence, his excellent diction, and his instinctive link with audience. Bosanquet, with his touch of the Regency buck, was an excellent foil to Gardner, bringing to the programme the sense of a man who had hurried to the studio from the heart of what was then seen very much as swinging London. I had reservations about Bosanquet as a newscaster over a long period. This was partly because the slight facial paralysis form which he had suffered since childhood continued to reassert itself when he was tired, giving a slur to his words which was the equivalent of a smudged print. But it was also because I valued his skills as a reporter and interviewer, and saw his place as being in the field as much as in the studio. But that first autumn I knew that we must establish the Gardner-Bosanquet combination as the cornerstone of *News at Ten*. I had expected some criticism from the press and the companies, for this flew straight in the face of their deeply held view that only a single major star could hold the programme together. But such was the momentum of *News at Ten* by then that the change passed virtually unnoticed, and the partnership was forged which was to carry the programme through its first decade. It was a partnership which, reinforced by Sandy Gall and Leonard Parkin, carried over into this longer news the note of relaxed authority which had been cardinal to ITN's earlier success. Peter Black noted this when he assessed our performance at the end of the year. 'It's the style of *News at Ten* that wins its following. Andrew Gardner looks comfortable, as if he is smoking a pipe. The BBC's disadvantage is that it can do nothing in the news line without feeling the weight of its forebears, all those occasions when the world waited for it to speak'.

This was to prove a remarkably durable quality. Twelve years later Philip Purser was noting that

> ... the newsreader's relationship to the stuff he peddles is of crucial importance. Richard Baker and Kenneth Kendall still handle it with invisible white gloves. On ITN the stout duo

of Reginald Bosanquet and Sandy Gall, especially, treat it convivally: even if the heavens are falling there should be time for a quick one before last orders.

It was a quality further developed by Alastair Burnet when he returned to ITN in 1976, and which gave him, especially during the exacting period of the Falklands War, a stature within British broadcasting comparable to that won by Walter Cronkite in the United States. It was to bring him not only public acclaim and affection, but a knighthood from the Queen, and the spiteful taunts of *Spitting Image*.

We were able to end the year with the first live news broadcast from Australia, which had been linked to the West Coast of the United States by a satellite in orbit over the Pacific. Prince Charles flew out to Melbourne, on his first overseas public engagement, to attend the funeral of the Australian Prime Minister, Mr Harold Holt, who had been drowned whilst surfing. It was a costly transmission, which came near to being frustrated when we learnt that the RAF plane in which Prince Charles was travelling was running ahead of schedule, and would touch down, and pass out of the range of our cameras before the brief satellite pass became available. But the RAF, who were in touch from London with the plane, proved co-operative, and delayed the landing until Diana Edwards-Jones in our control room was able to call over the line to the Air Ministry 'Cue Royal plane'. Down it swooped, visible on our monitors as it landed in the Australian sunshine twelve thousand miles away.

45

Colour, computers, and ENG

W ith the establishment of the half hour news television journalism in Britain came into its own. Not only did the public now regard television as their main source of news, but we were at last able to supply that news vividly and reasonably fully. Prior to 1967, significant though our coverage had been, we had neither the time nor the technology to do the task adequately. From now onwards television was able to anticipate the front pages of the next day's papers, to be the first as well as the main source of the main news of the day. From now onwards the householder who picked up a newspaper from beside the milk bottles on the doorstep, the worker who bought a paper from the corner shop, would almost certainly have gained a prior impression of its main contents from the screen the evening before. This was the real revolution brought about by *News at Ten*, a development far more significant than the changes in techniques or in timing which had made possible our expansion from a bulletin to a programme. It was not a phenomenon unique to British viewing. It had already become marked in the United States. Theodore H. White, the American journalist turned historian, in the third of his massive studies of The Making of a President, wrote in 1968:

> If one had to locate the precise date of television's dominance in American life, one would have to choose, certainly the fall of 1963, when, on September 2nd, the half-hour evening news shows were established on the national networks – a date as significant in American history asthe Golden Spike that linked the Union Pacific and Central Pacific to give America its first continental railway in 1869.

Though big technological developments were to follow, with the arrival of colour, of ENG cameras, and of computerised graphics, and though further long news programmes, culminating in *Channel 4 News*, were to gain time, the watershed had been crossed on that sweltering summer night in 1967, with the first edition of *News at Ten*. From then on, television was to be the dominant medium in Britain for daily news.

Fig. 23. Mobile satellite dish.

The value of the longer news was demonstrated vividly in 1968, a year which rivalled 1963 for high drama. The Tet offensive in Vietnam; Johnson's decision not to run again for President; the assassination of Robert Kennedy; the anti-Vietnam War riots in Grosvenor Square; the crushing by Soviet tanks of the Dubcek regime in Prague; and the RUC attack on civil rights demonstrators which, caught by the cameras, gave the IRA the excuse to launch the bloody campaign which continued for 25 years; these were all stories for which television was the medium par excellence. They were ideally suited to coverage by the technique of the film news package. This established itself as the basic method for reporting news on television, elbowing aside live interviews and studio discussions, and turning *News at Ten* into a mosaic of reporters' stories on film cemented together by spoken news from the newscasters. It was a pattern adopted too by the BBC, as it steadily lengthened the *Nine O'Clock News*, until it lasted at least twenty five minutes.

In 1968 I gave up the Editorship of ITN to become Deputy Chairman of Yorkshire Television, the new programme company set up in the 1967 reshuffle of programme contracts. I was succeeded by Nigel Ryan, who held the post until 1977, when he went off to a top job in NBC News in New York. He in turn was succeeded by David Nicholas, first as Editor and then as Chairman, until 1991, winning a knighthood along the way. His successor wasStewart Purvis.[1]

The early years of Ryan's editorship saw the next major advance in the technology of television news, the introduction of colour. Colour was first used in a British television news programme on 7 March 1968, in the BBC 2's *Newsroom*. When it came into use on BBC 1 and ITN in 1969, it added greatly to the impact of film coverage. As Nigel Ryan put it, 'colour meant a great deal more than just the same old news stories but with the blood showing red'. It conveyed more information to the viewer. This was strikingly so in coverage of sport. With colour the ball could be more clearly seen, and the differing shirts of opposing players more easily identified. Golf was one sport which gained greatly when viewers could see the green of the fairways, of trees, and of the greens themselves, and the contrasting beige of sand in the bunkers, and red and yellow of fluttering flags. Indeed some sports for the first time became worth transmitting on television. Foremost amongst these was snooker, virtually meaningless in monochrome, but soon to prove fascinating in colour.

One of the early effects of colour was to make the war in Vietnam seem even more horrible. Vietnam was revealed as a country of flamboyant oriental colours, with dark green jungles and vivid blue skies. In such a setting the reddish glare of napalm and the fiery spurts of tracer fire stood out with hideous clarity. And when in 1980 the Soviet Union sent its forces into Afghanistan, the reality of their arrival, strenuously denied at the time from Moscow, was made all the more clear because of the stark background of snow-covered mountain ranges looming against a blue sky, beyond the massed ranks of olive grey Soviet tanks on the edge of Kabul airport.

The next big step was the introduction, late in the 1970s, of the electronic ENG (Electronic News Gathering) camera. It not only produced a high quality picture, but by doing away with the need to process film, it enabled a news programme to include material shot only minutes earlier. Its material could also be injected from one of the multitude of Post Office inject points in different parts of the country, or through a links van. From overseas taped material could be edited on the spot, and transmitted by satellite. And electronic editing took less time than film editing. By the time of the Gulf War a further new tool was in the broadcasters' hands – a portable transmitter, like a huge metal golf umbrella, which could enable reporters in the field to transmit direct to a satellite, and so link up immediately with their home base.

A computerized electronic graphics system greatly improved the use of diagrams, maps and statistics. This was a development of cardinal importance in providing information which is not readily susceptible to pictorial treatment, such as reports on inflation, or tax changes, or trade figures. In the past such diagrams had to be hand drawn. In all General Elections prior to October 1974 the broadcasters had, for instance, to use either printed or hand drawn captions to give the voting figures in separate constituencies – a huge task involving the work of scores of artists, ranged in rows in the background of the Election News studio. Computers now do that in an instant.

---

1   In 1995 Richard Tait became Editor in Chief, ITN, Stewart Purvis becoming Chief Executive.

The revolution in these techniques was brought about by Paul McKee, a consultant in computer techniques working for ITN. By adapting a computer designed to display permutations of knitting patterns, he was able to show on the screen, in an instant, multi-coloured and animated diagrams. The system was first used in the General Election in the autumn of 1974. The value to daily news of such electronic techniques for all types of screen graphics was quickly realized. Today an electronics graphics suite is a major element in every television newsroom – and is indeed perhaps the most striking change in the behind the screen operations since the earliest days of television news.

These technological advances strengthened the claim of television news for more air-time. In 1972, when broadcasting hours were extended, Nigel Ryan won for ITN the right to transmit twenty minutes of news at lunchtime. He had to fight for every minute of it, in the face of the same antagonism from the programme companies as had greeted the bid for *News at Ten*. The concept of a news and discussion programme at lunchtime had been pioneered by BBC Radio, who in 1965 had begun The *World at One*. Presented by a former Editor of the *Daily Mail*, William Hardcastle, it had developed a pattern of following the news with interviews and background material, to bring out the significance of the hard facts of the news. Though the programme was accused of blurring at times the boundary between news and comment, it steadily gained prestige, and politicians and other would-be shapers of public opinion came forward readily to be interviewed. Nigel Ryan saw that a comparable programme on television would enable ITN to bring back the element of interpretation which had been part of the early *News at Ten*. He found an excellent presenter in Robert Kee, whose thoughtful and rigorous interviewing made the studio interview a key element in the programme, reviving memories amongst older hands of the Robin Day interviews of the early days. In due course the programme won more time, and in 1976 became *News at One*. When Kee left, Leonard Parkin took over, and then Peter Sissons who, on *News at One*, developed the skills which were to win him fame as the anchor man of *Channel Four News*.

A further major development came in 1982, with the introduction of a fifty minute news programme, at 7pm, on weekdays on the newly established Channel 4. It was produced by ITN, under the editorship of David Nicholas (now Sir David) who had taken over from Nigel Ryan in 1977. After experimenting with various formats, the programme settled down, with Stewart Purvis as its editor, into a pattern which combined coverage in considerable depth of two or three of the main stories of the day with summaries of other news items. It widened news values to include coverage of arts and literature, and used studio interviews extensively. Its in-depth treatment was reminiscent of that of *Panorama* in its heyday.

The 1980s also saw the emergence of two further television news services on offer to United Kindom viewers, those of the breakfast time ITV company, TV-am (later to be replaced by GMTV), and the rolling news of Rupert Murdoch's satellite channel, Sky News. On cable two further news services are now on offer: Channel One in London offers a 24 hour a day service, and Super Channel brings the NBC News from the United States to European viewers. The decade also saw a closer integration of news and current affairs within the BBC with the appointment of John Birt as Deputy Director-General. Birt at once reaffirmed the need for impartiality in news, and set about developing a greater degree of interpretation of the news to counter the 'bias against understanding' which he and Peter Jay had proclaimed, 20 years earlier, as the characteristic of television news. One outcome of this policy was the placing of *Newsnight* at the regular hour of 10.30pm on BBC 2.

The most significant development in television news in the 1980s came, however, in the United States, with the establishing by Cable News Network (CNN) of the first 24 hour rolling news service to use satellites to transmit its service, first across the United States, and then around the world. CNN became, as a result, the first news service which is also a news agency. Subscribers in countries around the world can record items from CNN broadcasts, and use them in their own news programmes. This has made it a major rival to the two specialist international television news agencies, Visnews and Worldwide Television News, which until then had dominated the field of supplying news in pictures to television stations throughout the globe.

The first agency to supply newsfilm to television stations was set up in 1953, when the American wire service, United Press International, joined forces with Fox Movietone News to provide film of news events to television stations. They won customers not only in the United States, but in Europe, where the BBC in particular became a major outlet for their product. By the end of the 1950s UPI Movietone was a highly prosperous business, taken by virtually all European stations, and widely used in the United States.

In 1955 the BBC decided to form their own newsfilm agency, and offered the fledgling ITN a share in the project. But ITN had at that stage no money for such ventures. When the BBC in 1956 came back with a formal invitation to join the British Commonwealth International News Agency – BCINA, ITN had already become sufficiently competitive to decide to go its own way.

BCINA comprised three public broadcasters – the BBC, CBC of Canada, and ABC of Australia – and the commercial Rank Organization, whose cinema newsreel, Universal News, was being driven to the wall by television. It soon changed its name to the more commercially sensible one of Visnews. After a difficult start, it soon became commercially viable, winning as customers virtually all the public service television services in Europe. To keep up its competitive position, ITN linked up with CBS to sell a syndication service of newsfilm. This proved hard going, because there were then virtually no commercially financed stations in Europe.

By the early 1960s Visnews had ousted UPI from its place as the leading supplier of international news on film. In 1965 the BBC cancelled their contract with UPI, and two years later UPI were dealt a deadly blow when ABC News in the United States not only ceased to subscribe to their service, but refused any longer to send it out over their electronic network.

In the 1950s most of the film supplied by these agencies had gone out by air freight. But as Eurovision, and then Intervision (which linked the Iron Curtain countries) provided a means of distributing film electronically, a process already under way in the United States, electronic distribution became essential.

But it was also expensive, particularly in the United States. UPI therefore turned to ITN, and proposed a merger of ITN's syndication service with UPI. This came about in 1967. The new agency called itself UPITN – a clumsy title for the general public, but one which, to the news editors of television stations, had the ring of quality from two established news organizations.

UPITN had some difficult early years, the more so because they soon had to face ever higher delivery costs, as transmission of newsfilm by satellite began to supplant distribution by electronic cable. UPITN went through a number of changes in its ownership, and in the 1980s changed its name to WTN – Worldwide Television News. It is now owned predominantly by ABC of America.

WTN and Visnews dominated the market throughout the 1980s, until CNN came on the scene. On 1 June 1980 Ted Turner, owner of a small television station in Atlanta, Georgia launched the first 24 hour, round the clock news service, which was distributed by satellite to cable stations throughout the United States. It was, after a hard early struggle, swiftly successful. By 1990 it was being received in 53 million homes in the United States, and in 84 different countries. This worldwide distribution made it, very effectively, the third great international television news agency.[1] This global outlet has given CNN a significance beyond that of being a mere purveyor of news. It has become an instrument of diplomacy, being utilized as a means by which governments can convey messages not so much to the governments of other countries, but direct to their peoples. Saddam Hussein in particular tried to use it in this way during the period leading up to the outbreak of the war in the Gulf. Its role in conveying, in August 1991, Boris Yeltsin's defiance of the coup against the reformers in the Soviet Union, has passed into history. Tele-diplomacy has indeed come a long way since Robin Day, in a sunlit garden in a Cairo suburb, set about interviewing President Gamal Nasser.

---

1   From 1995 onwards the CNN service has been challenged, particularly in the Far East, by the BBC's television news service, BBC World, transmitted by satellite.

46

Under attack

As television news became, more and more, a power in the land it increasingly aroused criticism. The first complaints were not that news items were too violent, but that they were too mild. Criticisms were voiced against softer stories which had been part of the newsreels' calendar, and which had been continued into television. New Year's Eve traditionally brought scenes of crowds, excited but orderly, in Trafalgar Square and Piccadilly Circus; Bank holidays meant a predictable fare of crowded railway stations and airports, of traffic jams – with Exeter bypass, in those pre-Motorway days a much filmed black spot – of packed beaches at Blackpool and Margate. Shrove Tuesday was pancake races at Olney, and May Day was a scene of choristers greeting the dawn from the top of Magdalen Tower. The Queen's birthday brought ritual filming of the Royal Horse Artillery firing the salute in Hyde park. On Christmas Day, an ITN reporter would be detailed to bring his bathing shorts, and be ready to join the swimmers across the icy Serpentine.

Television news editors competed to vary this fare, rather than abandon it. ITN preened itself on finding a new angle when it filmed not just the usual Royal birthday guns in Hyde Park, but the previously unfilmed ceremony of firing a cannon at the Tower of London. And we envied the BBC a scoop when on Spring Bank Holiday they came up with an entirely new scene, the villagers at Cooper's Hill in Gloucestershire rolling a cheese down a steep hill to commemorate their traditional rights to the common land on the hill.

Such pictures were useful in filling the bulletins at Christmas and other holidays periods when film from overseas was still scarce, and communication slow. And they were cheap to cover, being predictable and close at hand. But by the end of the 1950s they had begun to attract criticism, and gradually lost their place in the news schedules, to be replaced by harder – and harsher – scenes. Yet these softer stories had their merits. The events they portrayed, together with the great national sporting occasions like the Cup Final and the Derby and Wimbledon and Test matches, provided, unintentionally and yet usefully, a common annual pattern of familiar events which help to express a sense of national identity and cohesion. They formed a part of the fabric of British life as the British people had come to see it. The predictability of these stories, year after year, was reassuring, in a way which the last night at the Proms later came to be. And, soft or not, they reminded people that life was not merely crises and disasters, accidents and riots and wars.

As we moved into the 1960s, the pendulum swung the other way, and television news was increasingly criticized for showing too much violence. Certainly the amount of violent action in news programmes had increased. With news cameramen on station all over the world, and with transmission improving, first through land lines across Europe and the United States, and then with satellites, the volume of up-to-the-minute news film increased dramatically. A substantial part of that increase was of scenes of violence. The fighting in Algeria, the civil war in the Congo were, for instance, marked by acts of great brutality. A decade earlier these might well have gone unrecorded, or at the most made the subject of a still picture. But now they were caught by the camera, and relayed night after night into the sitting rooms of the land.

The half hour news, with its quantum leap in the time for news, had brought a quantum leap also in the time for violent news. One argument I had constantly – and sincerely – advanced for the half hour news was that it would give us a chance to set the news in perspective immediately. Yet the characteristics of the programmes which, in the crucial early days, had won over the audience and won over the critics had been the vivid, on the spot coverage as with Argylls in Aden and the mercenaries in Rwanda. In August 1967, some six weeks after the start of *News at Ten*, I received a letter from a Leicester City Councillor protesting about the amount of violence we were showing. In the days of the shorter news we had received complaints about individual scenes of violence, but never about the quantity of such constant element in the letters we received.

Violence in news was only one aspect of the wider issue of violence in all types of programmes, an issue which has been the subject of debate, research and regulation throughout the past thirty years. But for television news the argument had particular force, for it threw doubt on the validity of the moving picture as a form of journalism, and on the camera as a journalist's tool. One of the first to raise these doubts was the great ITN pioneer, Robin Day. In an article in the magazine *Encounter*, in May 1970, Robin Day (he did not become Sir Robin until 11 years later) warned that television is not only a powerful means of communication, but a crude one, which strikes at the emotions rather than at the intellect. He later stated that he had come to feel that 'television, with its enormous power to project violence and unreason, had a heavy responsibility to present reasoned and civilized argument. The electronic journalism of TV should do more than transmit 'bloody good pictures'.

> With its appetite for visual sensation, its tabloid dependence on pictures, television had an inherent tendency to distort and to trivialize. Disaster, violence, disruption, were the staple ingredients of TV's diet. Television's appetite for them was insatiable. This appetite, this lust for visible action and violent happenings, is itself an invitation to create more of the same for TV to project.[1]

Over the years criticism of television news has concentrated largely on this impact as a

---

1   Sir Robin Day, *Grand Inquisitor.*. Weidenfeld and Nicholson, 1989, p. 284.

visual medium, on the power of the picture. The first argument is that, by showing violence on the screen, it inspires or incites further copycat violence in real life. This first emerged as an issue inn the early 1960s, when rival groupings of youths, Mods and Rockers, brought a new element to Bank Holiday coverage by clashing in leather coated mobs on beaches and seaside promenades. The commentators and the leader writers put this down to the new phenomenon of television. The police warned us that rival mobs watched the lunchtime television bulletins to see where their rivals were gathering and could best be targeted, and asked us to cut down detail of where the motor cycle columns of the gangs were heading. We did so, but the punch-ups continued, providing a staple part of Bank Holiday coverage until uglier and more deadly violence took its place on the screen.

The issue of television news as an instigator of such troubles came to the fore, in the starkest form, when rioting broke out in the Watts District of Los Angeles in the summer of 1965. An enterprising American network covered the riots with an outside broadcast camera in a helicopter. The helicopter circled over the scene, and broadcast its pictures live. A number of rioters and looters who were later arrested testified that they had been drawn to the area of the riots by this on-screen publicity. The American networks drew from this the lesson that live coverage of rioting or other violent scenes should not take place, a ban all three networks observed punctiliously when similar riots, essentially racial in character, later occurred in Detroit. Full coverage was accorded to the Detroit troubles in the regular news bulletins, but no live coverage was shown. The police were sure this has helped to keep the rioting in check, and this self imposed rule has since been followed by United States broadcasters. In Britain the copycat effect came under discussion during the riots in Brixton in 1983. ITN had some vivid film looters smashing a shop window and stealing televisions sets. This was not only shown in bulletins, but used in discussion programmes, and was blamed for further looting which followed.

A second main charge against television news is that, by its nature, it encourages people to embark upon violence to gain the huge publicity of having their acts broadcast to millions. Should television news help the men of violence by showing actions mounted deliberately in order to win a place in the news bulletins? This was the dilemma which had faced me in those very early days over the film of the ambush mounted by the Algerian guerrillas. It was a dilemma which was soon to face television news editors day after day. Peaceful demonstrations like the Aldermaston march soon gave way to acts of violence, ranging from digging up the Headingly Test wicket to draw attention to a man's imprisonment, to the bombings and shootings which became the daily news fare from Ulster. A striking proof that such acts were mounted to catch the eye of the cameras came in a documentary made by ATV in 1970. A sequence filmed in a flat in the Bogside area of Londonderry showed young men preparing petrol bombs for use against the police the next day, whilst on a television set in a corner of the room they watched on the news the scenes of that days's rioting, whooping with delight every time the yellow flames of fire bombs could be seen curving across the screen towards the police. Here indeed was an instance of television news providing 'the oxygen of publicity', as Sir Leon Brittan was later to argue.

In the face of such evidence, should news editors suppress reports of events – deliberately staged events? In 1968 in Amsterdam television did stop showing scenes of hippy riots in the centre of the city. Finding their actions unreported, the rioters stopped. And there are instances of similar suppression of news by the press and broadcasters in Britain. Bomb scares are no longer reported on BBC News or on ITN. In kidnapping cases, all news has been withheld until the matter has been resolved. During the Balcombe Street siege of IRA terrorists, and the Iranian Embassy seige, news programmes did not show scenes which the authorities thought might help those under siege.

It would be a great error, however, to deduce from these particular cases that pictures of violence, however contrived that violence may have been, should be withheld to discourage those who resort to violence. There is a clear distinction between the self censorship by the media of information where publication would clearly put lives at risk, and the withholding of information because of some general effect its publication might have. For one thing, one cannot be sure what the effect of withholding information may be. Holding back news that a riot has broken out in a particular area might discourage further rioters flocking to the spot. But equally it might mean that motorists and others who, forewarned, could have avoided the area were caught up in the rioting. The only rule an editor can follow is to publish unless there are compelling reasons, readily understood by the public, for not doing so. The cases I have cited, such as those of kidnapping, all had two factors in common. The ban was short lived; and it was clear that lives were at risk. These are reasons which the public can clearly understand, and so not result in any loss of public trust in the honesty of the news. And that trust is essential, not only in the interest of the news services, but in the interests of society. A supply of trustworthy news is as vital to a modern democracy as is a supply of good fresh water. The long ugly story of the years of violence in Northern Ireland makes this clear. Despite all the difficulties and dangers which have been involved, both the BBC News and ITN continued to give the news, not to suppress it, and rumour and false propaganda were as a result kept in check.

A third main charge against television news is that pictures can distort. Film of a punch-up on the edge of an otherwise peaceful meeting can give the impression that the whole affair was riotous. This is a very real problem for television news. No more misleading adage was ever enunciated than the statement that the camera cannot lie. The camera is a razor sharp instrument which has to be used with care, an instrument which can as readily distort the truth as portray it. Because the impact of the picture has such force, because in Wordsworth's words the eye is 'the most despotic of the bodily senses', pictures can mislead unless they are presented with care. This is plain from the arguments about coverage of clashes in the Miners' strike of 1984, where either the police or the miners could be presented as villains, according to which scenes have been caught by the cameras.

Television editors can offset bias by using commentary to give explanation, and by setting the scenes in context. But the best method is to ensure full coverage, so that pictures are available to tell the whole story. But that takes copious resources. In 1977 the siege of Grunwick, the small film processing plant blockaded by trade union pickets, became a testing ground for the use, or abuse, of union power. On the main day of the siege, ITN deployed no fewer than 14 camera crews to ensure that it secured a fully rounded picture.

But such full coverage can be difficult to achieve, particularly if war and censorship prevents cameramen getting to the scene. The absence of pictures can distort, as much as does their misuse. The classic case of such distortion was provided by the sufferings of the people of Cambodia under Pol Pot. For a decade, during the Vietnam War, the sufferings of the people of Cambodia, like those of South Vietnam, had been portrayed every day on our screens, filmed in all the sharp colours of those lands. With the fall of the two countries under Communist control in 1975 they disappeared as abruptly from the screen, and from the consciousness of the outside world, as if Indo-China were a spacecraft which had passed on to the dark side of the moon. We saw, and came to know, nothing of the sufferings of the South Vietnamese in the concentration camps, given the mocking title of re-education camps. In the case of Cambodia, the distortion of the truth was even worse, because there genocide was being carried out by the Khmer Rouge on a scale equal to that of the Nazis. It was to remain hidden until the conquest of the country by South Vietnam opened the door again to cameramen.

Similar distortion existed in the West's reporting of life behind the Iron Curtain until the era of *Glasnost*. Before Gorbachov's day, camera were admitted to the countries of the Communist bloc only on terms which ensured that the outcome would be highly selective material favourable to Communism. The economic weakness of Communism, the appalling pollution and damage to the environment which it brought in its train, and above all the lack of liberty and freedom were never effectively portrayed on television until Gorbachov allowed a remarkable degree of freedom to foreign journalists. With the collapse of Communism, this freedom was spread over all Eastern Europe, and is firmly established throughout the former Soviet Union. The area of the world open to television coverage has increased by at least 30 per cent since 1989.

A fourth criticism of television news is that, in its lust for pictures, it underplays or ignores stories which do not lend themselves to visual treatment. This is the main thrust of Sir Robin Day's criticism. He has argued that 'television could cover riot, a war, a revolution, an assassination, more vividly than any newspaper. But television tended to give much less explanation of the reasons behind these events. Television producers must recognize that the most important developments are not primarily visual'.[1]

Technology has done something in recent years to help cope with this problem. Electronic graphics, now available at the touch of a button, can provide diagrams and maps and charts to explain and illustrate news, such as developments within the European Union, which deals with ideas and concepts rather than action. But the best corrective for this problem and indeed for the problem of ensuring that the picture does not lie, is the journalist's oldest tool, the word. Well written scripts, well phrased interviews, clear verbal explanation have a major role to play in news programmes, and can offset other inherent dangers in this age of pictures.

Another vitally important corrective to these limitations of television news is the longer news in depth programme, and above all the fully researched full length documentary. The documentary is television's best instrument for probing and explaining a major issue. In it the combined and complementary powers of the picture and the word can be fully utilized. Studio discussions, interviews in depth, and immediate on-the-spot in-

---

1   Sir Robin Day, *op.cit.* p. 285.

Fig. 24. Stewart Purvis, Editor in Chief, ITN, 1991–95.

quiries in the news are all of value. But the most effective technique of all is the major documentary.

Unfortunately it is a weapon television has failed to use on many of the key issues of the past thirty years. Any student who cares to scrutinize the programmes set out in the programme journals for that period will find, for instance, that neither the BBC nor

ITV mounted any critical inquiry in the 1960s into high rise housing. It took the Ronan Point disaster to bring the issue on to the screen. Until then the producers had been prepared to have high rise housing acclaimed as the approved architecture of the brave new world. Similarly no probing has been done, in documentary form, until recently into the nature and effect of modern progressive teaching methods. It was not television which exposed the nature of the teaching, or the lack of teaching, at the William Tyndale School in Islington in 1976 which led working class mothers en masse to take their children away from the school. It took a £100,000 public inquiry, with all the panoply of QCs and formally questioned witnesses, to bring into the open the conditions which had prevailed at the school. *Panorama* made some recompense by reconstructing this inquiry, using actors and working from the transcript. But since then, parents seeking knowledge of what state schooling is really like have learnt more from *Grange Hill* than from the documentary makers.

There have been other strange gaps. No full scale inquiry was launched by the BBC, or by any ITV company, into the structure and powers of the trade unions during the period, form 1964 onwards, when they threatened to become a law unto themselves. Within ITV the only documentaries on this vital issue were two fairly modest efforts from a regional company, Anglia, one of which found its way on to the network only after strong opposition. Similarly the Parliamentary struggle over the closed shop in 1976 attracted little or no in depth examination on television, even though a closed shop in journalism could have struck at freedom of the press and broadcasting. The newspapers saw the danger, and fought the proposal, but the documentary producers walked by on the other side. Nor was the situation in Ulster probed effectively during the years leading up to the start of the IRA campaign in 1969.

These are serious gaps, which have left the daily news programmes exposed, more than need have been the case, to the argument that television news lacks depth. Fortunately, in Channel Four News, ITN has now an instrument under its own hand which it can use – and does – to help remedy this situation. On the BBC,too, *Newsnight* does a valiant task night after night.

The impact of the visual image has not been the only aspect of television news to arouse criticism. In the mid-1970s both BBC News and ITN were attacked for their editorial stance, and in particular for their claim to report impartially. This was in part a knock-on effect from an attack on the principle of impartiality which had been mounted at the time by current affairs producers, who were restive at the constraints imposed on them. They scoffed at impartiality as involving artificial concepts of balance denounced neutrality as being the equivalent of being neutered, and saw impartiality at best as being an unattainable ideal, if not a delusion. Their campaign had – and continues to have – considerable success. The broadcasting authorities yielded to this pressure, first by ruling that treatment of an issue of public concern could be balanced across a series. Then they agreed that opinionated programmes could be permitted if these were clearly labelled as the opinions of a particular person. This led in practice to a balance being struck, not between different sides of a particular issue, but between people of different views, even if they were dealing with different issues. Truth, it seems, is adequately served if John Pilger is given time to put his own strongly opinionated views on Cambodia, and then within the same series Auberon Waugh is allowed to be rude about the

Fig. 25. Trevor McDonald, Newscaster, *News at Ten*, 1990–present day.

British working class. So strongly entrenched has this concept of a free-for-all in current affairs and documentaries become – that is, a free-for-all for the very few who can get access to the screen – that the idea of a balance of news views, except on immediate political and industrial issues, has largely gone by the board.

In the midst of these changing attitudes in current affairs, both BBC News and ITN have held obdurately to their belief in impartiality as a guiding principle for news. In 1976 this attitude came under attack from a prestigious academic quarter – the University of Glasgow. Their Media Group, in two books *Bad News* (1976) and *More Bad News* (1980) argued that the impartiality claimed by television news applied, at most, to only a particular spectrum of views and news, confined to what they termed the consensus, and that in fact the news services merely reflected and reinforced the power structure within which they operated. It was not always easy to determine, through their socio-logical terminology, the exact accusation of the Glasgow Group, but to broadcast jour-nalists their case seemed to be that journalists delude themselves if they believe they can be objective or fair. Whether journalists know it or not, these critics insist, they are blinkered in their approach to the news by their background and experience, or, in short, by their class. Even the most manifestly objective of journalists is, by this credo, unconsciously a propagandist.

Within the academic world, in the swiftly widening field of media studies, the assertions of the Glasgow Group had considerable influence, until they were challenged and undermined by a detailed critique of their work and their methods by Professor Martin Harrison, Professor of Politics of of the University of Keele.[1] Within broadcasting, they did not shake the faith of the BBC News or of ITN in the principles of impartiality or in their news values, but they did influence early programming on Channel 4. Jeremy Isaacs shrewdly gave those who argued for a different attitude to news, an opportunity to put their ideas to the test in a weekly programme, *The Friday Alternative*. It had only a short life. It could not find enough alternative news to interest the viewers, nor enough bias in existing news services to make the charges against them stick. The programme faded from the screen, and the argument about impartiality in news has, at least for the time being, faded away.

One major reason for that may lie in the nature of the news with the newsrooms have had to grapple across the past two decades. These have been the years of highly sensitive issues such as the Falklands War and the Gulf War and Miners Strike of 1984. When passions run high, when broadcast news is dealing with events which shake society to its depths, objectivity and fairness, which go hand in hand with impartiality, are what the public instinctively seeks from broadcast news. The moment when the news comes under the glare of close and informed scrutiny, the moment when people's live and their homes and possessions can be affected by the accuracy and fairness of the news, any hint, any shade of editorializing becomes unacceptable.

---

1   Martin Harrison, *TV News. Whose Bias?* Polity, 1985.

47

Summing up

A gainst these defects of television news must be set its virtues. These are substantial, geniunely enabling journalists to present a more truthful picture of events. The probing interview has proved to be an invaluable tool for broadcast journalism, on radio as well as on television. It is used today as unhesitatingly by the most junior reporter on a local radio station as by the Grand Inquisitors of Sunday lunchtime. It flourishes despite two recent defects. One is the determination of some politicians not to answer the question put to them, but to launch into a prepared statement of their own. This is an attempt to put the clock back, to return to the pre-1955 days when the politicians would come on the air only on their own terms. But firm and patient questioning can counter this tendency.

The other defect comes from the side of the broadcasters. It is what John Birt, the BBC's Director General, recently stigmatised, when he attacked 'reporters who pretend that answers and remedies are obvious; that everyone in the world but them is an incompetent fool, overbearing interviewers who sneer disdainfully at their interviewees'. Such methods are much more common on radio than on television. They distract attention from what should be the object of the interview, to get at the truth, and are an abuse of the right to cross-question those in power which was won back in those early days of the mid-1950s. Nevertheless, the probing interview remains an invaluable journalistic instrument.

The other great gain of television news has been the capacity to let people see for themselves what is happening, to provide first hand evidence by which the public can make their own judgements. Television journalism has not only provided fuller and clearer information, but has been a force for liberty.

One striking example of this came in August 1968, when television showed the world the truth of the Soviet invasion of Czechoslovakia to put down the Dubchek regime. Brave Czech cameramen filmed the advance of the tanks, and the opposition of the crowds in the street, and then smuggled their first can of film out of the country by dropping it, wrapped in brown paper, into the car of a tourist near the Austrian border. Later pictures were sent out by a secret transmitter hidden in a van. The scenes which

Fig. 26. Cameraman at broken bridge in Iraq.

the cameras recorded of jeering, weeping, angry crowds shouting protests and abuse at Soviet troops, or hurling stones and rubble at the tanks, the fires rising from buildings, shelled by invaders, the crumpled bodies of the dead by the roadside, provided evidence beyond any doubt that this was an invasion, not the arrival of a welcome ally. It left in the West the enduring impression that the Soviet Union was, whatever its protestations about detente, a brutal dictatorship.

A year later television news conveyed other, more constructive scenes in a way no other medium could match, when it showed the actual moment of man's first landing on the moon. When on the evening of July 20 1969 the cameras could show, live, the moment when Neil Armstrong's boot groped its way down the ladder of Apollo Eleven's landing module, and stirred the grey dust of the moon's surface, they provided a level of reporting hitherto unknown.

Historians may indeed decide that television news' finest hour will be the part it has played, since 1988, in bringing about the end of Communism in the Soviet Union and the satellite states. The Soviet Communist Party had recognized early on the power of this new visual medium, and had set about harnessing it to their own purposes. Strict censorship of all news and current affairs behind the Iron Curtain had ensured that television strengthened the iron grip of the Party. Except in East Germany, where the programmes from the West could be seen, this grip was firmly maintained until, in July 1988, Mikhail Gorbachov decided to use television cameras in the interests of his policy of Glasnost. He saw that television could give him a way of getting his message directly to the people, and so enable him to circumvent the grip of the Communist Party hardliners on public opinion. He did so by broadcasting live the proceedings of the Nineteenth Party Conference, held in Moscow in June-July 1989. Gorbachov's speech to the Conference started an avalanche of reform, and he ensured that all three and a half hours of it were carried into the homes of the people on prime time television.

This bypassed at a stroke the massive apparatus of Party censorship, enabling the public to observe, and so share in the reforms which he proposed. The wave of support for Gorbachov which this released strengthened his hand against the hardliners. The precedent for live coverage which had been established was continued, ensuring that later proceedings of the new Congress of People's Deputies, of the new Supreme Soviet, and of the Russian Parliament, were widely televised.

When the wave of change reached the Eastern European satellites, television news was to play an equally significant part. This was most clearly seen in Czechoslovakia. The Communist authorities there met the first wave of demonstrations in the Autumn of 1989 by tough police repression, and by continued censorship of television news. But police violence was counter productive, stimulating further protests. On 23 November matters came to a head. The television staff in Prague demanded the right to provide live coverage of the continuing demonstrations in Wenceslas Square, and to show film of brutal police action a week earlier, censored at the time. When the Czechoslovak Government yielded to this demand, the revolution became unstoppable. Within a few weeks even more dramatic scenes were to be broadcast in Romania, where the outside broadcast cameras showed, live, to an astonished nation, the spectacle of Ceaucescu being howled down, and then retreating from the balcony in Bucharest from which he had been haranguing the crowds.

Eighteen months later the cameras were to come to the aid of Boris Yeltsin in Moscow. These were great blows for freedom, and they were struck by television news. The new journalism had come a long way since it took its first tentative steps barely four decades ago.

Index

930855